NEW KOSHER CUISINE
FOR ALL SEASONS

NEW KOSHER CUISINE
FOR ALL SEASONS

Edited by

Ivy Feuerstadt

&

Melinda Strauss

TEN SPEED PRESS
Berkeley, California

1☉

TEN SPEED PRESS
P.O. Box 7123
Berkeley, CA 94707

Cover design by Terri Barel Eisenberg
Text design by Font & Center Press

Library of Congress Cataloging-in-Publication Data

New kosher cuisine for all seasons / edited by Ivy Feuerstadt and Melinda
  Strauss : foreword by Mollie Katzen.
      p.   cm.
  Includes index.
  ISBN 0-89815-559-2
  1. Cookery, Jewish. 2. Cookery (Natural foods) I. Feuerstadt,
Ivy. II. Strauss, Melinda.
TX724.K64 1993   93-2373
641.5'676—dc20   CIP

FIRST PRINTING 1993
Printed in the United States

4 5 6 - 00 99 98

This book is dedicated to my husband,
Nelson Wasserman, whose love and friendship
I will cherish forever.
— *Ivy Feuerstadt*

All of us associated with the Solomon Schechter
Day School of Greater Boston miss Nelson
Wasserman very much. His love for the school
was a reflection of his own personal odyssey
toward a more involved and fulfilling Jewish
life — an odyssey that occupied him
for most of his adult life.

A brilliant businessman and a committed
Schechter board member, Nelson was, above all,
a devoted husband and father. He gave more to
his wonderful family during his short life than
many who live much longer.

May his memory be for us a blessing.
— *Rabbi Joshua Elkin*

Proceeds from the sale of this book
will benefit the Solomon Schechter Day School
of Greater Boston.

"For the Lord your God
is bringing you into a good land
a land of WHEAT and
BARLEY, of VINE and
FIG TREES and
POMEGRANATES
a land of OLIVE TREES
and HONEY...And you shall
eat and be full and you shall bless the
Lord your God for the good land
He has given you."

Deuteronomy 8: 7-10

CONTENTS

TABLE OF ESSAYS

FOREWORD

This delightful collection expands and enriches our notions of what we think of as kosher cuisine. It joyfully celebrates all sorts of occasions, including but not limited to Jewish festivities, and has something for just about everyone who enjoys cooking good food and serving it to loved ones. Deeply rooted in tradition, these recipes are thoroughly, as my grandmother would have said, "modern." They reflect our increasing knowledge and sophistication about food and the complexities of our everyday lives, within which we strive to be motivated — and to find the time — to cook healthful, delicious meals for our families, friends, and selves.

My own upbringing in a kosher home profoundly and forever influenced my attitudes towards the blessings of the table. The dietary laws of Kashrut taught me that food — and the privilege of eating — should be regarded with the utmost awareness and respect, as they have been down through the centuries. All memorable occasions, most notably and frequently the Sabbath, with its very special meal every Friday sundown, centered around particular foods. And the preparation of them was regarded as a near-sacred activity.

Sometimes considered unfashionable, the observance of Kashrut is making a comeback among young Jewish families across the nation. Many are turning (or returning) to their roots as part of a broader quest to find meaning and connectedness in this difficult and rapidly changing world. We seek to impart strength to our children by celebrating with them certain powerful traditions. And our traditions surrounding food more than symbolize the continuity of life, which is no small subject!

To all those who, for whatever reason, seek to relish and enjoy such gifts, I recommend this collection. But whether you keep kosher or not, whether you are Jewish or not, these menus will provide you with many easy, accessible, and wonderful meals.

Mollie Katzen

PREFACE

f one is good, two is better!

It had been nine years since the Solomon Schechter Day School of Greater Boston's publication of the successful *From Soup to Nosh: A Modern Kosher Cookbook,* and our school community had been asking for a sequel. In planning the new cookbook, we recognized that as we began the 90s, our eating habits had changed — to consider fat, sodium, and cholesterol, not just calories; to reduce our consumption of red meat in favor of other sources of protein; and to select whole foods with high nutritional value.

We weren't sure what we would receive in response to the call for recipes. What we found confirmed our hunches — that families are enthusiastically using whole foods and natural ingredients. As a result, you will not find recipes in this cookbook that contain pareve soup mixes, non-dairy creamers, jello, and other artificial staples from a less health-conscious era. None of our ingredients contain preservatives or additives, and we have included many tasty and versatile ingredients such as tofu, soy milk, and vegetable stock (bouillon), available in supermarkets as well as natural food stores and Oriental markets.

Readers familiar with whole foods know that natural cooking can often mean last-minute preparation by the cook. However, this cookbook contains many make-ahead dishes to accommodate the traditional household on Shabbat and the Festivals, and to free up all cooks so that they may enjoy their families and guests. Even stir-fry dishes can be cooked ahead and reheated. And there are a great many pareve and vegetarian selections to permit maximum flexibility in kosher menu planning. Of course, as of this writing, all name-brand ingredients used here are certified kosher.

Above all, apart from their nutritional value, make-ahead convenience, and pareve versatility, our recipes are simply delicious! Our contributors are people who love good food, and who love to cook. Each recipe is kitchen-tested — prepared and tasted by devoted cooks who know food. No recipe has been repeated from Schechter's *From Soup to Nosh,* so that *New Kosher Cuisine for All Seasons* can be used as a companion cookbook.

The format of this cookbook is dictated by the seasons. Most recipes are included in menus for either traditional Jewish holidays or traditionally American celebrations. Additional recipes are included in a miscellaneous section at the back of the book. All the recipes can be used by kosher cooks.

It is in the Jewish tradition to show affection by cooking for one's loved ones. This cookbook provides new ways to express our love and maintain our health. *B'tayavon!*

NOTE: The following symbols highlight the recipes and menus to make kosher cooking clear and easy:

Pareve   Meat   Dairy   Pesach

ACKNOWLEDGMENTS

We wish to acknowledge with gratitude the following people who assisted with this project.

First, this cookbook benefitted in untold ways from the expert artistic hand of Terri Barel Eisenberg who designed the cover and all the artwork, including the Hebrew and English calligraphy. Amelia Welt Katzen guided the book to and through publication and final editing. Rena Gray Fein organized and oversaw the recipe testing. Joan Leegant helped to edit the book, and Nancy Grodin kept track of administrative details. A special thanks to Mollie Katzen for her advice, encouragement, and, of course, her recipe.

Joni Schockett and Marilyn Sandberg, co-editors of *From Soup to Nosh: A Modern Kosher Cookbook,* paved the way for a second cookbook. Rabbi Dan Shevitz provided untiring computer consultation to help produce the index; he and Sol Eisenberg translated information from a diversity of computer formats so that this book could be produced. Craig Greenwald of *The Butcherie* in Brookline, Massachusetts, provided us with up-to-date information on the availability of *kosher l'Pesach* products. Marlene Leffell answered our questions about nutrition, and developed the useful evaluation form that was completed for every recipe. Michael Bohnen, Bob Dancy, and Les Fagen helped us untangle publishing legalities. Harvey Freishtat and Neal Farber, past presidents of our school, encouraged us and probably believed, as we did, that the cookbook would be completed during their terms!

The following friends helped in many ways, and their support is greatly appreciated: Dan Bricklin, Lora Brody, Rabbi Joshua Elkin, Ann Falchuck, Varda Farber, Joan Gadon, Rabbi Richard Israel, Caryl Levine, Estelle Linder, Lois Nadel, Bill Novak, Judy Rin, David Strauss, Moshe Waldoks, Nelson Wasserman, and Esther White.

The following volunteers were our dedicated recipe testers. Some spent short but productive hours in their kitchens, and others spent days. We are grateful to all of them and their families for contributing to this "kitchen-tested" cookbook.

Julie Arnow	Sheryl Dropkin
Sara Abramovitz	Ruth Ehrlich
Hannah Aroesty	Cathy Felix
Linda Bick-Helfgott	Rita Feuerstadt
Joyce Bohnen	Janice Goldstein
Madeline Bronitsky	Hilary Greenberg
Asaf Cohen	Jill Grossman
Robyn Cohen	Simon Helfgott
Susan Creditor	Miriam Hoffman
Jone Dalezman	Sharon Jacobs
Rachel Dibner	Linda Jason

Esther Kletter
Heni Koenig-Plonskier
Roselyn Kolodny
Nadine Krasnow
Annette Koren
Beth Lang-Nadel
Susan Levin
Davida Manon
Carol Mersky
Chana Meyer
Lisa Micley
Linda Germaine Miller
Sara Ravid
Arlene R. Remz
Judy Rin
Susie Rodenstein

Lisa Rosenfeld
Judy Rubinger
Edith Russman
Robert Russman-Halperin
Wendy Russman-Halperin
Amy Sands
Diane Schildkraut
Fran Morrill Schlitt
Donna Schweon
Susan Schenberg
Larry Sternberg
Judy Taub
Ruth Tepper
Roz Weiner
Debby Zigun

Our plea for typists was graciously answered by the following people. These friends became our word-processing lifesavers. We are forever indebted to them for their initial work, and for the many times they corrected their disks.

Harriet Cole
Faith Friedman
Carol Ghatan
Deborah Guthermann
Linda Jason

Melanie Katz
David Lee-Parritz
Diane Schildkraut
Katie Weinger
Debby Zigun

We want to thank all the cooks who submitted their personal and prized recipes. We are sorry that we could not use them all; however, they are securely tucked away in case there is yet another cookbook in the future. Last but not least, *todah rabah* to the Schechter community for its energy and excitement throughout the duration of this project.

Ivy Feuerstadt and Melinda Strauss
Newton, Massachusetts

INTRODUCTION

Thought for Food

"...וַיֶּחֱזוּ אֶת הָאֱלֹהִים וַיֹּאכְלוּ וַיִּשְׁתּוּ"

"...and they beheld God, and did eat and drink." *(Exodus 24:11)*

The *Torah* has just been given; the sin of the Golden Calf has not yet
been recorded. Moses, Aaron and his children, and the seventy elders of
Israel are invited up to the holy mountain. There they experience a vision
of the Divine Glory. We can only dimly imagine it. What does
it mean to see God? And what is their reaction? Do they fall on their
faces? Utter hymns of praise? Merge with the cosmic consciousness?
No; they have lunch.

The incongruity did not escape the classical commentators. Rashi
(the medieval French rabbi and scholar, Rabbi Shlomo Yitzhaki) attempts
to apologize for the apparently sacrilegious behavior: "Do you think that
they ate food? No, they 'feasted their eyes' on the presence of God." But
I think we need not be embarrassed by Moses and his party. We are
being taught that there is a relationship between food and theology that
is far more profound than the gastronomic Judaism of later generations.

What is the source of energy for the world? The source of energy
for all things is God, of course. But the Almighty generally works
through the food chain: big fish eat little fish. Through the combined
miracles of photosynthesis, cell reproduction, human biology, and good
kosher restaurants, we are sustained each day: "You open Your hand and
satisfy all that lives" *(Psalms 145:16)*. One medieval commentator sug-
gests that when Moses, Aaron, Nadav, Avihu, and the seventy elders
ascended the holy mountain, they were at such a lofty spiritual height
that they by-passed the normal channels; they were physically sustained
directly from God. At that moment they perceived God not only with
their intellects and emotions, but with their viscera as well: "Taste, and
experience how good is the Lord!" *(Psalms 34:9)*. The normal boundary
between the spiritual and the physical was shown to be illusory; theology
and cuisine were intertwined. To be human was understood in its fullest
meaning: seeing God, they understood that human beings are in God's
image, and the sacred feast is a perfectly appropriate religious response
to holiness.

It is in this spirit that we can understand the celebratory side of
Yom Kippur. On that day, we remind ourselves that eating is not just a
physical requirement, but a way to experience God's bounty. Hunger, ful-
fillment, want and plenty: these are all windows through which we can

glimpse the Glory. By transcending biology for 25 hours, we too by-pass the food chain and gain our physical nourishment directly from God. This is an occasion for celebration: the fasting of atonement is just half of the ritual of the day: the eve of the Day of Atonement is, according to tradition, to be spent in feasting!

My great aunt Tante Meryashe, of blessed memory, certainly intuited this intertwining of the spiritual and the prandial when she prepared her recipes; all her written instructions used the standard *Yahrzeit* glass as the accepted unit of measure: one *Yahrzeit* glass of flour, a half *Yahrzeit* glass of sugar. To be sure, this synergy is not an excessively subtle point. It's just that when it occurs to us, we usually dismiss it as inauthentic. And, of course, there is that annoying ascetic religious tradition that denies the holiness of the body and sees self-denial as the only path to God. Thankfully, the Sabbaths and festivals of the calendar mitigate against such moroseness.

God is the author of human biology, and we can experience God's presence through our most basic needs and sensations. The procurement, preparation, serving, and enjoyment of food have always been opportunities for a religious encounter. One's table is an altar, one's meals a sacrifice. An old tradition instructs the pious to make their coffins out of their dining-room tables — what better possession to accompany us to the True World than the instrument of hospitality to strangers, of sweet Sabbath melodies, of the celebration of our holy seasons, of words of *Torah* and blessings offered over tea and cake. Moses perceived that standing in the presence of God was a celebration and called for a feast. The reverse is also true: mealtime is an opportunity to stand before God.

Rabbi Dan Shevitz

MENU PLANNING

Appetizers

Baba Ghanouj ~ 282
Ceviche ~ 228
Chopped Liver ~ 132
Easy Gefilte Fish ~ 116
Herring in Sour Cream ~ 33
Kreplech ~ 8
My Grandma's Yaprakes (Turkish
    Style Stuffed Grape Leaves) ~ 242
My Mother's Sweet and Sour Fish ~ 6
Nut and Mushroom Paté ~ 283
Sue's Salmon Roll ~ 140
Tuna-Horseradish Dip ~ 136
Zucchini Pancakes ~ 69

Breads

Banana Bread or Muffins ~ 151
Bran Oatmeal Muffins ~ 85
Carrot Muffins ~ 77
Carrot, Zucchini and Apple
    Muffins ~ 84
Challah ~ 5
Corn Bread Muffins ~ 95
Gougère ~ 86
Nana's Coffee Rolls ~ 166
No Knead to Stay Around the House
    Challah ~ 25
No-Knead Whole Wheat
    Challah ~ 20
Pineapple Bread Pudding ~ 81
Pumpkin Bread ~ 78
Zucchini Bread ~ 24

Chicken

Barbecued Chicken Marinade ~ 178
Bourbon Chicken ~ 199
Chicken Soup ~ 7
Chicken Verdicelieo ~ 218
Chicken with Artichokes ~ 308

Chicken with Cashews ~ 309
Chinese Noodles with Chicken ~ 310
Cinnamon Honey Chicken ~ 9
Cold Sesame Stick Chicken
    Sandwiches ~ 232
Grilled Chicken Caribbean ~ 179
Lo Mein ~ 258
Low-Cholesterol Chicken Curry ~ 311
Low-Sodium Peanuty Chicken ~ 312
Mother's Glorified Veal Chops ~ 219
Noah's Favorite Chicken ~ 274
No-Fail Chicken ~ 208
Orange Chicken ~ 67
Polynesian Chicken ~ 209
Shabbat Chicken ~ 245
Spicy Oriental Chicken Salad with
    Creamy Peanut Sauce ~ 257
Stir-Fried Chicken with Peanuts and
    Hot Peppers ~ 313

Desserts (Dairy)

Apricot Dairy Hamentaschen
    Filling ~ 106
Apricot Squares ~ 39
Banana Bread or Muffins ~ 151
Banana Yogurt Cake ~ 103
Bible Fruit Salad ~ 142
Brown Rice Pudding ~ 152
Chocolate Mousse Torte ~ 135
Cran-apple Crisp ~ 50
Cranberry Crunch ~ 58
Danish Pastries ~ 76
Easy and Delicious Chocolate
    Cake ~ 324
Fresh Fruit Cream Cheese Tarts ~ 167
Grape Freeze ~ 129
Hot Pear Soufflé ~ 332
Italian Plum Cake ~ 200
Lace Wafers ~ 125
Mom's Famous Apple Pie ~ 45
Pineapple Bread Pudding ~ 81
Plantation Cake ~ 38

Desserts (Pareve)

Fish

Kugels

Tofu Dinner ~ 306
Tofu Loaf ~ 307
Tofu with Vegetables ~ 297
Vegetarian Stuffed Cabbage ~ 120

Orange Brown Rice ~ 49
Saffron Rice ~ 246
Thanksgiving Loaf ~ 60

Pasta

Rice

Salads

Vegetables

ROSH HASHANAH DINNER

Serves 10

Kiddush Wine

Challah (shaped into traditional round loaves) ~ 5

Apples and Honey

My Mother's Sweet and Sour Fish ~ 6

Chicken Soup ~ 7
with Kreplech ~ 8

Cinnamon Honey Chicken ~ 9

Bubbie Katie's Tsimmis — double recipe ~ 10

Julienned Zucchini and Summer Squash Sauté

Taiglach ~ 11

Honey Spice Cake ~ 12

Kiddush Wine

Challah (shaped into traditional round loaves) ~ 5

Apples and Honey

Pesto Stuffed Mushrooms ~ 13

Salmon en Papillote — triple recipe ~ 14

Orange Bulgar Pilaf Salad — double recipe ~ 16

Steamed Broccoli Garnished with Sautéed Sliced Almonds

Carrot Salad — double recipe ~ 16

Taiglach ~ 11

Honey Spice Cake ~ 12

A Matter of Standards

In retrospect, her kitchen was tiny. A freestanding sink with a porcelain drainboard, an apartment-sized Frigidaire, a stove, and a pair of wooden cupboards — you wouldn't call them cabinets — with maybe twenty-five or thirty inches of counter beneath them. And a formica table where I sat in the afternoons, along with any of the other grandchildren let loose in the neighborhood.

From that viewing spot, I watched, her back to me as she stood at her workspace, the sink-drain-countertop circuit, and churned out vast quantities of food: a hundred pieces of gefilte fish, gallons of soup, pans of stuffed cabbage, cakes. Maybe it was Rosh Hashanah, maybe it was Passover. There would be her six children with their spouses, each with two or three kids, plus miscellaneous relatives. We would all eventually be seated at a table that ran from the foyer through the living room and into the bedroom, set with bright red, depression glassware that ran down the table like ribbons.

She'd cook, I'd sit, and every once in a while, she'd turn around, face me and hold out an offering. "Here, *bubbala*, a piece for you." Honey cake or maybe sponge, mandelbrot or a cookie. I ate appreciatively — she did not press food upon us, believed in moderation — she turned back, and I continued my watch from the table, smelling the soup on the stove, hearing her chopping on the board, and gazing upon the efficient motions of her back, the apron ties running down her housedress.

She was not a talkative woman, which was fine with me since my mother, one of her four daughters, was. She didn't fuss or coo, or utter hysterical *"oy gevalts!"* if someone in her building, or ours across the alley, went to the hospital, or if another family took the big step and moved out of the Bronx to Westchester or Long Island. Manners and moderation were important to her. So were standards. Like the correct length of a hem: I modeled every new dress for her approval, stiffly posing in her living room with the Ed Sullivan show on in the background while she scrutinized me with her seamstress's eye, a pin in her mouth, and said something to my mother like, "Nu, Selma, it's too long. A half an inch and it will be perfect."

Of course, her high standards also applied to food. By 1960, when most of her children had moved to the suburbs, we began having family celebrations in one of the more spacious houses, at first only on Thanksgiving, and later on Passover, when the daughters insisted it was too much for her. That first year — she was seventy, I was ten — my rich uncle, a six-foot-six obstetrician whose hobbies ran to needlepoint and gourmet cooking, made the meal. Among its many features were banana fritters and asparagus vinaigrette. My grandmother was not impressed. She raised her eyebrows, shrugged, and told me discreetly he had it all backwards. "What, this is cooking? He cooks the fruit and leaves the vegetables cold? Feh."

From her point of view, the family meals probably went downhill from there. My gourmet uncle continued to experiment on Thanksgiving, and Passover was moved to our suburban house with its large dining room and fancy white dishes holding a purchased-once-a-year-kosher-turkey-for-grandma which she wouldn't eat anyway. ("She doesn't trust me!" my mother cried to me in the kitchen.) It was slipping away from her and she knew it: the traife kitchens, the families all far-flung, the jarred gefilte fish, her grandchildren with the gentiles, even the arbitrary hemlines. She'd sit at our spacious table in the carpeted dining room and pick at her food. I ate my mother's second generation cooking: soup, turkey, brisket, coleslaw, sweet potatoes with marshmallows. It wasn't really so different. But I'd glance over at my grandmother picking at the hard-boiled eggs my mother had made for her in the special saucepan kept in the closet for her visits, and see her staring down the length of the table. Looking for bright red ribbons, looking for something familiar, looking for what we'd lost.

Joan Leegant

"Taking" Challah (Hafrashat Challah)

Before baking challah (or any other bread), we remove a piece of the dough, no smaller than the size of an olive, and say this *bracha*:

בָּרוּךְ אַתָּה, יְיָ אֱלֹהֵינוּ, מֶלֶךְ הָעוֹלָם, אֲשֶׁר קִדְּשָׁנוּ בְּמִצְוֹתָיו,
וְצִוָּנוּ לְהַפְרִישׁ חַלָּה.

"Blessed are You, Lord our God, King of the Universe, who has sanctified us with *mitzvot* and commanded us to separate *challah*."

We then burn the dough on the floor of the hot oven.

The word *challah* originally refers not to the whole loaf, but to the piece of dough that is separated. *Challah* is not taken from a batch of dough which is less than three and a half pounds. If the quantity is in doubt, *challah* may be separated without a *bracha*. If one forgets to separate *challah*, the bread may still be eaten.

In Numbers 15:17-21, God commands Moses to bid the Israelites set aside a piece of dough, called *challah*, as a tax for the benefit of the *kohanim* (priests). Although nowadays the *kohanim* may not consume this gift, the custom has prevailed for centuries, in identification with the ancient system of self-taxation of the Jews of Israel. Many households keep a *tzedaka* box handy, and use the occasion of "taking" *challah* as an opportunity to contribute to an appropriate charity.

Rabbi Dan Shevitz

Challah

P

Joan Gadon

Baking this challah puts me in the spirit of Shabbat and the chagim — the house smells festive. I love to bake it with a friend.

4 packages dry yeast (about 3 tablespoons)
3 cups warm water
1 cup vegetable oil
11 cups all-purpose flour
4 eggs, beaten

³/₄ cup sugar
4 teaspoons salt
1 egg beaten with ¹/₂ teaspoon sugar
Sesame seeds

In a bowl, mix the yeast, 1¹/₂ cups warm water and oil, and set aside.

In a large bowl, mix the flour, eggs, sugar, salt, and remaining 1¹/₂ cups warm water. Add the dissolved yeast mixture, mix together and knead well. If using an electric kneader, do not knead for more than 5 minutes or the bread will taste too "yeasty." Cover with a towel and let rise 1¹/₂ hours.

Preheat oven to 375°.

Punch down, "take" challah (*hafrashat challah*, see page 4) and divide into six loaves. Divide the dough for each loaf into three equal parts. Roll each portion into a rope about 1 inch in diameter on a lightly floured board. Braid the three ropes together beginning in the middle and working toward one end. Invert and braid toward the other end. Press the ends together very firmly and seal them with a little water, or tuck ends under securely.

Place all six challots on cookie sheet sprayed with vegetable oil, and let rise again uncovered for another hour. Brush on the glaze of egg and sugar and sprinkle with sesame seeds. Bake for 25 minutes.

The loaves freeze well.

Yields 6 large challot

Variation: For Rosh Hashanah, add 1 cup golden raisins. Instead of braiding the dough, roll each piece into a snake and shape it into a circle or spiral. Bake the challot in a baking pan rather than on a cookie sheet.

My Mother's Sweet and Sour Fish

 Rabbi Richard J. Israel

This is a wonderful cold Yom Tov dish. It tastes best made with lake trout (our family is from the Midwest) which is available elsewhere in the country, although it can be expensive, unless it arrives in the arms of a visiting relative. The fish can be served as an appetizer or as part of a larger meal. It is also a wonderful snack or light meal served simply with bread and butter. The taste improves as the refrigerated fish sits in its juice for a few days. It can be kept frozen in its liquid for a long time so I make it whenever I get a good buy on the right fish. It can be cooked in the summer and eaten on Sukkot or later. Warning: if served outside on a warm day, the wasps will love it!

My mother got this recipe from her mother, who in turn probably got it from hers. It is a simple recipe, but one whose smell always declares Yom Tov for me. An 80-year-old friend to whom I recently served it said, "It has such a Jewish taste! I haven't had it since I was a little girl." I am not sure what a Jewish taste is, but this one comes with so many memories that she might be right.

4 medium or large onions, sliced

3 pounds (or more) 1-inch steaks from a fatty fish such as lake trout or salmon

1 teaspoon salt

1/2 teaspoon pepper

1 bay leaf (optional)

1 cup golden raisins

2 tablespoons sour salt/citric acid, less if used in rock form (available in the kosher section of supermarkets)

2 cups sugar (sugar and sour salt can be reduced up to one-half for a milder flavor)

Place onions on the bottom of a large pot. Add fish, salt and pepper, optional bay leaf, and raisins and enough cold water to cover the fish. Bring to a boil, cover, and boil gently for 30 minutes. Add sour salt, reduce heat to a simmer, and cook covered for another 30 minutes. Add sugar and continue simmering covered for 1 to 1 1/2 hours until the fish is tender (overcooking may make it tough).

Remove from heat, remove bay leaf, and cool. Freeze fish in its liquid or transfer all to a serving dish and refrigerate. Serve cold.

Serves 6–8

Chicken Soup

  Rita Feuerstadt

6–7 quarts cold water
1 ½–2 pullets, cleaned
and cut into eighths
(depending on size)
1 leek, trimmed and rinsed
carefully to remove grit
2 parsnips, whole or cut into
chunks

6 carrots, whole or cut into
chunks
3 celery stalks, including leaves
3 onions, peeled and left whole
1 bunch fresh dill, tied together
for easy removal
Kosher salt and pepper, to taste

Bring water to boil in a very large pot. Add the pullets and remaining ingredients. Cover pot and simmer about 2 hours, skimming the fat occasionally, until the chicken is tender. Remove chicken, vegetables, and dill. Let soup cool to room temperature.

Refrigerate until cold and remove the fat that has congealed on top. Reheat the soup, adding the chicken meat and/or vegetables, if desired. Taste and adjust seasonings.

Serve with kreplach (recipe follows) if desired.

Serves about 16

Kreplech

 Helen Santis

These are delicious and provide a great way to use leftover meat. The dough is very sticky: be patient, the result is well worth the effort.

1 tablespoon chicken fat
5 eggs
1½ pounds ground roasted meat (leftover turkey, veal brisket, or beef)
4 cups all-purpose flour

1 teaspoon salt
1 teaspoon sugar
1 cup cold water
6 quarts water
1 tablespoon salt

In a bowl, combine chicken fat, 1 egg, and meat, and set aside.

To prepare the dough, place flour on a cutting board or in a bowl. Form a well in the flour and add 4 eggs, salt, and sugar. Blend while slowly adding the one cup of water. Cut dough into 4 pieces and roll out each piece with a rolling pin until it is about ¼-inch thick. Cut the rolled dough into 2-inch squares. Place 1 teaspoon of meat mixture in each square, then fold into a triangular shape. Press the edges together to seal.

Bring the water and salt to a boil in an 8-quart pot. Drop the triangles in, 10 or 12 at a time. Cook for 10 minutes, then remove from boiling water. At this point kreplach may be a) eaten, or b) dropped into chicken soup. (They can also be baked and served as hors d'oeuvres. If baking, par-boil them until they are soft but not completely cooked, about 5 minutes, smear them with chicken fat or margarine, and bake for 10 minutes at 350° until golden brown or crispy.)

Once removed from boiling water and cooled, kreplech can be frozen. Place them on a foil-lined cookie sheet, not touching each other. When frozen, store in plastic bags.

Yields about 5 dozen

Cinnamon Honey Chicken

   Deborah Guthermann

This is one of our favorite Shabbat "company" dinners. Start marinating the chicken the night before.

Marinade:

1¹/₂ cups dry sherry (use cooking sherry for Pesach)
2 tablespoons cinnamon
1 cup honey
¹/₃ cup lime juice

Zest of one lime
2 large cloves garlic, crushed
Salt and freshly ground black pepper, to taste
3 3-pound chickens, cut into eighths

To prepare the marinade, mix together sherry, cinnamon, honey, lime juice, lime zest, garlic, salt and pepper.

Arrange chicken pieces in a single layer in a shallow, nonaluminum, ovenproof pan. Pour marinade over the chicken, turning pieces to coat well. Refrigerate overnight, longer if desired, turning pieces occasionally.

Preheat oven to 350°.

Drain marinade and reserve. Bake chicken uncovered for 40 to 50 minutes, depending on size of pieces, basting with marinade and turning once or twice. If you like crispy skin, bake a little less and then broil until done.

Serves 8, at least

Bubbie Katie's Tsimmis

 Linda Bick-Helfgott

Good for any holiday!

6 large carrots, sliced on the diagonal
1 cup pitted prunes
2 sweet potatoes, cut into chunks

1/2 cup honey or 1/4 cup sugar
2 tablespoons pareve margarine
1 teaspoon all-purpose flour
1/2 cup cold water

In a medium-sized pot, place carrots, prunes, and sweet potatoes with enough water to cover. Cook uncovered over medium heat until the vegetables are tender, about 20 to 30 minutes. (Do not let them get too soft.) Add honey and margarine.

Preheat oven to 350°.

Place the carrot mixture in a 2½-quart casserole. Combine flour and water and pour on top. Bake until most of the juice is evaporated and carrots stick together, about 45 minutes. (It may take a little longer.)

Serves 4–6

Taiglach

 Jane Ravid

This honeyed dessert is made by Lithuanian Jews for happy occasions.
It is especially appropriate for Rosh Hashanah, expressing hope for a sweet
new year.

4 cups all-purpose flour
1 1/2 teaspoons baking powder
6 eggs
2 teaspoons sugar
3 tablespoons vegetable oil
1 tablespoon lemon or
   orange zest

1 1/2 cups honey
1 cup sugar
2 teaspoons powdered ginger
1 cup chopped walnuts
1/2 cup shredded coconut
   (optional)

Sift flour with baking powder. In a medium bowl mix together, in
order, eggs, sugar, oil, zest, and flour mixture until smooth and soft,
but firm enough to knead with your hands. Roll into balls about
2-inches in diameter, then into long ropes 1/2-inch in diameter, and
cut into 1/2-inch pieces.

    Preheat oven to 375°.

    Bring honey, sugar, and ginger to boil in a wide ovenproof pan.
Drop the dough pieces into pan. Bake for 20 minutes, keeping the
door closed. Remove pan, add nuts, and stir carefully with a wooden
spoon to separate the pieces. Return to oven and bake 45 minutes to
1 hour, until golden.

    Wet a board with cold water and pour the cooked mixture onto
it. Sprinkle with optional coconut. Cool. Break up and trim pieces
before serving.

Serves 10

Honey Spice Cake

 Nurit Kussell

This is a delicious honey cake and it only uses one bowl for the batter.

4 eggs
1 scant cup sugar
1 ounce whiskey
1 teaspoon ground allspice
1 tart apple, grated
½ cup corn oil
1 cup honey
1½ teaspoons orange zest

⅓ cup strong coffee
Scant ¼ cup orange juice
2⅔ cups all-purpose flour
4 teaspoons baking powder
2 teaspoons baking soda
1½ cups raisins
⅓ cup ground walnuts

Preheat oven to 350°.

Combine all ingredients in the bowl of an electric mixer and beat at medium speed until well blended. Bake in a large greased tube pan for 50 minutes or until a toothpick inserted comes out clean.

This cake freezes well.

Serves 12–14

Pesto Stuffed Mushrooms

 Ivy Feuerstadt

This pesto also makes a delicious sauce for pasta — there's enough here for six servings. Just blend a tablespoon or two of the hot water in which the pasta was boiled into the pesto, toss with pasta, and serve.

3 cloves garlic
2 cups fresh basil leaves
1/2 cup olive oil
1/4 cup freshly grated
   Romano cheese
1/4 cup freshly grated
   Parmesan cheese

Kosher salt, to taste
1/2 cup butter, softened
4 tablespoons pine nuts
20 large mushrooms for stuffing

Mince garlic in food processor. Add basil, olive oil, cheeses, and salt. Blend until completely smooth. Add butter and blend. Stir in the pine nuts by hand.

Preheat oven to 350°.

Clean and stem the mushrooms. Fill the mushrooms caps with pesto and bake for about 10 minutes until hot and bubbly.

Pesto freezes well, so make extra and pour it in ice cube trays, then pop the frozen cubes into ziplock bags. You'll have pesto all year long!

Serves 10, yields 1 1/2–2 cups pesto

Salmon en Papillote

Jean Jacques Paimblane, Executive Chef,
Legal Sea Foods, Boston, Massachusetts

Not only salmon, but trout, flounder, whiting, virtually any white, firm-fleshed fish tastes especially delicious when cooked en papillote, *or in a package. The steam generated within the paper wrappers keeps the fish moist and succulent. Then the entire package is placed before your guest, who opens it up and is met with all the marvelous aromas trapped within.*

Parchment paper works the best for your packages. It can be purchased in a specialty kitchen store. Your next choice would be brown butcher's paper; but not brown paper bags, which are chemically treated. Cut four sheets of paper. Each sheet, when folded in half, should be 2 to 4 inches longer and wider than your fillets — you don't want to crowd the ingredients. Fold the paper, and trace half a heart on it, with the fold running through the middle of the heart, using the entire paper. Cut out the heart. Repeat with the other three pieces of paper.

The fish-filled packages can be held in the refrigerator for several hours. Remove 30 minutes before cooking to allow them to come to room temperature.

1 carrot	2 pounds salmon fillet, divided
1 stalk celery	into 4 pieces
1 leek	4 teaspoons dry white wine
9 tablespoons butter	1 tablespoon minced fresh
Salt and pepper, to taste	parsley
4 teaspoons minced shallots	Melted butter

Preheat oven to 375°.

Cut carrot, celery, and leek into julienne, about ⅛ inch wide by 2 to 3 inches long, to make ½ cup each. Place the carrot in a small sauté pan with 2 tablespoons butter and a light sprinklng of salt and pepper. Sauté over medium-low heat for 2 minutes. Add celery, cook for 2 more minutes, then add leek. Sauté until all the vegetables are cooked, but still quite firm. Remove pan from heat, cover, and allow vegetables to steam so that they will not toughen.

Butter ½ of one paper heart, using about 1 tablespoon butter. Season lightly with salt and pepper, and sprinkle 1 teaspoon shallots on each buttered half. Place a fillet atop shallots, season lightly with salt and pepper, cover with ¼ of the julienned vegetables. Moisten with 1 teaspoon of wine and dot with 1½ teaspoons of butter. Garnish with a scant teaspoon of minced parsley. Repeat for each heart. Fold the unbuttered half of the heart over the fish. Beginning at the seam, seal each package by making narrow folds an inch or two in length around the perimeter. Each fold will serve to anchor the preceding one. The last fold can be double-sealed by turning the point of the heart up upon itself.

Butter a cookie sheet or other ovenproof pan with the remaining tablespoon of butter and set the four fish packages onto it. Bake for 12 minutes. Serve each guest an entire package accompanied by a small dish of melted butter.

Serves 4

Orange Bulgar Pilaf Salad

 Barbara Linder

1 large onion, chopped
4 tablespoons olive or
  corn oil
2 cups raw bulgar
Rind of two large, brightly
  colored oranges
3½ cups hot vegetable broth
⅓ cup currants

Salt and pepper, to taste
½ cup pine nuts, toasted

Garnishes (optional):
½ cup parsley, chopped
½ cup scallions, chopped

Sauté the onions in oil in a medium-sized pot over low heat until soft. Add bulgar and orange rind and cook for one minute. Add the broth and currants and simmer until all the liquid is absorbed, about 5 to 10 minutes. Fluff pilaf with a fork and let cool. Add salt and pepper while cooling — this dish needs salt. When cooled, add pine nuts. Garnish with parsley and scallions, if desired. Best served at room temperature.

Serves 4–6

Carrot Salad

  Judy Adnepos

4 cups grated carrots
½ cup raisins
¼ cup cider vinegar

¼ cup honey
¼ cup plain nonfat yogurt
½ cup light mayonnaise

Place the carrots and raisins in a bowl. Whisk together the remaining ingredients and pour over the carrots. Mix well and refrigerate for several hours.

Serves 6

EREV YOM KIPPUR DINNER

Serves 4

*To ensure an easier fast, the pareve menu includes simple, hearty foods
that are low in protein and fat, high in carbohydrates, and caffeine-free.
This meal can be made ahead, with the exception of boiling the water for
the pasta, broccoli and tea. May you have an easy fast!*

גמר חתימה טובה

gamar hatimah tovah

No-Knead Whole Wheat Challah ~ 20
Mushroom Barley Soup ~ 22
Pasta with Creamy Peanut Sauce ~ 23
Steamed Broccoli
Zucchini Bread ~ 24
Herbal Tea

No Knead to Stay around the House Challah ~ 25
Homemade Tomato Soup ~ 26
Whole Roast Chicken
Oven Roasted Potatoes ~ 27
Steamed Broccoli
Cortland Apple Pie ~ 28
Herbal Tea

Fast Food

Fasting is no fun. It isn't supposed to be. But it is held in high esteem by many religious traditions and health regimens. On a major holy day like Yom Kippur, even Jews who wouldn't think of entering a synagogue will nevertheless fast because they believe it to be good for either the body or the spirit, or both. In the Jewish religious tradition, the discomfort that is produced by neither eating nor drinking is thought to have instructional value, to help us reflect on our human frailty. This does not mean that Jews are intended to make themselves as miserable as possible on Yom Kippur. Yet the discomfort some people experience is so extreme, they forget why they are fasting.

Not only is eating wisely tricky, so is fasting wisely. Here are some strategies that may make the day a little easier, leaving you less aware of physical aspects of the fast than the spiritual ones.

It may be hard to believe twenty or so hours into a fast but, if stranded without food in the wilderness, most healthy adults could survive well over a month without eating. Most of the unpleasantness does not come from lack of food, but from lack of fluid. The solution therefore is to superhydrate beforehand. "Camel up" before a fast by drinking a great deal the prior afternoon — perhaps two quarts well in advance of your final pre-fast meal. At the time, you may feel you are going to float away. Before the fast is over, you will be glad you did it. Diluted orange juice is good here, as is water. Beer or other alcoholic beverages, however, will dehydrate you.

Although you should drink a lot before a fast, you do not need to stuff yourself with food. Eat a normal meal but emphasize carbohydrates like potato or noodle dishes, not proteins or fats. Carbohydrates bond with water, so your body can go on drinking them in when it needs to during your fast. Proteins do not. Most of the dramatic but limited weight loss people on high-protein diets experience is water that protein molecules cannot hold on to or bring into the system. You want that water around during a fast.

I have heard of grandmothers in Europe who fed their families immense starch meals for the better part of the week before a fast and then, at the final meal, encouraged everyone to eat heavy meat dishes. The carbohydrates taken early would provide the necessary water reservoir. The last-minute meat meal would give the comfort of a full stomach for a number of hours. This kind of pre-fast diet might have been suitable, a celebration of souls, for a culture in which meat was a rarity and people were close to involuntary fasting through much of the year. What people who still eat this way before a fast have to consider is whether they really want to take on all those calories.

Fast food need not be hopelessly bland, but go easy on the salt and pepper, which may make you thirsty. Season with non-irritating spices and herbs.

The nausea and headaches often complained of during a fast are likely as not the results of caffeine withdrawal. If you are a heavy coffee or cola drinker, start tapering off a week or so before the fast, since withdrawal is less of a problem while you are eating and drinking regularly. Unless you are used to a great deal of caffeine, one cup less a day, with the day before the fast being caffeine-free, will usually do it. Using decaffeinated coffee during this period may help you fool your system.

A brief fast is not a quick weight-loss scheme. An average adult will burn 2,000 to 2,500 calories, about two-thirds of a pound, during a twenty-four-hour fast. It doesn't take long at all to put that back on again. A couple of pieces of cheesecake and you will be just about even. Most of the weight loss that you see on the scale the day or two after a fast is fluid that you will quickly replace.

After the fast, be careful not to gorge yourself. Since the body protects itself from starvation when you are not eating by slowing down the rate at which it burns food, the calories you take on right after a fast will stay with you a lot longer than those acquired when your metabolism is once again functioning at full speed.

These suggestions will not prevent you from experiencing the fast. If you are not eating or drinking for twenty-four to twenty-six hours, there is no chance you will forget that you are fasting. But it is important for you to be able to focus on some soul-searching and prayer, rather than on your complaining stomach.

So prepare yourself for fasting, both physically and spiritually, and in the words of one of the traditional greetings, have an easy fast!

Rabbi Richard J. Israel, adapted from an article published under this title in The Kosher Pig *(Alef Design Group, 1993).*

No-Knead Whole Wheat Challah

 Alisa Israel Goldberg

This recipe is a version of one which came to me from our good friends Ellie and Josh Cohen. Ellie and Josh like to use a variety of flours, including whole wheat, rye, oat and soy, along with the white. My version is a simplified one, using only whole wheat and white flours, but you might like to experiment with some of the others. Ellie and Josh also double the recipe, freezing what they don't use right away. However, I have found that this is such an easy and relatively quick recipe that I don't mind making it fresh each time.

The instructions below read "knead," belying this recipe's title. I have used the term only for lack of a better way to describe how to squish and pat the dough until it comes together. The dough really doesn't need to be, nor should be, truly kneaded.

The resulting challah has a dense, almost cakey texture, and is best served warm.

3 packages dry yeast (about 2 tablespoons)
1 tablespoon brown sugar
$^3/_4$ cup warm water
3 cups whole wheat flour
3 cups unbleached white flour (more, if necessary)
$1^1/_2$ teaspoons salt

3 eggs
$^2/_3$ cup vegetable oil
$^1/_2$ cup water
$^1/_2$ cup honey
1 egg beaten with 1–2 teaspoons water
Sesame seeds

Mix yeast and brown sugar with warm water in a bowl. Let stand for about 5 minutes or until mixture starts to bubble a bit. If it doesn't bubble, it's not working: try again.

Meanwhile, in the bowl of an electric mixer, mix the flours and salt. Set aside. In another bowl, mix eggs, oil, water, and honey. Set aside.

When yeast has proofed (bubbled), add to flour and salt mixture and mix on low speed. With mixer going, add egg mixture and continue mixing on medium speed until the dough has come together. If necessary, add unbleached white flour as you are mixing. The dough will remain fairly soft, but it shouldn't be sticky.

Turn the dough out onto a counter or a board, and knead it a few times just to smooth it out. Form it into a ball. This "kneading" should not take more than one minute. Place the ball of dough in a large, well-oiled bowl, turning the dough to oil all the surfaces. Cover with a towel and let rise in a warm, non-drafty place for about two hours, or until doubled in size.

Preheat oven to 325°.

"Take" challah (*hafrashat challah*, see page 4). Divide the dough into loaves. I usually make 2 medium-large loaves and 2 small rolls. Then divide the dough for each loaf into 3 equal parts. Roll each portion into a rope about 1-inch in diameter on a lightly floured board. This dough can take a lot of rolling to get it smooth enough to braid. I often end up just braiding the cracks underneath where they won't show as much. Braid the three ropes together beginning in the middle and working toward one end. Invert and braid toward the other end. Press the ends together very firmly and seal them with a little water.

Place on a lightly greased baking sheet. Brush the tops of the loaves with the egg and water glaze, then sprinkle with sesame seeds.

Bake for about 30 to 40 minutes. Small rolls will take less time. Challah is done when both top and bottom are browned and it makes a hollow sound when tapped. If after about 30 minutes the outside is browning too quickly, turn the oven down to 300° and/or cover challah with foil and continue baking.

Challah freezes quite well. Wrap it up in foil while it is still warm, wrap again in a plastic bag and freeze. When ready to serve, defrost, remove plastic, and heat up in the foil wrapping.

Yields 2 medium loaves and 2 small loaves

Mushroom-Barley Soup

 Robbie Fein

This soup is great before a fast, with just a little tamari sauce.

9 cups water
1 large onion, chopped
2 celery stalks, chopped
   (including leaves)
2–3 carrots, chopped
1 cup barley
8 ounces mushrooms, sliced

1 teaspoon tarragon
1/4 teaspoon thyme
1/4 teaspoon garlic powder
Pepper, to taste
2–3 tablespoons tamari sauce
   (more to taste or enough to
   lend brown color to soup)

Bring water to boil in a large pot and add the onion, celery, carrots, barley, and mushrooms. Simmer 1 1/2 hours, covered. Add herbs and spices and simmer another 30 minutes, covered. Add tamari sauce and heat for a few minutes, but do not boil.

When reheating, the barley will soak up more liquid, so add more water, tamari sauce, and garlic powder to taste.

Serves 6

Pasta with Creamy Peanut Sauce

   Brenda Freishtat

1 pound pasta
1 1/2 cups creamy peanut
  sauce (see below)

Cook pasta according to directions. Toss pasta with sauce and serve immediately.

Serves 4–6

Creamy Peanut Sauce

   Brenda Freishtat

When making the peanut sauce, you can use vegetable broth to make it pareve. It tastes great on noodles as a cold pasta salad.

1/2 cup smooth, creamy
  peanut butter
1/3 cup chicken or vegetable
  stock[1]
1/4 cup tamari or soy sauce
4 tablespoons toasted
  sesame oil
2 tablespoons garlic, minced
2 tablespoons peeled and
  minced ginger root

2 tablespoons sugar
2 tablespoons red wine vinegar
1–2 teaspoons hot pepper oil, or
  to taste (be careful, the sauce
  gets hotter as it sits out)[2]
1/4 cup plain, whole soy milk
  (available in natural food
  stores)

Blend all the ingredients except the soy milk in a food processor until smooth. Add soy milk and blend until smooth.

Yields 1 1/2 cups

[1]Erev Yom Kippur Dinner: use 1/3 cup warm water instead
[2]Erev Yom Kippur Dinner: omit hot pepper oil

Zucchini Bread

 Varda E. Farber

This is a great recipe for gardeners who have too many zucchini all at once. Deliciously moist, it can be served as a bread or as a simple cake.

3 eggs
1½ cups sugar
¾ cup vegetable oil
1 tablespoon vanilla extract
2 cups grated zucchini
1 cup all-purpose flour
1 cup whole wheat pastry
   flour or whole wheat flour

1 tablespoon cinnamon
2 teaspoons baking soda
1 teaspoon salt
¼ teaspoon baking powder
½ cup nuts, chopped
½ cup raisins

Preheat oven to 350°. Grease two loaf pans. In a large bowl, beat eggs until frothy. Add sugar, oil, and vanilla and beat until thick and frothy. Stir in zucchini, flours, cinnamon, baking soda, salt, and baking powder. Fold in nuts and raisins.

   Pour into loaf pans. Bake for about 1 hour or until a tester inserted in the center comes out clean. Cool 10 minutes in the pan, then transfer to a rack.

   This bread freezes well.

Yields 2 small loaves

No Knead To Stay around the House Challah

 P   Joan Leegant

2 cups lukewarm water
1/2–1/3 cup honey
1 teaspoon salt
2 packages dry yeast (about
   1 1/2 tablespoons)
3 eggs
1/2 cup vegetable oil

6 1/2–7 cups flour, more if needed
   (use all unbleached white or
   up to 2 cups whole wheat)
1/2 cup raisins (optional)
1 egg yolk mixed with
   1 tablespoon water
Sesame or poppy seeds (optional)

Mix water, honey, and salt in a small bowl. Sprinkle in the yeast and mix. Leave yeast mixture for about 5 minutes, until it bubbles.

To make by hand, mix eggs and oil in a large bowl; add yeast mixture and stir. Add flour and optional raisins, mixing well.

If using a food processor, process eggs and oil for a few seconds. Add 5 cups of flour at once, then process for about 5 to 10 seconds. Add remaining flour and process until dough forms into a ball. Once it has done so, add enough extra flour so that it isn't too sticky to get out of the processor. Do not knead the dough. Mix in optional raisins.

Oil a large bowl. Place dough into bowl, turning it once to evenly oil all surfaces. Grease a piece of waxed paper, place greased side on top of the dough, then cover the bowl with a towel. Place in refrigerator overnight.

Punch down the risen dough. Let it rest a few minutes while you grease cookie sheets. Divide dough in half, "take" challah (*hafrashat challah*, see page 4), then divide the dough for each loaf into 3 equal parts. Roll each portion into a rope about 1-inch in diameter on a lightly floured board. Braid the three ropes together beginning in the middle and working toward one end. Invert and braid toward the other end. Press the ends together very firmly and seal them with a little water. Cover and let rise for 1 hour.

Preheat the oven to 350°.

Brush the loaves with the egg and water glaze, sprinkle with seeds, and bake for 30 to 35 minutes. Challah is done when top and bottom are browned and it sounds hollow when tapped.

Yields 2 loaves

Homemade Tomato Soup

  Hilary Greenberg

This is a perfect light first course for a meat meal. A real change from the usual. Can easily be doubled.

$^1/_2$ cup minced onion

3 tablespoons pareve margarine

2 large fresh tomatoes, chopped

2 cups chicken stock

1 cup dry white wine

Pinch of sugar (optional)

$^1/_4$ cup fresh mint leaves, chopped

Sauté onion in margarine over medium heat until just soft, add tomatoes and heat through. Purée in food processor. Strain through a sieve to remove seeds.

Combine in a pot with chicken stock, wine and optional sugar. Simmer for about 15 minutes.

Garnish with fresh mint leaves.

Serves 4

Oven Roasted Potatoes

  Alisa Israel Goldberg

3 pounds potatoes,
  preferably small and new
6 tablespoons unsalted
  pareve margarine or butter
3 tablespoons olive oil
4 cloves garlic, crushed

$1/2$ teaspoons dried thyme
$1^1/2$ teaspoons dried rosemary
$1^1/2$ teaspoons paprika
Dash of cayenne pepper
Salt and pepper, to taste

Preheat oven to 400°.

Scrub potatoes and cut into chunks if large. Put margarine and oil in roasting pan, and place in oven until margarine melts. Remove from oven. Add garlic, thyme, rosemary, paprika, and cayenne. Add potato chunks and toss to coat well. Roast, stirring occasionally, until tender inside and starting to brown outside, about 40 minutes. Season with salt and pepper and serve.

Serves 4–6

Cortland Apple Pie

  Alisa Israel Goldberg

This pie is particularly mouthwatering served à la mode with pareve "ice cream."

3³/₄ cups all-purpose flour
¹/₂ teaspoon salt
14 tablespoons pareve margarine
4–6 tablespoons iced water
3 pounds Cortland apples, peeled, cored, and sliced (if Cortlands are not available, use Northern Spy, Staymans, Winesap, or Baldwin)

¹/₂ cup plus 1 tablespoon sugar
2 teaspoons cinnamon
¹/₂ teaspoon nutmeg
2 teaspoons vanilla extract
³/₄–1 cup golden raisins
1 egg, beaten

To prepare the crust, combine 3 cups flour, salt, and margarine in food processor and mix until crumbly, about 5 seconds (or use a bowl). Add only enough iced water to form a rough dough (you may not need it all). Turn the dough out. Divide in half, form each into a patty, wrap in plastic wrap, and refrigerate for at least ¹/₂ hour.

Combine apples, remaining flour, ¹/₂ cup sugar, spices, vanilla, and raisins. Let stand at room temperature until dough is ready.

Preheat oven to 400°.

Roll out half the dough on a floured surface and place it in a 10-inch pie plate. Spoon in filling mixture. Roll out other half, lay over pie, and pinch the top and bottom crusts together gently to seal. Crimp decoratively if desired. Cut 3 or 4 slits into the upper crust. Bake for 40 minutes and remove from oven.

Brush crust with beaten egg, sprinkle with remaining sugar and return to oven. Bake for another 10 to 15 minutes until you can see the juices bubbling in the slits on top and the crust is golden brown.

Serves 8

Variation: Use whole wheat flour for sprinkling on the counter and rolling pin when rolling out the dough to add a bit of color and texture.

BREAK FAST BUFFET

Serves 18–20

*This extensive buffet can be made two days in
advance for quick reheating and serving. The baked
desserts can be made ahead and frozen.*

Aunt Pearl's Noodle Kugel

Until I went to college, I had never even heard the word "kugel." I grew up in a home where the culinary traditions were Swiss (my mother to this day speaks with a French accent), rather than Jewish.

We did, however, maintain connections to the Rumanian heritage of my father's family. Aunt Pearl, the eldest sister in a family of seven children in which my father was the baby, had an unchallenged reputation as the best cook of all the family.

When Aunt Pearl married Uncle Lou, she stepped out of the garment district into a well-heeled life that epitomized that of the German Jews who had settled in New York City in the late nineteenth century. Aunt Pearl and Uncle Lou belonged to Temple Emanuel, a flashy monument to the great wealth of these immigrants, constructed by German reform Jews right on Fifth Avenue. They had an apartment on Central Park West, down the block from the Plaza Hotel, and a beach house next to the dunes in Lido Beach, Long Island. Most important, they had a Thursday night subscription to the Metropolitan Opera, with ninth row orchestra seats. Yet, despite the fancy life they led, Aunt Pearl's house in Lido always smelled of her cooking — exotic, eastern European Jewish cooking.

My younger sister fully appreciated my Aunt Pearl's special talents at a very early age. I was too fascinated with the mysteries of her green linoleum kitchen to ever fix on what we ate there. I was distracted, for example, by Aunt Pearl's ritualistic charring of an eggplant on the gas burner of her stove. The secret and essential prelude, she informed me, to making her famous "potle jella" (eggplant relish). Meanwhile, my sister clamored for Aunt Pearl's noodle pudding. She ate quantities of the stuff, while I suspiciously eyed the raisins.

After several consecutive visits during which we were served my sister's "favorite dish," I began to come around, although I was slow to admit its virtues publicly. I wondered about its place in the food universe. It seemed odd to me that I was eating "pudding" alongside my main course. In those days, raisins and slivered almonds were unlikely accompaniments to a vegetable. And noodles were supposed to be slippery and hard to maneuver, not heavy and easily stabbed. But the sweet and fragrant consistency of the dish was comforting. Its spicy aroma filled the house, beckoning to us. And it gave my sister and me welcome relief from the thick, garlicky slices of pot roast with which it was served.

The noodle pudding delighted our senses and filled our stomachs, but now I see that Aunt Pearl's faithfully remembering to cook it each time we visited was, above all, an act of love.

Amelia Welt Katzen

Aunt Pearl's Noodle Kugel

 Amelia Welt Katzen

After searching our recipe files in vain for a scrap that might reveal Aunt Pearl's recipe for noodle pudding, my mother turned up the following recipe from her own dog-eared notebook. This noodle pudding, since it is dairy, can't give anyone relief from the pot roast, but it's great for breaking the fast on Yom Kippur.

2 eggs
2 apples, sliced
1 cup golden raisins
$\frac{1}{2}$ cup broken walnuts or
   almond slivers
$\frac{1}{3}$ cup vegetable oil
1 cup lowfat cottage cheese

1 cup lowfat plain yogurt
1 tablespoon sugar
$\frac{1}{2}$ teaspoon cinnamon
$\frac{1}{2}$ teaspoon nutmeg
$\frac{1}{2}$ teaspoon salt
1 pound medium noodles,
   cooked and drained

Preheat oven to 350°.

In a large bowl mix all the ingredients, except noodles. Fold in the noodles and put into a greased 9 x 13-inch baking dish.

Bake covered for 30 minutes. Uncover and bake an additional 10 minutes.

Serves 10–12

Cheese and Spinach Casserole

 Karen Montner-Silverman

This tasty casserole has been a dinner favorite for many years (even my kids love it!). The cheeses form a delicious "crust" when baked.

3 eggs
2 cups cottage cheese
1 cup grated Swiss cheese
1 cup grated Cheddar cheese
6 tablespoons flour —
  ½ unbleached white,
  ½ whole wheat (substitute
  matzoh meal for Pesach)

1 teaspoon garlic powder
1 teaspoon salt
10 ounces fresh spinach torn
  into bite-sized pieces, or
  frozen chopped spinach,
  defrosted, and squeezed dry
½ cup wheat germ (use matzoh
  farfel for Pesach)

Preheat oven to 350° and grease a 9 x 13-inch pan.

In a large bowl, mix eggs, cheeses, flours, garlic powder, and salt. Add spinach to bowl and combine. Spread into pan, press and smooth with a spoon. Sprinkle wheat germ on top and bake for 35 to 40 minutes.

This casserole freezes well.

Serves 10–12

Herring in Sour Cream

  Melinda Strauss

This recipe feeds a lot of people as part of a brunch or lunch buffet. It needs a few hours to sit in the refrigerator for the flavors to blend and will keep well for several days. This dish goes very well with small, thin slices of pumpernickel bread.

1 32-ounce jar herring in wine sauce, drained
1 cup light sour cream (use regular sour cream for Pesach)
1 cup plain yogurt
4 tablespoons light mayonnaise (use regular mayonnaise for Pesach)
1 tablespoon fresh lemon juice

¼ cup sugar
1 small red onion, grated
1 or 2 scallions, green parts only, chopped

Garnishes: (optional)
Tomato wedges
Sliced hard-boiled eggs
Parsley

Cut herring into bite-sized pieces. In a large nonaluminum bowl, combine all ingredients, except for garnishes, and refrigerate. Garnish as desired before serving.

Serves 8–10 for buffet portions

Tomato Quiche

 Leslie Blachman

1 8-inch thin pie crust
1¼ cups grated Swiss cheese
1 8-ounce can stewed
   tomatoes, drained
1 egg
1 cup milk
½ teaspoon salt

¼ teaspoon white pepper
¼ teaspoon nutmeg
2 medium tomatoes, thinly
   sliced
¼ cup freshly grated Parmesan
   cheese
¼ cup fresh parsley, chopped

Preheat oven to 350°.

Prick holes in pie crust and bake for 15 minutes. Let the pie crust cool.

Sprinkle 1 cup of Swiss cheese on top of the crust. Place canned tomatoes on cheese.

Combine egg, milk, salt, pepper, and nutmeg in a bowl. Pour into the pie crust. Place tomato slices on top. Sprinkle on grated Swiss and Parmesan cheese, then the parsley. Bake for about 40 minutes or until quiche is set.

Serves 4–6

Carrot Pudding

 Ronda Jacobson

2 tablespoons onion, chopped
2 tablespoons butter
1 pound carrots, peeled and
cut into chunks

20 "Ritz-style" crackers
3/4 cup grated cheese

Preheat oven to 325°.

Sauté onion in butter until translucent, and set aside. In a saucepan, cover carrots with water and simmer until tender; reserve cooking water. Purée all the ingredients, including one cup of the carrot cooking water, in food processor.

Bake in a small greased casserole for 30 minutes. Serve hot or at room temperature.

This pudding freezes well.

Serves 8

Cucumber Salad with Fresh Dill

  Brenda Freishtat

3 English or 1 pound
pickling cucumbers
1 tablespoon salt
1 tablespoon sugar
1/2–1 teaspoon pepper

3 tablespoons wine or tarragon
vinegar (use red wine vinegar
for Pesach)
1 tablespoon fresh dill or
parsley, minced

Rinse and drain cucumbers. Trim ends and cut in half lengthwise. Scoop out seeds if necessary. Cut into slices 1/4-inch thick. Place in colander, add salt and toss. Leave to sit at room temperature for one hour.

Rinse cucumbers and pat dry. Place the cucumbers in a bowl, add rest of ingredients and toss. Refrigerate for one hour.

Serves 6–8

Chickpea Salad

 P   Esther Kletter

This is a flexible recipe. If I don't have pimiento, I use red pepper for color, or increase the green pepper and celery a bit. Sometimes I use a little less mayonnaise and horseradish. It can be doubled easily and lasts several days in the refrigerator. Also, kids like it.

1 19-ounce can chickpeas, rinsed and drained

¼ cup pimiento, chopped

½ cup green pepper, chopped

½ cup celery, chopped

Salt and pepper, to taste

½ cup mayonnaise

2 tablespoons white horseradish

Mix all ingredients together in a large bowl and chill.

Serves 3–4

Salmon Muffins

 Melinda Strauss

These pretty muffins are light, airy, and low in cholesterol. They are a good addition to a brunch.

1 cup cooked brown rice
¼ cup grated Cheddar cheese
1 6¾-ounce can skinless and boneless salmon, drained
5 tablespoons light mayonnaise
¼ apple, peeled and finely chopped

1 tablespoon lemon juice
¾ teaspoon sugar
2 teaspoons tamari sauce
1 teaspoon spicy brown mustard
3 egg whites

Preheat oven to 375°.
   In a large bowl, combine all ingredients except egg whites.
   Beat egg whites with mixer until stiff. Fold into salmon mixture.
   Coat 6 muffin tins with oil, and fill with salmon mixture. Bake 40 minutes or until golden brown. Let cool in the pan for 10 to 15 minutes, then loosen with a spoon to remove.

Yields 6 muffins

Plantation Cake

 Roberta Hoffman

A very delicious and moist cake.

1 1-pound jar cooked prunes
2½ cups all-purpose flour
1 teaspoon baking soda
1 teaspoon salt
1 teaspoon allspice
1 teaspoon cinnamon
1 teaspoon nutmeg
1 cup pecans, finely chopped
1½ cups sugar
3 eggs, well beaten

1 cup vegetable oil
1 cup buttermilk

Vanilla glaze:
½ cup sugar
¼ teaspoon baking soda
¼ cup buttermilk
¾ tablespoon light corn syrup
¼ cup margarine
½ teaspoon vanilla extract

Preheat oven to 350°. Grease and flour a 9-inch tube pan (12-cup capacity).

Drain prune liquid into a 1-cup measuring cup. Pit prunes carefully, cutting each into 3 to 4 pieces, and add to the liquid until prunes and juice together fill 1 cup. Set aside.

Sift together flour, baking soda, salt, allspice, cinnamon, and nutmeg. Stir in pecans and set aside.

Place the eggs in a large bowl and slowly beat in the sugar until the mixture is fluffy and light. Add oil, then buttermilk. Stir in prunes with liquid. Beat in flour mixture a third at a time until well blended. Pour into prepared pan, spreading evenly.

Bake 55 minutes or until top springs back when pressed (may need up to 1 hour 5 minutes). Cool 10 minutes in pan.

Meanwhile prepare glaze by combining all ingredients except vanilla in a small saucepan. Heat slowly and stir until boiling. Boil 2 minutes. Remove from heat and stir in vanilla.

Loosen edges of the cake and turn onto rack to cool completely. (At this point, cake can be frozen without glaze.) Drizzle or brush glaze on top as soon as cake is removed from pan.

Serves 10

Apricot Squares

  Rita Feuerstadt

These even taste great right out of the freezer.

2 12-ounce boxes of dried apricots, cut into pieces (scissors work well)
3/4 cup sugar
1 cup water
1 cup walnuts, finely chopped
1 1/2 cups all-purpose flour

1 cup oatmeal (not instant or quick)
1 teaspoon baking soda
1 cup brown sugar
1/4 pound butter or pareve margarine
1 teaspoon vanilla extract
1 egg

Combine apricots, sugar, and water in a small saucepan and simmer, uncovered, until all the water has evaporated, about 10 minutes. Remove from heat, mixing occasionally as apricots cool. When cool, add walnuts.

Preheat oven to 350°. Grease and flour a 12 x 8-inch baking dish.

In medium bowl, combine flour, oatmeal, and baking soda. In a food processor or mixer, cream brown sugar, butter, vanilla, and egg. Mix in flour mixture. Spread half of this batter into the baking dish. Place the apricot-walnut mixture on top. Spread remaining batter evenly on top. Bake for about 25 minutes or until brown. Cool in pan, then cut into squares.

Serves 8–10

Chocolate Crunchies

 Judy Gray

1 cup all-purpose flour
$^1/_2$ teaspoon baking powder
$^1/_2$ teaspoon baking soda
$^1/_2$ teaspoon salt
$^1/_2$ cup pareve margarine, softened
$^1/_2$ cup brown sugar
$^1/_2$ cup granulated sugar

1 egg
2 ounces unsweetened baking chocolate, melted
$^1/_2$ cup uncooked quick oats
$^1/_2$ cup shredded coconut
$^1/_2$ cup semi-sweet chocolate chips

Preheat oven to 350°.

In a small bowl, combine flour, baking powder, baking soda, and salt.

In a large bowl, combine margarine, brown sugar, granulated sugar, and egg. Beat until creamy. Blend in the unsweetened chocolate. Add flour mixture, oats, and coconut; mix until well blended. Add chocolate chips. Drop by slightly rounded tablespoonfuls onto ungreased cookie sheets.

Bake for 10 to 12 minutes. Remove cookies from pan onto cooling rack. When cooled, store in an airtight cannister so cookies will stay crunchy.

Yields about 2 dozen 2-inch cookies

DINNER IN THE SUKKAH

Serves 6–8

Kiddush Wine
No-Knead Whole Wheat Challah (*see Erev Yom Kippur Dinner* ~ 20)
Eggplant Roulade ~ 42
Ziti with Roulade Tomato Sauce ~ 43
Lentil Soup ~ 44
Steamed Green Beans
Mom's Famous Apple Pie ~ 45

Kiddush Wine
Challah (*see Rosh Hashanah Dinner* ~ 5)
Pumpkin Black Bean Soup ~ 46
Lamb with Eggplant ~ 47
Orange Brown Rice — double recipe ~ 48
Pea Salad — double recipe ~ 48
Etrog Marmalade ~ 49
Cran-apple Crisp ~ 50

After Simchat Torah you can use your *etrog* (the citron that is carried on Sukkah and waved in the synagogue with the *lulav,* a branch made of palm, myrtle, and willow boughs) to make Etrog Marmalade, page 49.

Eggplant Roulade

 Anne Waldoks

This recipe came to me via my mother and our cousin Betty, the "gourmet cook" in the family. Betty and her husband would spend a Sunday every now and then making the tomato sauce in this recipe to be used, frozen, or given as special gifts. The sauce makes more than is needed for the eggplant so, with the extra, you could do what my cousin Betty did. . . .

Sauce:
4 large onions, chopped
1 celery stalk, chopped
2 carrots, grated
2 cloves garlic, chopped
2 tablespoons olive oil
2 tablespoons vegetable oil
3 16-ounce cans whole
  tomatoes with juice
12 ounces tomato paste
1 bay leaf
1½ cups red wine or water
2 cups water
Salt and pepper, to taste
Sugar, to taste

½ teaspoon dried oregano
½ teaspoon dried basil

2 large eggplants
1 tablespoon salt
All-purpose flour for dredging
Vegetable oil for frying
1 pound skim ricotta cheese
½ cup grated Parmesan cheese
1 10-ounce package frozen
  chopped spinach, defrosted and
  squeezed dry
1 tablespoon fresh parsley
1 tablespoon dried oregano

To prepare the sauce, sauté onions, celery, carrots, and garlic in the oils. When soft, add tomatoes, tomato paste, bay leaf, wine, water, salt, pepper, and sugar. Simmer 2 hours uncovered, stirring occasionally. Add more water if necessary (should be fairly thick). Add oregano and basil. Cook another ½ hour. Correct seasonings. The sauce may be cooled and frozen at this point.

Cut eggplants lengthwise (not in rounds) into ½-inch slices. Do not peel. Each eggplant usually makes six slices. Sprinkle 1 tablespoon of salt over all the slices, weight with heavy object, and allow to stand for 15 minutes. Rinse and pat dry each slice, and dredge lightly with flour. Heat at least 1 inch of oil in skillet over medium-high heat. Fry each slice until crisp on both sides. Drain well on paper towel.

Preheat oven to 350°.

In a bowl, blend together all the remaining ingredients. Spoon mixture onto eggplant slices and roll.

Place in a 9 x 13-inch baking dish seam side down. Pour enough sauce over rolls so that bottom quarter rests in sauce. Bake for 45 minutes.

Yields 12 eggplant rolls,
yields 8 cups sauce

Variations: Eggplant slices may be broiled instead of fried to cut down on oil.
¹/₃ cup of sautéed mushrooms, carrots, and onions may be added to the filling.

Ziti with Roulade Tomato Sauce

  Anne Waldoks

1 pound ziti
1¹/₂ cups Roulade Tomato Sauce (see page 42)

Cook ziti according to directions. Toss pasta with warmed sauce and serve immediately.

Serves 6–8

Lentil Soup

 Melinda Strauss

This thick soup can be prepared in advance to serve on cold nights in the sukkah.

4 quarts water
1½ teaspoons salt
2½ cups brown lentils, rinsed
¼ cup olive oil
2 onions, chopped
5 cloves garlic, thinly sliced
2 large bay leaves

½ teaspoon cinnamon
½ teaspoon ground cloves
½ teaspoon powdered ginger
1½ teaspoons ground cumin
¼ cup fresh parsley, chopped
Salt and pepper, to taste
2 tablespoons pareve margarine
Fresh parsley or cilantro, chopped, for garnish

Bring water, salt, and lentils to boil in a large pot, lower heat, and simmer uncovered for 1 hour.

Heat olive oil in a sauté pan. Add onions, garlic, and bay leaves and sauté until onions start to turn golden. Add cinnamon, cloves, ginger, and cumin. Lower heat and sauté, stirring, for 2 minutes. Add this mixture to lentils. Add ¼ cup parsley. Simmer uncovered for 1 hour, stirring occasionally.

Remove bay leaves, then purée most of the soup in small amounts in a blender or food processor, leaving only some lentils whole for texture. (For a chunkier soup, do not purée.) Return soup to pot, add salt, pepper and margarine. Garnish with parsley or cilantro.

This soup freezes well.

Yields 14 small or 7 generous servings

Mom's Famous Apple Pie

 Amelia Welt Katzen

My mother, Leonce Welt, now of Massapequa Park, New York, but origi-nally from Fribourg, Switzerland, comes from a culture that dictates that the evening meal be small, and the main meal served at noon. Even though our American lifestyle could never fully accommodate that tradition, Sunday nights always benefited from her conviction that the lighter the evening meal, the better we'd sleep. One of my favorite meals as a child (and as an adult as well) had apple pie as its main course. My mother served it with a simple homemade vegetable soup. The flavors complement each other beautifully.

1 9-inch pie crust, unbaked

1/4 cup sugar, or less

Cinnamon, to taste

6 Cortland apples (if not available, try Northern Spy, Staymans, Wine-saps, or Baldwin), peeled, cored and cut in eighths

2 eggs

1/4 cup milk (or cream, if you do as the Swiss)

1/4 teaspoon salt

2 tablespoons all-purpose flour

Preheat oven to 425°.

Sprinkle the pie crust with half the sugar and a generous amount of cinnamon. Arrange the apple slices in concentric circles in the pie crust. (If you use apples that are sweeter than Cortlands, drizzle with lemon juice.) Sprinkle the remainder of the sugar over the apples.

If you're not going to bake the pie right away, cover with plastic wrap. Don't proceed to the next step until just before you want to pop the pie into the oven.

Using a wire whisk, make a custard by beating the eggs with the milk, salt, and flour. When the mixture is smooth, pour it evenly over the apples, making sure to moisten each of the apples a little.

Sprinkle generously with cinnamon. Bake for 15 minutes. Lower the oven temperature to 350° and bake for another 30 minutes. The pie is done when bubbling and lightly browned.

Serves 6–8

Pumpkin Black Bean Soup

 Judy Adnepos

A hearty, filling autumn soup. The garnish is needed to liven up the color of the beans.

2 cups black beans
3 tablespoons pareve
 margarine or vegetable
 oil
1 1/2 cups chopped onions
3 large cloves garlic,
 chopped
1 1/2 teaspoons salt
1 8-ounce can tomatoes,
 drained
1 1/2 cups canned pumpkin
3 1/2 cups vegetable stock

1 tablespoon cumin
2 tablespoons red wine vinegar
2 tablespoons dry sherry
1/2 teaspoon freshly ground black
 pepper

Garnishes:
Red bell pepper, chopped
Parsley, chopped
Coriander, chopped

Cover beans with 4 cups of water and soak in the refrigerator overnight.

Drain and rinse beans and place in a pot, with enough water to cover. Simmer for about 1 1/2 hours, until just soft (all the water may not be absorbed).

While the beans cook, melt the margarine in a skillet and sauté onions and garlic with salt until soft. Set aside.

Drain cooked beans and chop with tomatoes in a food processor until some of the mixture is puréed and some chunky. Return beans to pot and add the sauté and remaining ingredients, except for garnish. Mix well and simmer for 20 minutes. Adjust seasonings to taste. Garnish generously and serve.

Serves 6–8

Lamb with Eggplant

 Joan Gadon

I use the shoulder cut of the lamb with the bone for this dish. It's best made the day before you want to serve it.

2 tablespoons vegetable oil
3 pounds lamb shoulder (not including the bone), well trimmed and cut into 1-inch cubes
4 medium onions, chopped
1 large eggplant, cubed

$^1/_2$ teaspoon garlic powder
1 teaspoon basil
$^1/_4$ teaspoon pepper
1 16-ounce can tomatoes, with juice
1 teaspoon sugar
$^3/_4$ cup red wine

Preheat oven to 350°.

In a large ovenproof casserole, heat oil. Brown lamb, add onions and cook until onions are soft, about 10 minutes. Add eggplant, seasonings, and the bone (if one was included with your chosen cut). Add remaining ingredients. Bake covered for 1$^1/_2$ hours or until lamb is tender.

Serves 6

Variation: If you like firmer eggplant, add it after the lamb has been cooking for 45 minutes.

Orange Brown Rice

  Ann Daitch

This dish is even more festive for being low in cholesterol.

2¹/₃ cups water
1 cup brown rice
1 tablespoon pareve
   margarine (optional)
1¹/₂ teaspoons salt
¹/₂ pound carrots, grated

1 medium onion, grated
¹/₂ cup slivered almonds
¹/₄ cup orange juice concentrate,
   thawed
¹/₄ cup scallions, chopped,
   for garnish

In a large saucepan, bring the water to a boil. Add the rice, margarine, salt, carrots, and onion. Stir and cover. Cook over low heat until all the water is absorbed, about 50 minutes. Stir in almonds and orange juice concentrate. Garnish with scallions.

Serves 6

Pea Salad

  Nancy Gans

A very easy make-ahead salad for company or picnics.

1 10-ounce package frozen
   small peas, defrosted
1¹/₂ tablespoons onion,
   chopped
2 celery stalks, sliced
1–2 tablespoons
   mayonnaise, to bind

1 small jar pimientos, drained
   and sliced (optional)
¹/₂ cup dry roasted peanuts
   (optional)

Steam peas 1 to 2 minutes, drain and cool. Combine with onion, celery, optional pimientos, and mayonnaise in a serving bowl. Refrigerate for several hours. Just before serving, add peanuts.

Serves 4–6

Etrog Marmalade

 Melinda Strauss

Etrog, or citron, has a distinctive taste, and this recipe uses less sugar than jam recipes so that the taste comes through.

1 etrog
6 cups water

³/₄ cup sugar

Wash etrog and trim off the ends. Slice and remove as many seeds as possible. Chop into very small pieces, including peel. (Chopped etrog should equal about 1 cup for the amount of sugar in this recipe.)

Add fruit to water and refrigerate for 12 hours. Place fruit and water in a saucepan, bring to a boil, and simmer uncovered for 20 minutes. Drain fruit. Add remaining water, and refrigerate again for 12 hours.

Mix fruit, water, and sugar in a saucepan. Bring to a boil and simmer uncovered for 1¹/₂ hours, until the water becomes syrupy and the fruit becomes clear.

Yields 10 ounces

Variation: For a more traditional marmalade, add 1 cup of chopped orange and double the water and sugar.

Cran-apple Crisp

 Alisa Israel Goldberg

6–8 apples (MacIntosh are good)

2 cups raw or frozen cranberries

2 tablespoons sugar

$1/2$ teaspoon cinnamon

1 cup flour (all-purpose, whole wheat pastry, or combination)

$1/2$ cup packed brown sugar

$1/2$ cup butter or margarine

Preheat oven to 425°. Grease a shallow baking dish (I usually use a 10 or 12-inch quiche dish).

Peel, core, and slice apples. Place in baking dish. Spread cranberries on top, as evenly as possible. Mix sugar and cinnamon, sprinkle on top.

Combine flour, brown sugar, and butter in food processor until crumbly. Sprinkle over cranberries and apples, patting down if necessary. Bake for 20 to 30 minutes, until top is golden brown. Serve with vanilla pareve "ice cream," if desired.

Serves 6

THANKSGIVING DINNER

Serves 8–10

Roast Turkey
with Grandma Epstein's Turkey Stuffing ~ 53
Green Beans with Cashews ~ 54
Whole Baked Onions ~ 55
Fruited Sweet Potato Casserole ~ 56
Holiday Chutney ~ 57
Cranberry Crunch ~ 58
Bourbon Balls ~ 59

Thanksgiving Loaf ~ 60
Sandy's Carrot Kugel ~ 61
Brussels Sprouts with Cashews — double recipe ~ 62
Tangerine Sweet Potato Casserole ~ 63
Gingered Pear and Cranberry Sauce ~ 64
Cranberry Crunch ~ 58
Bourbon Balls ~ 59

Tanksgivnig

Faran azah min yuntif
Vos es heyst Tanksgivnig Day;
Dos shtamt fun yeneh tzeiten
Ven dos land is vild gevehn.

M'hot nit gezehn keyn heiskelach
Keyn gassen und keyn shtedt;
Fun teiereh depotment stores,
Is gor shoin obgeredt.

Vos ken ich eich dertzelehn
Fun die mentshen fun dos land?
Nur roiteh Indianer
Mit ah tomahok in handt.

Tzu dieseh echteh vildernish,
Drei hundert yohr tzurik,
Kumt ohn tzufohren dort ah shif -
An emeser antik.

'Sis ongepakt mit mentshen
Vos m'zucht ah neieh heym;
As chotchbeh voinen in ek velt,
Abi getrei tzu Got aleyn.

Men ruft zey epis Pilgrims,
Und zey zeinen gut und frum;
Antloifen fun der alter velt,
Doh kuken zey arum.

Aklal, der ershter vinter,
Oi, nit far eich gedacht;
'Sis nebach ah rachmohnes
Vos zey hoben mitgemacht.

Fun frosten beyz und bitter,
Fun hunger und fun tzar,
Is bald ah halber oilim
Geshtorben yenem yohr.

Tzum sof hot zich der Oibershter
Af die reshteh derbarimt;
Die neshohmeh hot er zey derkvikt,
Die glieder zey dervarimt.

Bekitzer, men hot obgelebt,
Mit naches zich bekant;
Azoi vie Got hot zey gebentsht,
Hoben zey ihm gedankt.

Simches hot men gepravet,
Maicholim ohn ah mons;
Die Indianer eingebeten,
Tzu tcholint, tzimmis, kvas.

Tzeit dan, af yeder yohrtzeit
Fun Pilgrims, olav hasholem,
Danken Mir Got — er shenkt uns
Gezundt, parnosseh, yohren.

Bei uns is oichet yuntifdig,
Men halt nur in eyn kochen;
'S tut zich af tishen und af benk,
Mit fieleh guteh zachen.

In yeder hois kumt zich tzugehn
Die teiereh mishpocheh;
Men freyt zich, und men kormet zich,
Mit mahzel und mit brocheh.

Tanksgivnig past geradeh sheyn
Die Amerikaner bieneh;
Veil Pilgrim-helden hob'n beshtelt
Die goldeneh medineh.

From Gut Yontif Gut Yohr,
Marie B. Jaffe (Citadel Press, 1976)

Grandma Epstein's Turkey Stuffing

 Wendy Russman-Halperin

This recipe was created by my grandmother and is moist and delicious. During the 1940s she entered the recipe in a newspaper contest and won first place — two free movie passes!

10 slices whole wheat bread
2 cups wheat cereal flakes
20 pareve "Ritz-style" crackers
1 1/4 cups chicken stock
1 cup onion, chopped

1 cup celery, chopped
1/3 cup vegetable oil
3 eggs, beaten
1/2 teaspoon salt
3 carrots, grated
1 cup walnuts, chopped

Preheat oven to 300° and dry the bread in it for 15 minutes. Set aside to cool.

In a large bowl, crumble together bread, cereal, and crackers. Add chicken stock to crumb mixture. Let stand to absorb. (If any stock remains, pour it off.)

Sauté onion and celery in oil until soft. Add to the bread mixture. Then add the eggs, salt, and carrots and stir to combine. Add walnuts.

Stuff turkey and bake. This stuffing can also be baked in a covered casserole for 30 minutes at 350°.

Yields about 8 cups stuffing,
enough for a 12–14 pound turkey

Green Beans with Cashews

 Taren Metson

My family enjoys this every Thanksgiving.

2 pounds fresh green beans
4–6 tablespoons pareve
   margarine

2 teaspoons lemon juice
1 cup salted cashews
Salt and pepper, to taste

Bring a large pot of salted water to boil. Add beans, bring water back to boil, and slowly boil, uncovered, for 3 to 5 minutes, until tender but still crisp. Immediately pour into colander and run under cold water until beans are cool. Pat dry. At this point they may be covered and refrigerated.

Before serving, bring beans to room temperature. Melt margarine in large pan. Add beans, lemon juice and cashews. Cook over moderately high heat, stirring and tossing gently, until heated through. Season with salt and pepper.

Serves 8–10

Variation: Use one cup macadamia nuts instead of cashews.

Whole Baked Onions

   Lois Nadel

12 even-sized boiling onions
2–3 cups chicken stock
¼ teaspoon paprika
2 tablespoons pareve
   margarine, melted

⅓ cup bread crumbs (use
   matzoh meal for Pesach)
¼ cup ground toasted pecans

Peel onions and simmer in enough chicken stock to cover for 30 minutes.

Preheat oven to 375°.

Drain the onions (save liquid for other uses). Place them in greased baking pan. Mix the paprika with the melted margarine and brush over the onions. Mix the bread crumbs and ground pecans and sprinkle over the onions. Dot with more melted margarine if desired. Bake for 20 minutes or until lightly browned.

Serves 6

Variation: Add herbs of your choice to the crumb mixture.

Fruited Sweet Potato Casserole

 Lois Nadel

8 medium yams or sweet potatoes, unpeeled

12–16 ounces dried mixed fruit (depending on how much you like it)

1 cup fresh orange juice

6 tablespoons orange liqueur

1/4 teaspoon freshly grated nutmeg

1/4 teaspoon allspice

1/2 teaspoon cinnamon

1/2 cup dark brown sugar

1/4 cup honey or maple syrup

2 tablespoons pareve margarine

1 orange, thinly sliced, with peel

3 tablespoons apricot preserves, melted

Boil potatoes until they pierce easily with a fork, about 20 minutes. Drain, and peel when cool. Slice about 1/4-inch thick and place in a 9 x 12-inch casserole that has been well coated with margarine.

Preheat oven to 350°.

In a saucepan, simmer the fruit with the orange juice, orange liqueur, spices, sugar, and honey about 20 minutes, or until tender. Pour over the potatoes so that some of the fruit is arranged attractively on top. Dot with margarine and bake about 60 minutes, until soft and gooey.

When almost done, place orange slices on top and brush with apricot preserves. Bake about 10 minutes more.

Serves 6–8

Holiday Chutney

 Esther White

1 20-ounce can unsweetened
  pineapple chunks
2 cups sugar
1 pound cranberries
1 cup golden raisins

¹/₂ teaspoon cinnamon
¹/₄ teaspoon ginger
¹/₄ teaspoon allspice
1 cup walnuts, coarsely
  chopped

Drain juice from pineapple and combine juice with sugar, cranberries, raisins, and spices. Simmer in a saucepan for 15 minutes or until cranberries are tender. Add pineapple and walnuts and transfer to a serving bowl. Refrigerate until chilled.

This chutney can also be frozen. It's delicious served with chicken or turkey.

Serves 6–8

Cranberry Crunch

  Faith Friedman

Cranberries are one of the three fruits native to America — the other two are Concord grapes and blueberries.

1¼ cups raw cranberries
¼ cup brown sugar
¼ cup walnuts or pine nuts, chopped
1 egg

½ cup granulated sugar
½ cup whole wheat pastry flour
⅓ cup melted butter or pareve margarine

Preheat oven to 325°.

Grease a 9-inch pie plate and layer the cranberries on the bottom. Sprinkle with brown sugar and nuts.

In bowl, beat the egg until thick. Gradually add the granulated sugar, beating until blended. Stir in flour and melted butter, blend well.

Pour this mixture over the cranberries. Bake 45 minutes.

Serve cut into wedges with ice cream or pareve "ice cream."

Serves 6

Bourbon Balls

   Sara Abramovitz

This is an old family recipe handed down by my great grandmother via Bohemia. In our family these were always an important (integral!) part of every simcha. *They are even good frozen for a quick "lift."*

1¾ cups vanilla wafer crumbs, dairy or pareve
1 cup pecan pieces
4 tablespoons unsweetened cocoa
¾ cup sugar

⅓ cup bourbon whiskey or rum
3 tablespoons light corn syrup
Ground nuts, powdered sugar, cocoa, coconut, or instant coffee powder (optional)

Pulverize wafer crumbs very finely in a food processor. Place them in a large bowl. Pulverize the pecan pieces in the food processor to very fine crumbs and add to wafer crumbs in bowl.

Add all the other ingredients and work together first with a fork and then with your hands. Form into balls about 1-inch in diameter. Roll into ground nuts, powdered sugar, cocoa, coconut, or coffee powder.

Balls can be served cold or at room temperature. They also freeze beautifully in their plain state.

Yields 38–40 balls

Variations: Substitute walnuts or almonds for pecans. Add cinnamon, instant coffee, or coconut, to taste.

Thanksgiving Loaf

 Sara Abramovitz

This is a wonderfully rich offering for a vegetarian Thanksgiving. Its popularity began in the upper peninsula of Michigan and is on the road to spreading nationwide.

The specific quantities of rice and vegetables aren't crucial, and any other vegetables can be added, especially garlic and carrots. I often substitute mashed tofu for part of the grated cheese, even as much as 1 1/2 cups.

3 cups cooked brown rice
1/2 cup onion, chopped
1/2 cup celery, chopped
1 1/2 cup ground walnuts
1/2–3/4 cup mushrooms, chopped
1 tablespoon tamari sauce
1 teaspoon dried sage
Dash of pepper
2 cups grated cheese (Cheddar, Monterey Jack, or Swiss)
4 large eggs, beaten

Mushroom gravy:
2–4 tablespoons butter
1 cup mushrooms, chopped
3 tablespoons whole wheat pastry or all-purpose flour
1 tablespoon tamari sauce
1 1/2 cups milk

Preheat oven to 350° and grease a 9 x 5-inch loaf pan.

Combine all ingredients in a large bowl. Place in the loaf pan and bake for 1 hour.

Meanwhile, for the gravy, melt the butter (more for richer flavor) and sauté the mushrooms in a skillet over medium heat. Stir in flour and tamari. Slowly pour in milk, cook and stir until thickened, about 3 to 5 minutes. (More milk may be needed if prepared in advance because the gravy will thicken when refrigerated.)

Serves 6–8

Sandy's Carrot Kugel

 Hannah Aroesty

1 cup pareve margarine
³/₄ cup dark brown sugar
1 heaping teaspoon salt
1 teaspoon lemon juice
1 teaspoon vanilla extract
1¹/₂ cups all-purpose flour

1 pound carrots, steamed and
  puréed
1 teaspoon baking powder
1 teaspoon baking soda
3 eggs, separated

Preheat oven to 350°. Grease a 2-quart ring mold or small casserole.

Combine all the ingredients except the egg whites in a large bowl.

Beat the egg whites until stiff and fold into the mixture. Pour the mixture into the mold or casserole and bake. Cooking times will vary depending on the container: 40 minutes for the mold, 50 to 60 minutes for the casserole; or until the center is firm and a tester comes out clean.

Unmold the ring and fill with peas, or serve straight from the casserole, hot or warm.

Serves 6–8

Brussels Sprouts with Cashews

  Lois Nadel

Brussels sprouts are all too often neglected or disguised with heavy sauces. The intriguing taste of this dish belies its simple preparation. You can use basil or dill instead of savory.

2 pounds Brussels sprouts
¼ cup pareve margarine
½ teaspoon dried savory
Dash of pepper

2 tablespoons lemon juice
⅓ cup cashews, chopped
Whole cashews, for garnish
(optional)

Choose small, firm sprouts, and pull off any limp outer leaves. Trim ends and cut an "X" in each bottom to ensure even cooking. Place Brussels sprouts in a 3-quart saucepan with 1-inch of water. Bring to a boil and simmer, covered, for 10 minutes. Drain.

In the same pot, melt margarine and mix with all the remaining ingredients except whole cashews.

Return the sprouts to the pot and stir gently with a wooden spoon to coat with the sauce.

Serve garnished with a few whole nuts, if desired.

Serves 6–8

Tangerine Sweet Potato Casserole

 Brenda Freishtat

I make this dish every Thanksgiving.

2 pounds (6 medium) sweet
  potatoes, cooked, peeled
  and mashed
¹/₄ cup melted pareve
  margarine
6 tablespoons firmly packed
  brown sugar

3 tablespoons dark rum
¹/₂ teaspoon salt
4 tangerines, peeled and
  segmented
2 tablespoons pecans, chopped
15–20 kosher marshmallows
  (optional)

Preheat oven to 375° and grease a 2-quart casserole.

In a large bowl, whip together the potatoes, 2 tablespoons melted margarine, 4 tablespoons sugar, rum, and salt.

Cut the sections of 2 tangerines into bite-sized pieces. Remove all the pits. Fold into the potato mixture and turn into casserole dish. Arrange the remaining tangerine sections on top.

In a small bowl, combine the remaining margarine, sugar, and the pecans, and sprinkle this on top of the potato-tangerine mixture. Bake about 30 minutes, until heated through, adding the marshmallows, if using, to the top for the last 5 to 10 minutes of cooking.

Serves 6–8

Gingered Pear and Cranberry Sauce

 P   Barbara Linder

This delicious relish is served cold, and tastes best when made the day before it is served.

¹/₄ cup water
³/₄ cup sugar
¹/₂ teaspoon powdered ginger,
    or more to taste
2 medium pears, peeled and
    chopped

2 cups raw cranberries
Juice and zest of 1 lemon
¹/₄ cup almond liqueur, or less
    to taste

Combine water, sugar, and ginger in a saucepan and stir over medium-high heat until sugar dissolves. Bring to a boil and boil for 5 minutes. Add pears, reduce heat, and simmer 1 minute. Add cranberries, lemon juice, and zest. Simmer without stirring until berries pop. Cool and stir in almond liqueur.

Yields about 4 cups

CHANUKAH DINNER

Serves 12

Spinach Salad — double recipe ✿ 66
Orange Chicken — double recipe ✿ 67
Potato Pancakes — double recipe ✿ 68
with Applesauce
Zucchini Pancakes — double recipe ✿ 69
American-style Sufganiyot ✿ 70

Salat Hatzilim — double recipe ✿ 71
Broiled Swordfish — triple recipe ✿ 72
Potato Pancakes — double recipe ✿ 68
Zucchini Pancakes — double recipe ✿ 69
Israeli-style Sufganiyot ✿ 73

Spinach Salad

 Lois Nadel

Everyone always asks for this recipe, and it's great to bring in a beautiful antique bowl to a potluck or gourmet dinner. It has a sweet dressing that even kids like.

Celery seed dressing:
1 teaspoon celery seeds
1 teaspoon salt
1 teaspoon dry mustard
$^1/_2$ teaspoon paprika
$^1/_2$ cup sugar
1 teaspoon grated onion
$^1/_4$ cup plus 2 tablespoons apple cider vinegar
2 tablespoons raspberry vinegar
2 teaspoons fresh orange juice
1 teaspoon fresh lemon juice
$^3/_4$ cup corn oil

Salad:
$2^1/_2$ pounds spinach
1 large head Romaine lettuce (optional)
2 11-ounce cans mandarin orange segments, drained
2 pears, thinly sliced
1 red onion, thinly sliced in rings
$^1/_2$ cup walnut pieces, sautéed in a few teaspoons toasted sesame oil until lightly brown

To prepare the dressing, mix the dry ingredients in a medium bowl, then add the remaining ingredients except the oil. Add oil slowly, mixing with a whisk until the dressing becomes thick.

Tear or cut the spinach and optional lettuce into bite-sized pieces and place in a large salad bowl, then add the orange segments, pears, onion, and walnuts. Add enough dressing to moisten, and toss.

Serves 12

Orange Chicken

   Julie Arnow

2½ pounds chicken breast, boned and skinned
Salt and pepper, to taste
½ cup cornstarch
½ cup vegetable oil
3 egg whites
Vegetable oil for frying

Topping:
1 green pepper, chopped
1 red pepper, chopped
1 can sliced water chestnuts, rinsed and drained
1 lettuce, very thinly sliced

Sauce:
½ cup orange liqueur
½ cup orange marmalade
½ teaspoon Worcestershire sauce
½ teaspoon Dijon mustard
Crushed garlic, to taste
1 cup chicken broth
½ teaspoon chopped fresh ginger, or ½ teaspoon powdered ginger (optional)

Preheat oven to 350°.

Slice the chicken breasts into 3 x ½-inch strips — don't worry if you don't end up with uniform pieces — and place in a large bowl. Sprinkle with salt and pepper, then add the cornstarch. Mix thoroughly. Sprinkle with the ½ cup oil, and mix. Pour in the egg whites and mix.

Heat the oil in a large skillet over medium-high heat. Sauté the chicken pieces until golden brown. You will probably need to do this in several batches to avoid crowding the pan. Drain on paper towels. Place chicken in a 9 x 12-inch baking dish, and set aside while you make the sauce.

Combine the sauce ingredients in a medium pot, and bring to a boil over high heat. Boil for 2 to 3 minutes. Pour over the chicken in the baking dish. (At this point, the dish can be frozen or refrigerated for up to 24 hours.) Cover and bake for 20 to 30 minutes until bubbly.

Mix together the topping ingredients, and arrange — with as much elegance as you can muster — on top of the chicken. Serve immediately, or allow to cool.

Serves 4

Suggestion: Reserve a few pieces of chicken for the younger children. Serve them with ketchup and a toy in an old shoe box, and the children may be tricked into thinking that McDonald's has gone kosher!

Potato Pancakes

 P   Ivy Feuerstadt

5 large potatoes, peeled and
  cut into chunks
1 onion
2 eggs, well beaten
1¹/₂ teaspoons salt, or to
  taste

1¹/₂ teaspoons baking powder
3 tablespoons all-purpose flour
Vegetable oil for frying
Sour cream or applesauce
  (optional)

Chop potatoes finely in a food processor fitted with a steel blade, but
don't let them get mushy. Place in a colander and run cold water over
them for about 1 minute. Leave to drain. Chop onion finely in the
processor. Place the chopped onion in a large bowl, add the eggs, salt,
baking powder, flour, and potatoes. Mix well.

Heat ¹/₂ inch oil in a large skillet over medium-high heat. For
each pancake, drop a scant tablespoon of batter into the hot oil.
Flatten, if desired, and fry for 3 minutes on each side or until brown
and crisp. Serve immediately with applesauce or sour cream.

To freeze, place pancakes between sheets of waxed paper so they
don't become soggy. When frozen solid, transfer to ziplock bags.
Reheat in 450° oven for 10 to 12 minutes until crispy.

Yields 4–5 dozen very small pancakes

Zucchini Pancakes

 Ivy Feuerstadt

2 cups zucchini, coarsely
shredded (about 1 medium
zucchini)
2 large eggs, beaten
¼ cup onion, minced
½ cup unbleached
all-purpose flour

½ teaspoon baking powder
Salt, to taste
Oregano, to taste
Vegetable oil for frying

Place zucchini in a colander and press out as much moisture as possible. In a medium-sized bowl, mix eggs, onion, and zucchini. Add dry ingredients and mix. Heat oil on griddle or skillet over medium heat. Drop a scant tablespoon of batter into the hot oil. Flatten, if desired, and fry for 3 minutes on each side or until brown and crisp.

To freeze, place pancakes between sheets of waxed paper so they don't become soggy. When frozen solid, transfer to ziplock bags. Reheat in 425° oven for 10 to 12 minutes until crispy.

Yields 20–25 small pancakes

American-style Sufganiyot

 Julie Arnow

In Israel, it is traditional to make sufganiyot (jelly doughnuts rolled in sugar) on Chanukah. Deep fried in oil, these sweets symbolize the rededication of the Temple after it was defiled by the Assyrians. American-style sufganiyot are made without the jelly. These closely resemble doughnut holes.

³/₄ cup orange juice
¹/₂ cup butter or pareve
   margarine
5 tablespoons sugar
2 packages dry yeast (about
   1¹/₂ tablespoons)
4 cups all-purpose flour,
   more if needed

2 eggs, beaten
Dash of salt
1 tablespoon vanilla extract
Vegetable oil for frying
Mixture of 2 teaspoons
   cinnamon and ¹/₂ cup sugar
   for coating

Heat orange juice, margarine, and sugar in a small saucepan over medium heat until butter or margarine is melted. Mix and cool slightly. Transfer to a large bowl, add yeast and mix to dissolve. Add the rest of the ingredients and combine. Knead dough for about 10 minutes, adding flour if dough is too sticky. Place in a greased bowl, cover with a towel, and let rise in a warm place for about 30 minutes.

    Uncover bowl, punch dough down, and knead for a few minutes. Cover and let rise again in a warm place for another 30 minutes. Divide dough into ¹/₂-inch diameter balls, and deep fry in oil over high heat. Place cinnamon-sugar mixture in a paper bag, add each batch of sufganiyot to the bag as they come out of the oil, and shake to coat them. Best served warm.

Yields 80 small sufganiyot

Salat Hatzilim

  Judy Zomer

This eggplant salad can be served as part of the main course or as an appetizer, Israeli-style.

1 large eggplant cut into ½-inch slices

Vegetable oil for frying

1 medium onion, chopped

1 large clove garlic, minced, or to taste

1 8-ounce can tomato sauce (3 ounces tomato paste thinned with 5 ounces water)

¼ teaspoon salt, or to taste

Dash of pepper, or to taste

Dash of cumin, or to taste

Wash the eggplant. Sprinkle with salt, place in a colander and drain for 30 minutes. Rinse and pat dry.

Fry eggplant slices in oil over medium-high heat in a large skillet until golden brown on each side. Remove and place on paper towels to absorb the excess oil. (The eggplant can also be broiled in the oven — brush each side with oil, turn and cook until tender, and watch carefully so it doesn't burn!)

Sauté the onion and garlic in the same pan until tender. Add tomato sauce or paste mix. Add spices and cook until blended. Return the eggplant to the skillet and cook 5 additional minutes. Serve immediately.

Serves 4–6

Broiled Swordfish

  Rachel Goldstein

5 tablespoons olive oil
1 leek, rinsed very well and sliced
$1/4$ cup parsley, chopped
1 teaspoon dried basil
Salt and pepper, to taste
Juice of 1 lemon

$4^1/2$ pounds swordfish steaks (at the fish market, have the steaks butterflied to the skin in order to form a pocket)
4 slices lowfat mozzarella cheese

Heat 1 tablespoon oil in a medium skillet and sauté the leeks over medium heat until golden. Stir in parsley, basil, salt and pepper, and heat through. Remove from skillet and let cool. Preheat the broiler. In a small dish, combine remaining 4 tablespoons oil and lemon juice. Place a slice of cheese in the pocket of each steak and one fourth of the leek mixture. Brush with oil and lemon. Broil on one side for about 5 minutes. Turn, brush again with oil. Cook 8 minutes more, or until done.

Serves 4

Variation: I have also used sautéed mushrooms with the leeks and found it very tasty.

Israeli-style Sufganiyot

 Raquel Orbach

The Israeli version of latkes looks like American jelly doughnuts but tastes . . . oh, so much better. Anybody afraid of the words yeast dough or calories, or too liberated to spend a day in the kitchen, kindly turn to the next page.

2 packages dry yeast (about 1½ tablespoons)
2 cups warm milk
1 cup plus 2 teaspoons sugar
5 cups all-purpose flour
Dash of salt
6 egg yolks
1 teaspoon vanilla extract
Rind of small lemon or orange, grated

¾ cup butter, softened
¾ cup jam for filling
Vegetable oil for frying
Powdered sugar for topping
Vanilla sugar (made in Israel, found in kosher grocery stores, optional)

Mix the yeast with ½ cup warm milk and 2 teaspoons sugar. Set aside for 7 to 10 minutes. Mix flour, salt, and remaining sugar together in a large bowl. Make a well in the center and pour in yeast mixture, mix in the flour and cover the bowl with a towel. Let stand for 15 to 20 minutes. Add egg yolks, vanilla, lemon or orange rind, and butter. Knead into a soft dough with as much of the remaining milk as needed. Cover and let dough rise 2½ hours in a warm place.

Roll out dough ½-inch thick and cut into 3-inch circles. Let circles rise 1 hour. Heat 3 to 3½ inches of oil in a deep skillet or saucepan to 360° using a candy thermometer. Deep fry in oil on both sides, 3 to 5 at a time, until lightly browned. Remove from oil and drain on paper towels. When cool enough to handle, make a small cut on the side and spoon or pipe 1 teaspoon of jam in. Sift powdered sugar over sufganiyot, or mix powdered sugar and vanilla sugar together in equal parts and shake over sufganiyot.

Yields 3 dozen sufganiyot

CHANUKAH BREAKFAST BUFFET

Serves 10–12

Orange Juice

Bread Basket:
Danish Pastries ~ 76
Carrot Muffins ~ 77
Pumpkin Bread ~ 78
Cream Cheese and Jams

A Lighter Dairy Kugel ~ 79
Granola ~ 80
Potato Pancakes (*see Chanukah Dinners* ~ 68)
Pineapple Bread Pudding — double recipe ~ 81
Coffee, Tea, Hot Cocoa

Danish Pastries

 Arline Shapiro

Do not substitute margarine for the butter; it will not make as flaky a pastry. The dough needs to be refrigerated overnight.

²/₃ cup all-purpose flour
1 cup plus 3 tablespoons
   sugar
¹/₄ pound margarine
¹/₄ pound butter
3 eggs, separated
1 tablespoon dry yeast (2
   squares or about 2
   packages dry yeast)

Scant ¹/₂ cup milk
1 teaspoon cinnamon
1 cup walnuts, chopped
1 cup raisins

Sift the flour and the 3 tablespoons of sugar together in a large bowl. Crumble margarine and butter into flour and sugar mixture, and mix in 3 egg yolks (refrigerate whites). Dissolve yeast in milk in a small bowl and add to mixture. Mix thoroughly, cover and refrigerate overnight.

Preheat oven to 350°.

Beat egg whites with ³/₄ cup sugar until stiff.

Mix together in a small bowl the cinnamon and ¹/₄ cup sugar.

Divide dough into 6 parts. Roll each portion out to ¹/₄-inch thick, spread with egg whites, cinnamon and sugar, chopped walnuts, and raisins. Roll up like a jelly roll, folding the short sides over and rolling along the length of the dough. Cut each roll into 4 or more pieces and place, cut side down, in small, papered muffin tins. Bake for 30 to 35 minutes.

Yields 24 pastries

Carrot Muffins

 Gail Wolfe

A nice addition to the bread basket, these muffins are a good alternative to bread and rolls at any meal.

1 scant cup vegetable oil	½ teaspoon baking soda
½ cup brown sugar	1 teaspoon baking powder
1 egg	½ teaspoon salt
1 tablespoon water	½ teaspoon cinnamon
2 cups coarsely grated carrots	½ teaspoon nutmeg
1½ cups all-purpose flour	1 cup walnuts, chopped

Preheat oven to 350°.

Cream oil and brown sugar together in a large bowl. Add egg, water, and carrots and mix. Add flour, baking soda, baking powder, salt, cinnamon, and nutmeg. Blend well. Add nuts. Pour into greased muffin tins, filling the tins ³/₄ full. (Batter can be refrigerated at this point, but let stand at room temperature for one hour before baking.) Bake for 20 minutes.

The muffins can be prepared ahead and warmed on a cookie sheet for 10 minutes or frozen and thoroughly heated prior to serving.

Yields about 18 muffins

Variations: Substitute pecans for walnuts, and/or whole wheat flour for part or all of the flour.

Pumpkin Bread

 Varda E. Farber

This recipe was given to me by my friend Andrea Swenson, a well-known food stylist in New York City.

2¹/₂ cups all-purpose flour
1¹/₂ teaspoons baking soda
1¹/₂ teaspoons baking powder
1 teaspoon cinnamon
¹/₂ teaspoon nutmeg
¹/₂ cup butter, softened
³/₄ cup light brown sugar
³/₄ cup granulated sugar
1 teaspoon vanilla extract
3 eggs, at room temperature
1 15-ounce can pumpkin
  purée

¹/₃ cup sherry
1 cup nuts, chopped (optional)
¹/₃ cup raisins (optional)

Topping:
¹/₄ cup butter, softened
¹/₂ cup light brown sugar
¹/₂ cup all-purpose flour
¹/₂ cup nuts, chopped
¹/₂ teaspoon cinnamon

Preheat oven to 350°. Grease and flour two 9 x 5-inch loaf pans.

Sift together flour, baking soda, baking powder, cinnamon, and nutmeg in a large bowl. Set aside. In another large bowl, cream butter, brown sugar, granulated sugar, and vanilla, beating until light colored and fluffy. Beat in eggs, one at a time. Beat in pumpkin. Alternate adding flour mixture and sherry, mixing well after each addition. Fold in optional nuts and raisins. Divide between pans.

Crumble topping ingredients together in a medium bowl. Divide and sprinkle on top of loaves. Pat down lightly. Bake 50 minutes or until tester inserted in the center comes out clean.

Yields 2 loaves

A Lighter Dairy Kugel

 Varda E. Farber

4 tablespoons melted butter
or margarine
1/2 scant cup sugar
1 cup light sour cream
2 cups milk
1 pound lowfat cottage
cheese
1 pound lowfat ricotta
cheese
1/2 teaspoon salt

1 teaspoon vanilla extract
6 eggs, beaten
1 pound medium noodles,
cooked and drained

Topping:
1/4 cup brown sugar
1/2 cup slivered almonds
2 tablespoons butter, melted

Preheat oven to 350°.

In a large bowl, mix all ingredients together except the noodles. Fold in the noodles. Pour into a 9 x 13-inch buttered casserole dish. Combine topping and spread on noodles. Bake for 1 1/2 hours.

Serves 10–12

Granola

Peggy Glass, *Home Cooking Sampler: Family Favorites from A to Z,* (Prentice Hall Press, 1989)

We always have a large jar of granola available as a topping for plain cereal or yogurt. Each batch is delicious and unique because the ingredients vary slightly from one to the next. Add your own favorites to the roasting pan, keeping the ratio of dry to wet ingredients about 7 to 1.

8 cups old-fashioned or quick rolled oats
1 cup brown sugar
1/2 cup flour, preferably whole wheat
1 cup grated dry, unsweetened coconut
1 cup dry milk powder
1 cup wheat germ or bran or bran cereal
1 cup slivered almonds

1/4 cup sesame seeds
2/3 cup corn or vegetable oil
1/3 cup water
1/2 cup light corn syrup or honey
1/4 cup maple syrup
2 teaspoons vanilla extract
1 teaspoon salt
1 cup raisins or pitted dates, chopped (optional)

Preheat oven to 300°.

Combine dry ingredients in a large roasting pan and stir well. Heat the remaining ingredients, except raisins, in a saucepan and pour into the roasting pan. Toss to mix the ingredients thoroughly.

Bake until golden, stirring three or four times, about 1 to 1 1/2 hours. Turn out the granola on top of a flattened brown paper bag to cool completely. Mix in the raisins or dates, if using. Store in a large jar or airtight container.

Yields 16 cups

Pineapple Bread Pudding

 Ivy Feuerstadt

7 slices whole wheat bread,
crusts removed, cut into
cubes

1 20-ounce can crushed,
unsweetened pineapple,
with juice

1 cup packed light brown
sugar

4 eggs, beaten

2 teaspoons fresh lemon juice

$1/2$ teaspoon grated fresh
nutmeg

6 tablespoons unsalted butter,
melted

Preheat the oven to 325° and grease a 2-quart soufflé dish.

In a large bowl, combine bread and pineapple, and place in
soufflé dish. Using the same bowl, mix together brown sugar, eggs,
lemon juice, nutmeg, and butter and pour over bread mixture. Bake
until puffed and golden, about 40 minutes.

Serves 6–8

NEW YEAR'S DAY BRUNCH BUFFET

Serves 18–20

Mimosas of Orange Juice and Champagne

Bread Basket:
Carrot, Zucchini, and Apple Muffins ∾ 84
Bran Oatmeal Muffins ∾ 85
Gougère ∾ 86
Bagels
Cream Cheese and Jams

Brunch Casserole ∾ 87
Apple Walnut Quiche — double recipe ∾ 88
Spinach Cheese Pie — double recipe ∾ 89
Baked Broccoli ∾ 90
Fresh Pears with Raspberry Sauce ∾ 90
Bourbon Balls (*see Thanksgiving Dinners* ∾ 59)
Rugelach ∾ 91
Filo Fruit Strudel ∾ 92
Coffee, Tea, Hot Mulled Apple Cider

Carrot, Zucchini, and Apple Muffins

 Roberta Hoffman

3 large eggs
1 teaspoon vanilla extract
1 cup vegetable oil
2 cups all-purpose flour
2 cups grated carrots
1¼ cups sugar
1 cup grated zucchini
1 golden delicious apple, peeled and chopped

¾ cup golden raisins
¾ grated coconut
½ cup walnuts, chopped
1 tablespoon cinnamon
2 teaspoons baking soda
1½ teaspoons grated orange peel
½ teaspoon salt

Preheat oven to 375°. Grease two muffin tins or use paper liners.

Beat eggs, vanilla, and oil in one large bowl, and mix remaining ingredients in a second large bowl. Stir flour mixture into egg mixture. Fill muffin cups ½ full. Bake about 25 minutes until tester inserted in the center comes out clean. Serve warm or room temperature.

Yields 24 muffins

Bran Oatmeal Muffins

 Marlene Leffell

These are low in cholesterol, low in saturated fat, and high in fiber, and kids love them when they're made into mini-muffins.

2 cups rolled oats
2 cups bran cereal
2 cups skim buttermilk
1 1/2 cups all-purpose flour
1/2 teaspoon salt
1 teaspoon baking soda
2 teaspoons baking powder
1/2 cup unprocessed bran, oat or wheat
1 cup canola oil
1/2 cup brown sugar
3 egg whites, beaten slightly

Optional additions:
1 large apple, chopped
1/2 cup raisins
1/2 cup dates or prunes, chopped
1/2 teaspoon cinnamon
Dash of nutmeg
or
1 cup blueberries or raspberries

Preheat oven to 400°.

Combine oats, bran cereal, and buttermilk in a large bowl. Set aside while sifting the flour, salt, baking soda, and baking powder into another large bowl. Add the unprocessed bran. Add oil, sugar, and egg whites to oatmeal mixture, then stir in dry ingredients. Add optional fruit and spices. Mix just long enough to moisten. Do not overmix or the muffins will be tough.

Spoon into greased muffin tins, filling each cup 3/4 full. Bake 15 to 20 minutes. Cool in pan for 5 to 10 minutes.

Yields 2 1/2 dozen mini-muffins or 1 dozen large muffins

Gougère

 Rebecca Milikowsky

This French cheese bread looks very fancy, yet is quick to make, and uses only two bowls or pans. It also tastes delicious and rich. I serve it on the side at a dairy dinner party or for a family dinner just with ratatouille or salad.

1 cup water	1 teaspoon Dijon mustard
1/2 cup butter	1/2 teaspoon dry mustard
1 cup all-purpose flour	1 teaspoon salt
4 eggs	Dash hot pepper sauce
1 1/2 cups grated Gruyère cheese	(optional)

Preheat oven to 450°. Lightly butter a small cookie sheet or baking dish.

In a medium saucepan, combine water and butter. Bring to a rolling boil over medium-high heat. Make sure the butter is completely melted. Add the flour all at once and mix with a wooden spoon until the mixture forms a ball and comes away from the sides of the pan. Remove from the heat, leave in the pan or transfer to a mixing bowl. Add eggs one at a time, beating after each addition until smooth and shiny. Blend in the remaining ingredients. Using half the dough, form a circle 9-inches in diameter, and place on the baking sheet. Repeat with the other half of the dough and place on top of the first layer. (I frequently stop at this point and cover with a tea towel.)

Bake for 10 minutes. Reduce the oven to 350° and bake 10 minutes more. Now lower the temperature to 325° and bake about 15 to 20 minutes, until puffed and lightly browned. Immediately poke all over with a fork to let out the steam. Slide onto a serving dish and cut into wedges. Serve immediately.

Serves 4–5 as a main dish

Brunch Casserole

 Alisa Israel Goldberg

This casserole is best assembled the day before the brunch.

4 cups cubed French bread
¼ cup melted butter
3 cups sliced mushrooms
4 cups grated Cheddar-type cheese (2 cups each Cheddar and Colby is good)
6 ounces lox or smoked salmon, chopped

8–10 scallions, chopped
8 eggs
4 cups milk
4 teaspoons Dijon mustard
1 teaspoon salt
½ teaspoon pepper
½ teaspoon paprika
¼ teaspoon cayenne

Place the bread in a glass, ovenproof lasagna pan and drizzle with melted butter. Scatter mushrooms, cheese, lox, and scallions over the bread cubes. Whisk remaining ingredients together in a large bowl, and pour over everything in the pan. Cover and refrigerate overnight.

In the morning, bake at 325° for about 1 hour, or until just firm and lightly browned.

Serves 8–10

Apple Walnut Quiche

 Relly Dibner

1³/₄ cups all-purpose flour
10 tablespoons margarine
1 teaspoon salt
4 tablespoons cold water
1 medium onion, chopped
3 cooking apples, chopped
3 cloves garlic, chopped
2 tablespoons vegetable oil
3 tablespoons red wine or
  sherry
¹/₄ teaspoon ground
  coriander

¹/₂ teaspoon ground cloves
¹/₂ teaspoon ground ginger
¹/₄ teaspoon dried thyme
Salt and pepper, to taste
2 cups grated hard mild
  Cheddar cheese
3 eggs, beaten (or 1 whole
  egg and 2 whites)
1 teaspoon mustard powder
¹/₂ cup walnuts, finely
  chopped

Preheat oven to 350°.

Mix the flour, margarine, and salt together in a bowl until the mixture resembles fine bread crumbs. Sprinkle on the cold water and mix until the dough forms a ball. Roll the dough out and line a 9-inch pie pan. Bake for 15 minutes. Set aside to cool while making the filling.

In a large skillet, sauté onion, apples, and garlic over medium heat in oil until just soft, about 15 minutes. Add wine, coriander, cloves, ginger, thyme, salt and pepper, and continue to cook 5 minutes more. Spread one cup of the cheese over the crust, spread apple mixture over cheese, and sprinkle remaining cheese on top. Combine eggs with mustard, pour over all, and sprinkle with walnuts. Bake for 50 minutes, or until the quiche is set.

Serves 4–6

Spinach Cheese Pie

 Wendy Russman-Halperin

A college roommate gave me this recipe, and we made it quite often in those days since it's fast, easy, and cheap. It can be prepared in advance and baked later.

1 tablespoon margarine or butter
1 cup minced onion
1 10-ounce package frozen chopped spinach, defrosted and squeezed dry
15 ounces ricotta or cottage cheese

2 eggs
3/4 teaspoon salt, or to taste
Dash of pepper
Dash of ground nutmeg
1/4 cup freshly grated Parmesan cheese
1 9-inch pie crust, pre-baked

Preheat over to 350°.

In a large skillet, melt butter over medium heat, add onion, and cook until soft. Add spinach and sauté for a few minutes more. Remove from heat. Mix remaining ingredients in large bowl. Add spinach-onion mixture and mix until it looks like green and white marble. Pour into pie shell and bake for 40 to 45 minutes until top is golden and filling is set.

Serves 4–6

Baked Broccoli

  Joyce Zakim

3 cups broccoli florettes
1/4 cup onion, chopped
6 tablespoons butter, plus 2
tablespoons extra for
topping
2 tablespoons all-purpose
flour (matzoh meal for
Pesach)

1/2 cup water
8 ounces Cheddar cheese
3 eggs, beaten
Salt and pepper, to taste
(optional)
1/2 cup wheat germ (matzoh
meal for Pesach)
1/2 teaspoon paprika

Preheat oven to 350°.

Steam broccoli until tender, drain and chop, and set aside in a large bowl.

In a saucepan, sauté onion in butter over medium heat. Stir in flour, add water, and cook over low heat, stirring until it comes to a boil. Blend in cheese. Add to broccoli. Add eggs, salt and pepper, if using, and mix. Turn into a greased 1 1/2-quart casserole. Cover with wheat germ, dot with extra butter, and sprinkle with paprika. Bake for 30 minutes or until lightly browned on top.

Serves 6

Fresh Pears with Raspberry Sauce

  Ivy Feuerstadt

2 10-ounce packages frozen
raspberries, defrosted
1/4 cup sugar, or to taste

1 teaspoon fresh lemon juice
9–10 pears

Place defrosted berries, including juices, sugar, and lemon juice in a blender or food processor, and purée. Refrigerate.

Halve and core the pears. Place in a serving dish skin side down. Pour sauce over the pears and serve.

Serves 18–20, sauce yields 2 1/2 cups

Rugelach

 Hazel Santis

These rolled-up pastries are equally perfect with morning coffee or afternoon tea.

1 cup sour cream
1 egg yolk
$^1/_2$ cup margarine
$^1/_2$ cup butter
$2^1/_2$ cups all-purpose flour
$1^1/_4$ cups sugar

2 teaspoons cinnamon
5 tablespoons raspberry jam
$^1/_2$ cup walnuts, chopped
$^1/_2$ cup dark or golden raisins, chopped

Have all the ingredients at room temperature. Mix the sour cream with the egg yolk and set aside.

Combine margarine, butter, and flour in a bowl or food processor until the mixture has the consistency of bread crumbs. Add sour cream mixture and process until dough forms. Cover with cling wrap and refrigerate overnight, or freeze for later use.

Preheat oven to 350°.

Mix sugar and cinnamon together. Dust $^1/_5$ of the mixture on a board or flat work surface, creating a circle about 8 inches in diameter.

Remove the dough from the refrigerator and cut into fifths. Roll one portion into a thin circle on top of the cinnamon mixture. Spread with a tablespoon of jam, sprinkle the rim of the circle with $^1/_5$ of the nuts and raisins. Cut into 12 wedges. Starting at the wide end, roll each wedge up snugly. Place on lightly greased cookie sheet. Repeat the process for the remaining dough.

Bake for 15 to 20 minutes, until golden.

Yields 5 dozen

Filo Fruit Strudel

Melinda Strauss

This recipe makes a low-sugar, low-cholesterol strudel that can be served as a side dish, but stands on its own for a guilt-free dessert with afternoon tea.

Work quickly and carefully with the filo dough, which is very fragile. As you remove each sheet, cover the remainder with a damp cloth to prevent them drying out and flying away.

<table>
<tr><td>

²/₃ cup dried apricots

²/₃ cup dried apples

1 cup apple juice, approximately

6 cups apples, peeled and chopped (use crisp, tart, varieties such as Granny Smith or Winesap)

1 cup currants

1 teaspoon cinnamon

¹/₂ teaspoon nutmeg

</td><td>

2 cups walnuts, finely chopped

³/₄ cup almonds, chopped

Grated rind of 1 lemon

1¹/₂ teaspoons vanilla extract

1 pound filo dough (defrost if frozen)

¹/₄–¹/₂ cup pareve margarine, melted

1¹/₂–2 cups pareve bread crumbs (white or whole wheat)

</td></tr>
</table>

Simmer the dried fruit in enough apple juice to cover until tender, about 10 minutes. Purée in a food processor, adding juice if necessary to make a thick paste.

Place apples in a large bowl and mix in currants, cinnamon, nutmeg, walnuts, almonds, lemon rind, vanilla, and dried-fruit paste. Set aside.

Gently remove one sheet of filo dough and lay it on a clean surface with one of the long sides towards you. Brush with melted margarine, spreading it thinly and evenly over the entire surface. Lay a second sheet down on top of the first and brush with margarine. Repeat with 6 more sheets, making a total of 8.

Sprinkle with ¹/₃ of the bread crumbs. Place ¹/₃ of the fruit mixture along one long side of the rectangle, 1 inch from the sides and bottom. Roll up as tightly as possible.

Preheat oven to 400°. Cut strudel roll into fourths and use a spatula to transfer to a 16 x 14-inch baking sheet. Repeat for two more rolls. Brush tops of strudels with melted margarine, and bake until browned, about 30 minutes. Best served warm.

Serves 12 generously

SUPER BOWL SUNDAY
TV DINNER

Serves 12

Popcorn, Pretzels, and Beer
No-Alarm Vegetarian Chili ～ 94
Corn Bread Muffins ～ 95
Chicken Salad — triple recipe ～ 96
Chocolate Crunchies (*see Break Fast Buffet* ～ 40)

No-Alarm Vegetarian Chili

   Melinda Strauss

Unlike other vegetarian chilis, this one is neither thin nor too heavy on the spices. Rich and flavorful, I find it's the soy that makes it so robust. Feel free to add more cayenne if you prefer your chili hot.

2 cups kidney beans
7 cups water
²/₃ cup soy granules or grits (found in natural food stores)
3 cups canned crushed tomatoes
3 bay leaves
3 tablespoons corn oil
2 cups onion, chopped
6 medium cloves garlic, crushed
1 cup green pepper, chopped

1 cup carrots, chopped
1 teaspoon dried basil
1¹/₂ teaspoons dried oregano
¹/₄ teaspoon ground cumin
¹/₂ teaspoon ground coriander
¹/₂ teaspoon chili powder
1 teaspoon cumin seeds
1 teaspoon salt
Dash of cayenne pepper, or to taste
Grated Cheddar cheese (optional garnish)

Rinse beans and soak in the water for 6 to 8 hours.

Bring beans and soaking water to a boil in a 4-quart soup pot. Cover and simmer 2 hours.

Add soy granules, tomatoes, and bay leaves, and simmer 30 minutes more, covered.

Heat oil in a skillet and sauté onion, garlic, green pepper, carrots, herbs, and spices over medium heat until onions brown, about 20 minutes. Add sauté to beans. Simmer uncovered for 20 minutes, stirring occasionally. Garnish with cheese if desired.

Freezes well.

Serves 6–8

Corn Bread Muffins

 Beth Lang-Nadel

1 1/2 cups all-purpose flour
4 1/2 teaspoons baking powder
1/3 teaspoon salt
1 1/2 cups fine yellow corn
    meal

2 eggs, beaten
Scant 1/4 cup honey
1 1/2 cups plain soy milk
8 tablespoons pareve margarine
    or butter, melted

Preheat oven to 375°.

Mix together flour, baking powder, and salt in a large bowl, and add corn meal. In another bowl, mix eggs, honey, milk, and margarine. Combine flour and egg mixtures, and beat until smooth, but don't overmix. Bake in a well-greased muffin tin for 20 to 25 minutes.

Yields 12 muffins

Variation: For a sweeter muffin, increase the honey to 1/2 cup.

Chicken Salad

 M   Phyllis Santis Stewart

1 whole poached chicken
  breast
1 celery stalk, cut into
  ½-inch slices
1–2 scallions, cut into
  ¼-inch slices
½ cup fresh dill, chopped
2 tablespoons tamari sauce,
  or to taste

1–2 drops hot oil (in Oriental
  section of supermarket)
1 small carrot, finely chopped
  and steamed
4–5 drops toasted sesame oil, or
  to taste (optional)
¼ cup mayonnaise, to taste

Cut chicken into ½-inch cubes and place in a large bowl. Add everything (including optional sesame oil) but the mayonnaise and toss gently. If you can, let the mixture stand in a covered container in the refrigerator for about an hour to let the flavors meld. Just before serving, add the mayonnaise.

Serves 4

TU B'SHEVAT SEDER LUNCH

Serves 10–12

No Knead to Stay Around the House Challah
(*see Erev Yom Kippur Dinners* ～ 20)
Noodle Kugel ～ 101
One Bowl Chinese Tuna Salad ～ 102
Banana Yogurt Cake ～ 103
Orange Chocolate Mousse ～ 104

A Tu B'Shevat Seder

J ewish tradition marks the fifteenth day of the month of Shevat as the New Year for trees ("tu" is the Hebrew word for fifteen), or Rosh Ha-shanah le-Ilanot.

A growing number of Jews today celebrate Tu B'Shevat by following a practice started by Jewish mystics in Tzfat (Safed) in the sixteenth century. Rabbi Isaac Luria and his followers would make a special seder, in many ways modeled on the Passover seder, in which four cups of wine were drunk and symbolic foods — in this case, all kinds of fruits, nuts, and seeds — were eaten. By eating various fruits and reciting the appropriate blessings, the mystics believed that the flow of holiness through the Tree of Life would be maintained.

Three groups of fruits are eaten at a Tu B'Shevat Seder, each representing one of the worlds of creation through which mystics believe that the divine flows: action, formation, and creation. Four cups of wine are drunk, each one representing a season. The first cup of wine, white wine with a drop of red wine added, symbolizes the winter, when nature is asleep and sometimes covered with snow. The second cup of wine, white with a small amount of red, symbolizes spring, when the sun begins to thaw the frozen earth. The third cup, mostly red with some white, is summer, when vegetables and fruit are abundant and we are reminded of the richness of life. The fourth cup, nearly all red with a drop of white, is autumn, when plants are preparing seed for the next cycle of nature, and the world provides nourishment for the coming generation.

With the return of Jews to the land of Israel, Tu B'Shevat has taken on a new character: Jewish Arbor Day, honoring the reclamation of the land. It marks the beginning of Israel's spring, and people all over the country plant saplings which will grow in the generations to come. Here in New England, Tu B'Shevat usually falls in mid-January and is an antidote to the winter blues, joining us in celebration with our kinsfolk in the land of Israel. If Tu B'Shevat falls on a weekday, the seder can be held on the nearest Shabbat, usually as a mid-day meal.

At the Tu B'Shevat seder, festive tables are laden with fruits and nuts, gleam with colored wines and grape juice, and are fragrant with flowers and spices. It is customary to enhance the Tu B'Shevat seder by singing songs and telling stories. This holiday reinvigorates our harmony with nature and, in a modern world, affords a wonderful opportunity to promote our ecological efforts.

Moshe Waldoks

כוס ראשון

Cup One

Pour the first cup of white wine with a single drop of red wine.

The first world: Assiyah (action) — Winter. This level represents our vulnerable lives as fragile and fleeting. The stark contrast of light and dark is symbolized by fruits with inedible shells (such as oranges, grapefruits, bananas, pomegranates, kiwis, nuts, served whole so they can be opened at the table). Blessing over fruits, fruits are eaten, blessing over wine (if the seder takes place on Shabbat, add morning Shabbat kiddush before blessing the wine), drink the first cup of wine.

ברוך אתה יי, אלהינו מלך העולם, בורא פרי העץ

ברוך אתה יי, אלהינו מלך העולם, בורא פרי הגפן

כוס שני

Cup Two

Pour the second cup of mostly white wine with a small amount of red or rosé wine.

The second world: Yetzirah (formation) — Spring. This level represents the less fragile, shadowy transition from cold to warmth. It is symbolized by fruits with inedible pits (plums, peaches, apricots, nectarines, dates, cherries, mangoes, etc.). Blessing over fruits, fruits are eaten, blessing over wine, drink the second cup. At this time lunch can be served, except for dessert, which can be served with the last cup of wine.

כוס שלישי

Cup Three

Pour the third cup of mostly red wine with some white or rosé wine.

The third world: Beriah (creation) — Summer. This level represents the unshielded light of creation, the fullness of life. It is symbolized by fruits which are entirely edible (figs, apples, pears, starfruit, raisins, etc.). Blessing over fruits, fruits are eaten, blessing over wine, drink the third cup.

כוס רביעי

Cup Four

Pour the fourth cup of red wine with a single drop of white wine.

The fourth world: Atzilut (emanation) — Autumn. This level represents the world beyond physical perfection, the afterglow of being fully alive, reaching the essence of one's being. It is symbolized by fragrant flowers and spices (roses, cinnamon, allspice, nutmeg, fragrant herbal teas). Blessing over spices:

ברוך אתה יי, אלהינו מלך העולם, בורא מיני בשמים

enjoy the fragrance, blessing over wine, drink the fourth cup. At this time dessert may be served.

Noodle Kugel

 Janet Chiel

12 ounces medium noodles
6 tablespoons margarine
3 eggs, beaten
1/2 cup lowfat vanilla yogurt
1/2 cup sugar, or more to taste
4 ounces evaporated milk

1/2 pound part-skim ricotta cheese
1 teaspoon vanilla extract
Graham cracker crumbs for topping
8 tablespoons margarine (optional)

Preheat oven to 350°.

Cook noodles and drain.

Place margarine in a 2 to 3 quart glass baking dish, and heat in the oven until it melts. Increase oven temperature to 450°. Combine eggs, yogurt, sugar, milk, ricotta cheese, and vanilla in a large bowl. Pour melted margarine into the batter and mix. Pour all the mixture into the baking dish. Top with graham cracker crumbs and pats of margarine, if desired. Bake for 10 minutes. Lower heat to 350° and bake for 50 minutes, or until lightly browned.

Serves 10

One Bowl Chinese Tuna Salad

 Lucille Smolens

This is a low-cholesterol, quick and easy main dish that everyone enjoys.

4 6^1/$_2$-ounce cans white tuna
  in water, drained
1 bunch romaine or red leaf
  lettuce, chopped
1 8-ounce can bamboo
  shoots, drained
1 8-ounce can water
  chestnuts, drained
1 12^1/$_2$-ounce jar three bean
  salad, drained
1 cup mushrooms, sliced

1 red bell pepper, chopped
3 celery stalks, sliced
3 hard-boiled egg whites,
  chopped
3 tablespoons no-cholesterol
  mayonnaise
1 tablespoon lemon juice
Salt and pepper, to taste
^{1}/$_4$ cup toasted almond slivers,
  for garnish

Toss all the ingredients, except for the almond slivers, together in a large bowl. Refrigerate for 1 hour. Top with almond slivers before serving.

Serves 10–12

Banana Yogurt Cake

 Carol Ghatan

¹/₂ cup margarine	Dash of salt
³/₄ cup sugar	2¹/₂ cups all-purpose flour
1 egg	3¹/₂ teaspoons baking powder
¹/₂ teaspoon baking soda	1 teaspoon vanilla extract
³/₄ cup yogurt, any flavor	¹/₂ cup dried fruits and nuts,
4 ripe bananas, mashed	chopped

Preheat oven to 350° and grease a 9-inch spring-form pan.

In a large bowl, cream margarine and sugar together. Add the egg and mix. In a small bowl, dissolve the baking soda in yogurt and add to the mixture. Add the remaining ingredients and mix. Pour into the pan and bake until a cake tester inserted in the center comes out clean, about 1 hour.

Serves 8

Orange Chocolate Mousse

  Gilbert and Davis Catering, West Roxbury, Massachusetts

12 ounces pareve chocolate bits or semi-sweet baking chocolate

4 tablespoons unsalted pareve margarine

Zest of 2 oranges

Dash of vanilla extract

2 tablespoons strong coffee

4 tablespoons orange liqueur (optional, omit for Pesach)

6 eggs, separated, at room temperature

Pinch of salt

1 cup sugar

Over barely simmering water in double boiler, slowly melt chocolate with margarine, zest, vanilla, coffee, and liqueur until smooth in a large bowl. Cool to room temperature.

While chocolate is melting, beat egg whites in a large bowl until frothy. Add pinch of salt. Continue beating egg whites while adding $^1/_2$ cup sugar. Beat until stiff peaks form.

In a separate bowl, whip yolks with remaining sugar until they double in volume and form a pale yellow ribbon.

Using a spatula, fold egg-yolk mixture into chocolate mixture. Then fold $^1/_4$ of the egg whites into the chocolate. Gently fold the remaining whites into chocolate mixture. Spoon mousse into serving dishes. Chill 2 to 3 hours.

Serves 10–15

A MISHLOACH MANOT BASKET FOR PURIM

Serves 24

*On Purim, two gifts or portions (traditionally, one of flour and
one of fruit or nuts) are brought to at least one friend
(Book of Esther, chapter 9). The messenger is often a young child
who is eager to help with the baking and decorating of the baskets.
The following recipes will make 2 dozen baskets (either dairy or pareve).
Paper plates covered with colored cellophane (or any
other invention) can be used instead of real baskets.*

Orange Hamentaschen Dairy Dough ～ 106
Prune Pareve Hamantaschen Filling ～ 106
Pareve Hamentaschen Dough ～ 107
Poppy Seed Pareve Hamentaschen Filling ～ 108
Prune and Apricot Hamentaschen Filling ～ 108
Coconut Balls ～ 109
Chocolate Chip Mandelbrot ～ 110
Chocolate Crunchies (*see Break Fast Buffet* ～ 40)
Nuts
Candies
Dried Fruits

Orange Hamentaschen Dairy Dough

 Ivy Feuerstadt

1 1/2 cups unbleached white
  flour
1/2 cup whole wheat pastry
  flour
1/2 cup honey coated wheat
  germ
2 teaspoons baking powder

1/4 teaspoon salt
3/4 cup sugar
1/2 cup unsalted butter
1 egg
Grated rind of 2 oranges
1 1/2 tablespoons orange juice

Mix flours, wheat germ, baking powder, salt, sugar, and butter in food processor or large bowl. Add remaining ingredients and blend. Cover and refrigerate several hours or overnight.

Preheat oven to 375°.

Roll out dough on a well-floured surface. Cut into 2 1/2-inch circles. Put 2 teaspoons of filling in the center of the circle, fold 3 sides toward the center and pinch the edges touching together to form a triangle, something like a tricorner hat. Bake for about 15 minutes, or until dough is lightly browned.

Yields 2 dozen hamentaschen

Prune Pareve Hamentaschen Filling

 Amelia Welt Katzen

3/4 cup pitted prunes
1 teaspoon orange rind,
  grated

1/4 cup almonds, ground

Purée the prunes, or boil them for 3 minutes in 1 cup water. Drain and chop into small pieces

Combine all ingredients in a bowl and use to fill pareve hamentaschen dough.

Yields 3/4 cup filling

Pareve Hamentaschen Dough

 P   Nancy Zibman

²/₃ cup sugar
¹/₂ cup pareve margarine
¹/₄ cup honey
1 teaspoon vanilla extract
3 large eggs, beaten
1¹/₂ cups whole wheat pastry
flour

2¹/₂ cups unbleached white
flour
2 teaspoons baking powder
1 teaspoon cinnamon
Dash of salt
¹/₂ teaspoon baking soda

Beat sugar with margarine in a bowl until light and fluffy. Blend in honey, vanilla, and eggs.

In a small bowl, mix flours, baking powder, cinnamon, salt, and baking soda. Add to honey mixture and stir until well blended. Chill at least 3 hours, or overnight. All or part of dough can be frozen for later use.

Preheat oven to 350°.

Roll out dough on well-floured surface. Cut into 2¹/₂-inch circles. Put 2 teaspoons of filling in the center of the circle, fold 3 sides toward the center and pinch the edges touching together to form a triangle, something like a tricorner hat. Bake on a greased cookie sheet for about 15 minutes, or until dough is lightly browned.

Yields 2 dozen hamentaschen

Poppy Seed Pareve Hamentaschen Filling

 Nancy Zibman

¹/₂ cup poppy seeds
³/₄ cup raisins
2 tablespoons honey

2 tablespoons pareve margarine, melted
2 teaspoons grated lemon peel

Combine all ingredients in a small saucepan and simmer over low heat, stirring constantly, until the margarine is melted and all the ingredients are combined. Let cool. Use to fill Pareve Hamentaschen Dough, page 107.

Yields ¹/₂ cup

Prune and Apricot Hamenstaschen Filling

  Arline Shapiro

1 pound dried prunes
1 pound dried apricots
1 orange, peeled and seeded

¹/₂ cup nuts, chopped (optional)
Sugar, to taste

Place fruit in saucepan, add water to cover. Bring to a boil, then simmer uncovered until fruit is plump and tender.

Drain and remove pits. Put cooked fruit and orange through medium blade of mini-food chopper or chop finely. Add nuts and sugar if desired. Use to fill Orange Hamentaschen Dairy Dough, page 106, or Pareve Hamentaschen Dough, page 107.

Yields 3 cups filling

Coconut Balls

 Toba Kimball

These are even great eaten straight from the freezer!

1 cup sugar
1¹/₂ cups dates, chopped
2 eggs
2 cups crisped rice cereal

1 cup walnuts, broken into
  pieces
2 teaspoons vanilla extract
2 cups shredded coconut

Mix sugar, dates, and eggs in a large skillet. Cook over low heat for 10 minutes and transfer to a large bowl. Add cereal, walnuts, and vanilla and mix together.

Moisten hands with water, shape into small balls, and roll in coconut. Refrigerate until serving.

These also freeze well.

Yields 50–60 balls

Chocolate Chip Mandelbrot

 Ivy Feuerstadt

The literal translation of mandelbrot is "almond bread," but this is a variation without almonds. This has become a favorite recipe of my family and friends.

1 cup sugar
1 cup corn oil
4 eggs
3 cups all-purpose flour
1¹/₂ teaspoons baking powder

1 teaspoon cinnamon
1 teaspoon vanilla extract
12 ounces pareve chocolate
  chips

Preheat oven to 350°. Grease and flour two cookie sheets.

In a large bowl, mix sugar, oil, and eggs. Add flour, baking powder, cinnamon, and vanilla. Mix well. Add chips and mix until dough comes together. It is very sticky! Divide the dough into five portions. Shape each one into an oval loaf. Place loaves two inches apart on the cookie sheets.

Bake in the middle of the oven about 20 minutes until tops are brown. Then remove from oven and cool about 10 minutes.

Meanwhile, raise the rack one notch and preheat broiler. Slice the mandelbrot into ¹/₂-inch thick slices. Turn the slices over and broil for about 30 seconds. Turn them over again and broil for another 30 seconds. Don't let them burn! Transfer to racks to cool.

Yields 4¹/₂ dozen

Pesach — Feast of Freedom

his general guide to food for Pesach is adapted from the Pesach Guide of the Rabbinical Assembly Committee on Jewish Law and Standards, accepted on December 12, 1984. However, consult your rabbi when any doubt arises. *Kosher l'Pesach* products with labels that do not bear the name of a rabbi, or one of the recognized symbols of rabbinic supervision, should not be used without consulting your rabbi.

Prohibited foods include the following: leavened bread, cakes, biscuits, crackers, cereal, coffees containing cereal derivatives, wheat, barley, oats, spelt, rye, and all liquids containing ingredients or flavors made from grain alcohol. Most Ashkenazic authorities add the following foods *(kitniyot)*: rice, corn, millet, legumes (beans and peas; however string beans are permitted). The Committee on Jewish Law and Standards has ruled unanimously that peanuts and peanut oil are permissible, as peanuts are not actually legumes. Some Ashkenazic authorities permit, while others forbid, the use of legumes in a form other than their natural state, for example, corn sweeteners, corn oil, soy oil. Some Sephardic authorities permit the use of *kitniyot* on Pesach.

Permitted Foods

The following foods require no *kosher l'Pesach* label if purchased before or during Pesach: fresh fruits and vegetables (for legumes, see above), eggs, fresh fish and fresh meat.

The following foods require no *kosher l'Pesach* label if purchased before Pesach: unopened packages or containers of natural coffee without cereal additives (however, be aware that coffees produced by General Foods are not kosher for Pesach unless marked KP); sugar; pure tea; salt (not iodized); pepper; natural spices; frozen fruit juices with no additives; frozen (uncooked) vegetables (for legumes, see above); milk; butter; cottage cheese; cream cheese; ripened cheeses such as Cheddar (hard), Muenster (semi-soft), and Camembert (soft); frozen (uncooked) fruit (with no additives); baking soda.

The following foods require a *kosher l'Pesach* label if purchased before or during Pesach: all baked products (matzoh, cakes, matzoh flour, farfel, matzoh meal and any products containing matzoh); canned or bottled fruit juices (these juices are often clarified with *kitniyot* which are not listed among the ingredients — however, if one knows there are no such agents, the juice may be purchased prior to Pesach without a *kosher l'Pesach* label); canned tuna (since tuna, even when packed in water, has often been processed in vegetable broth and/or hydrolyzed protein — however, if it is known that the tuna is packed exclusively in water, without any additional ingredients or additives, it may be purchased without a *kosher l'Pesach* label); wine; vinegar; liquor; oils; dried fruits; candy; chocolate-flavored milk; ice cream; yogurt and soda.

The following processed foods (canned, bottled, or frozen) require a *kosher l'Pesach* label if purchased during Pesach: milk, butter, juices, vegetables, fruit, milk products, spices, coffee, tea, and fish.

SUGGESTED PESACH RECIPES

Please note that many of these recipes have been adapted for Pesach. About three weeks before Pesach, choose the recipes you might like to prepare for the holiday so that you can buy the new spices you will need. Since there is a wide variation in practice and customs in Conservative Jewish observance, please consult your rabbi.

Appetizers

Baba Ghanouj ～ 282
Chopped Liver ～ 132
Easy Gefilte Fish ～ 116
Salat Hatzalim ～ 71
Sue's Salmon Roll ～ 140
Tuna Horseradish Dip ～ 136

Salads

Abigail's Eggplant Salad from
　Israel ～ 163
Beet Salad ～ 266
Carrot Salad ～ 16
Cheese and Egg Salad ～ 265
Cucumber Salad with Fresh Dill ～ 35
Cucumbers Vinaigrette ～ 180
Eggplant Salad ～ 132
Ginger Cucumber Salad ～ 190
Greek Israeli Eggplant Salad ～ 197

Soups

Chicken Soup ～ 7
Cucumber Yogurt Soup ～ 227
Homemade Tomato Soup ～ 26
Matzoh Balls ～ 118
Simple Vegetable Soup ～ 126

Main Dishes — Dairy

Baked Broccoli ～ 90
Broiled Swordfish ～ 72
Cheese and Spinach Casserole ～ 32
Eggplant Lamaze ～ 285
Herring in Sour Cream ～ 33
Microwave Poached Salmon ～ 287
Poached Salmon with Yogurt Dill
　Sauce ～ 288
Rolled Fish Fillets ～ 137
Salmon en Papillote ～ 14
Stuffed Sole for Passover ～ 127

Main Dishes — Pareve

Spring Pancakes ～ 299
Grilled Halibut Kabobs ～ 187
Microwave Poached Salmon ～ 287
My Mother's Sweet and Sour Fish ～ 6
Simple Sole ～ 303
Vegetarian Stuffed Cabbage ～ 120

Main Dishes — Meat

Cinnamon Honey Chicken ～ 9
Cinnamon Meatballs ～ 269
Greek Potato Moussaka ～ 290
Grilled Chicken Caribbean ～ 179
Lamb with Eggplant ～ 47
Orange Turkey Breast ～ 133
Shabbat Chicken ～ 245
Stuffed Breast of Veal ～ 295
Stuffed Cabbage ～ 207
Stuffed Celery ～ 277
Syrian Meat Balls ～ 296

Kugels

Bubbie's Cauliflower Kugel ~ 134
Grandma's Apple Kugel ~ 128
Pareve Matzoh Kugel ~ 119
Passover Fruit Kugel ~ 144
Passover Spinach Muffins ~ 141

Vegetables

Cauliflower Tiberias ~ 268
Easy Yummy Sweet Potatoes ~ 317
Fan Potatoes ~ 122
Oven Roasted Potatoes ~ 27
Potato Puff ~ 137
Whole Baked Onions ~ 55

Desserts

Bible Fruit Salad ~ 142
Carrot Cake for Pesach ~ 145
Chocolate Mousse Torte ~ 135
Fresh Strawberry Pie ~ 124
Grape Freeze ~ 129
Lace Wafers ~ 125
Orange Chocolate Mousse ~ 104
Plum Compote ~ 123
Raspberry Sauce ~ 90
Yali's Favorite Birthday Cake ~ 138

PESACH SEDER

Serves 16

Kiddush Wine

Traditional Seder Plate

Hard-Boiled Eggs, Chopped or Whole, with Salt Water

Easy Gefilte Fish ～ 116

Chicken Soup (*see Rosh Hashanah Dinners* ～ 7)
with Matzoh Balls ～ 118

Roast Capon

Pareve Matzoh Kugel — double recipe ～ 119

Vegetarian Stuffed Cabbage ～ 120

Steamed Asparagus with Lemon Wedges

Fan Potatoes ～ 122

Plum Compote — double recipe ～ 123

Fresh Strawberry Pie — double recipe ～ 124

Lace Wafers ～ 125

Kiddush Wine

Traditional Seder Plate

Hard-Boiled Eggs, Chopped or Whole, with Salt Water

Simple Vegetable Soup — double recipe ～ 126
with Matzoh Balls ～ 118

Stuffed Sole for Passover — triple recipe ～ 127

Grandma's Apple Kugel ～ 128

Steamed Asparagus with Lemon Wedges

Grape Freeze ～ 129

Fresh Strawberry Pie — double recipe ～ 124

Orange Chocolate Mousse (*see Tu B'Shevat Seder Lunch* ～ 104)

Easy Gefilte Fish

 Melinda Strauss

This is a recipe for intimidated cooks who believe that making gefilte fish from scratch is too much work (it calls for using a food processor). This dish keeps very well in the refrigerator for several days.

Here in the Boston area, some fish markets in Jewish neighborhoods stock freshwater fish right before Rosh Hashanah and Pesach — although there's always a danger they will run out several days before the holidays — and will special-order it at other times. Other markets take specific phone orders at least a month before the holidays, so call around well in advance. Regardless of how and when you purchase your fish, you must cook it the same day you buy it.

At the market, ask for a combination of whitefish, pike, and winter or buffel carp — about $8^1/2$ pounds of whole fish — enough to yield about $3^1/2$ pounds filleted. Ask them to grind it for you, tell you the exact weight of it after it's been ground, and to give you the heads, skin, and bones separately.

Since the weight of three whole fish won't be exactly $8^1/2$ pounds, the weight of the ground fish will vary. For 4 pounds ground, use the variations provided to adjust the amounts of the ingredients.

Fish head, skin, bones
6 onions, sliced
$3^1/2$ teaspoons salt
1 teaspoon freshly ground
   black pepper
2 quarts plus 2 cups water

Fish balls:
$1^1/2$ large onions
$3^1/2$ pounds ground fish

4 large eggs
1 cup ice water
$^1/2$ teaspoon sugar
$4^1/2$ tablespoons matzoh meal
$3^1/2$ teaspoons salt
1 teaspoon fresh ground black
   pepper
2 large carrots, julienned
Red or green leaf lettuce for
   garnish

To make the broth, combine head, skin, and bones in a very large (at least 8 quarts) pot with sliced onions, salt, pepper, and water. Bring to a boil, then simmer while preparing the fish.

Chop onions finely in a food processor, then add the rest of the ingredients, except the carrots and lettuce, and process for about 30 seconds. Let stand for 10 minutes.

Moisten hands with water, shape the mixture into balls or ovals, and gently drop into the simmering stock on top of all the stock ingredients. Partially cover and simmer over low heat for 1 hour. Remove cover and cook for 30 minutes more. Occasionally spoon broth over top balls if they get dry.

Let the fish balls cool in the pot, then carefully remove to a storage container. Strain broth. Save 1 cup in a small saucepan, and pour the rest over the fish. Heat the broth in the saucepan to simmer, add carrots, and cook until carrots are just tender, about 10 minutes. Add carrots to storage container, and refrigerate.

Serve fish, strewn with carrots, at room temperature, arranged on lettuce.

Yields about 42 palm-sized pieces or 55 small balls

Variation: For 4 pounds of ground fish, adjust these amounts as follows: Fish ball ingredients: 2 large onions, 5 large eggs, 3³/₄ teaspoons salt, 5¹/₂ tablespoons matzoh meal, same amounts ice water, sugar, and pepper.

Matzoh Balls

  Shirley Shulman

4 eggs, beaten	Dash of black pepper
1/4 cup safflower oil	1/2 cup seltzer
1 teaspoon kosher coarse salt	1 cup matzoh meal

Combine eggs, oil, salt, pepper, and seltzer in a large bowl and mix thoroughly. Add matzoh meal. Mix again to create a relatively stiff batter. Store covered in the refrigerator for 1 to 3 hours.

Remove from refrigerator. In a large pot,* bring about 2 quarts of salted water to a rolling boil. Have a bowl of hot water nearby in which to dip your hands. Form golf ball-sized balls and gently drop them into the pot. After sculpting each ball, dip your hands into the hot water; this creates a smoother and eventually fluffier ball. Balls should begin to float soon after they have begun to cook; they will puff up to the size of tennis balls. Cook partially covered for about 30 to 35 minutes. Test one to be sure the center is light in color and texture.

Remove matzoh balls from pot with a slotted spoon and place in a bowl. When cool, transfer to the refrigerator until ready to serve. Reheat balls in gently simmering chicken soup.

Yields 16 very large matzoh balls

*Editors' Note: For whiter color, many cooks use a white enamel pot to cook matzoh balls.

Pareve Matzoh Kugel

  Melinda Strauss

3 matzohs
6 eggs, beaten
$\frac{1}{2}$ cup sugar plus 1 tablespoon
$\frac{1}{2}$ teaspoon salt
$\frac{1}{2}$ teaspoon cinnamon
$\frac{1}{2}$ cup golden raisins

$\frac{1}{2}$ cup almonds, chopped and lightly toasted
4 tart apples, grated
Grated rind of 1 orange
$\frac{1}{4}$ cup pareve margarine, melted

Preheat oven to 350°.

Crumble matzohs into a bowl, cover with water, and soak until soft. In a separate bowl, mix eggs, sugar, salt, and $\frac{1}{4}$ teaspoon cinnamon until well blended. Squeeze water out of crumbled matzoh and add matzoh to egg mixture. Add raisins, almonds, apples and orange rind, and mix well. Pour mixture into a well-greased 1$\frac{1}{2}$-quart casserole.

Mix the remaining sugar and cinnamon together and sprinkle over the mixture. Drizzle margarine over the top. Bake until firm and lightly browned, about 45 minutes to 1 hour. This recipe can be doubled and baked in a 9 x 13-inch pan.

Serves 6–8

Vegetarian Stuffed Cabbage

  Melinda Strauss

Although the ingredients for the filling and sauce are different for Passover and everyday stuffed cabbage, the directions for rolling and cooking are the same, so both versions are included in this recipe. This is a good alternative main dish at a fleishig seder with vegetarian guests. It tastes best when made ahead and cooked again before serving.

Passover filling:
1 box matzoh, crumbled
  (I use mostly egg matzoh
  with some finely ground
  whole wheat matzoh)
4 cups vegetable stock
  or water
1/2 cup almonds, chopped
1/2 cup matzoh meal
1 large onion, finely chopped
4 large eggs, beaten
1/2 cup dark raisins
Salt and pepper, to taste

Passover sauce:
4 11-ounce cans *kosher
  l'Pesach* tomato mushroom
  sauce
4 1/2 cups vegetable stock
1 1/3 cups brown sugar
1 1/2 cups fresh lemon juice
2 cups dry white wine

Everyday filling:
1 1/2 cups barley
3 1/2 cups vegetable stock or
  water
1 tablespoon vegetable oil
1 teaspoon salt
3/4 cup pistachios, coarsely
  chopped
3 large eggs, beaten
2 medium onions, finely
  chopped
1/2 cup dark raisins
Salt and pepper, to taste

Everyday sauce:
2 1/4 cups tomato purée
2 1/2 cups vegetable stock
2/3 cup brown sugar
3/4 cup fresh lemon juice
1 cup dry white wine
1 8-ounce can tomato sauce

2 heads Savoy cabbage, or
  3 heads for Passover recipe
Lemon and tomato slices for
  garnish (optional)

To prepare Passover filling and sauce, combine all filling ingredients in a bowl and set aside. Combine all sauce ingredients in a bowl and set aside.

To prepare everyday filling and sauce, combine barley, stock, oil, and salt in a large saucepan and bring to a boil. Lower the heat, cover, and simmer for 40 minutes. Turn off heat and let stand covered for 30 minutes, or until all the water is absorbed. Stir in remaining filling ingredients and season to taste. Combine all sauce ingredients in a bowl and set aside.

Core each head of cabbage, and place in a large pot of slowly boiling salted water. Cover pot and simmer 15 minutes. Drain and cool until the leaves are comfortable to handle. Discard any torn outer leaves. Peel off a leaf and lay it down so that the inside faces you; if the bottom is too thick to roll, trim off some cabbage so that it is flexible.

Place leaf on a flat surface. Place about 2 tablespoons of filling at the core of the leaf, roll over once, tuck in both sides, and roll up all the way. Repeat until the filling is used up, using only the larger leaves — or about ²/₃ of each head.

Preheat oven to 350°.

Place rolls, flap down, in a 9 x 13-inch casserole, layering if necessary, and pour sauce over rolls. Reserve 1 cup sauce for basting and adding during first and second baking. Bake uncovered for 35 to 40 minutes, basting occasionally.

Remove from oven, allow to cool, and refrigerate overnight or longer, or freeze for later use (thaw before reheating).

Cook rolls again at 350° for 45 to 50 minutes, basting and adding sauce if needed. They can sit in a warm oven a while before serving. Garnish with lemon and/or tomato slices, if desired.

Yields about 35 Passover rolls, 20 everyday ones

Fan Potatoes

  Lois Nadel

This is one of those quick but fancy vegetable dishes that looks elegant enough for a dinner party. The potatoes can be peeled, sliced, and kept in ice water in the refrigerator to avoid last-minute rush.

16 baking potatoes
1 cup pareve margarine, melted

$^1/_2$ teaspoon paprika
Salt, to taste

Select baking potatoes of the same size. Peel and slice crosswise thinly, but be sure to leave a base of uncut potato. Wash in cold water and dry.

Preheat oven to 350°.

Spray a jelly-roll pan with a vegetable-oil spray and place potatoes on pan. Brush well with melted margarine and bake for 1 to 1$^1/_2$ hours (depending on size). Mix the paprika with the remaining margarine and use this to baste the potatoes often. As they bake, the slices open up like a fan.

Serves 16

Plum Compote

  Ann Daitch

A favorite dessert during Passover.

2 pounds plums	¹/₂ cup sugar
1 cup water	Juice of 1 lemon

Pit the plums and cut them into quarters (do not peel).

Combine water, sugar, and lemon juice in a saucepan, and bring to a boil. Add plums and simmer uncovered about 10 minutes, stirring occasionally, until fruit is soft.

Serve cold alone or spooned over ice cream or sponge cake.

Serves 8

Fresh Strawberry Pie

  Sena Yamuder, Izzy's Kosher Catering,
Warwick, Rhode Island

¹/₂ cup matzoh meal	5 pints fresh strawberries
¹/₂ cup walnuts, chopped	1²/₃ cup water
2 tablespoons sugar	2 cups sugar
Dash of salt	5–6 tablespoons potato starch
¹/₄ teaspoon cinnamon	
¹/₂ cup pareve margarine, melted	

Preheat oven to 375°.

Blend meal, walnuts, sugar, salt, and cinnamon in a small bowl. Add melted margarine. Mix well. Press into a 9-inch pie plate and bake for 10 to 15 minutes. Cool.

Wash and drain the berries.

To make the glaze, take 2 cups of smaller berries, cut them up and place in a medium pot. Add 1 cup of water, bring to a boil, and simmer for 3 minutes. Place sugar, ²/₃ cup water, and potato starch in a medium bowl and mix until smooth. Add to the berry mixture. Boil, stirring constantly for 5 minutes, until clear and thick. Cover and chill for 2 hours in refrigerator.

Put a layer of the glaze in the pie shell and arrange fresh berries over it. Pour glaze over. Alternate berries and glaze. End with a layer of glaze. Refrigerate or cool or serve immediately.

Serves 6

Lace Wafers

Sena Yamuder, Izzy's Kosher Catering,
Warwick, Rhode Island

*Haddar Products makes confectioners' sugar kosher l'Pesach for the frosting,
but if you can't find it, substitute the mixture below.*

*You can make sandwich cookies by doubling this recipe and using the
chocolate frosting as a filling.*

$^1/_2$ cup finely ground
blanched almonds

$^1/_4$ cup granulated sugar

1 tablespoon potato starch

$^1/_2$ cup melted butter or
pareve margarine

1 tablespoon milk or water

$^1/_2$ cup chocolate chips

$^1/_2$ cup confectioners sugar
(or $^1/_2$ cup less $1^1/_2$ teaspoons
granulated sugar mixed with
$1^1/_2$ teaspoons potato starch,
ground to a powder in a
blender)

1 tablespoon water

Preheat oven to 350°. Grease a cookie sheet and dust with potato
starch or cake meal.

Grind the almonds using the steel blade of a food processor.
Mix in the other ingredients. Drop mixture on cookie sheet by
$^1/_2$ teaspoonfuls about 3 inches apart. Bake 8 to 10 minutes or
until lightly browned. The batter will spread and become very thin
and lacy.

Cool on the pan not longer than 1 minute. Remove carefully with
a wide spatula to a wire rack.

Meanwhile, melt chips in a saucepan over low heat. Add sugar
and water and mix well. Remove from heat. Frost cookies when cool.

Yields 2 dozen cookies

Simple Vegetable Soup

  Amelia Welt Katzen

1 onion
6 carrots
2 large potatoes
2 large celery roots or
  parsnips
2 celery stalks
4 tablespoons pareve
  margarine

4 cups water
2 cups vegetable bouillon
2 tablespoons fresh parsley,
  finely chopped
Salt and pepper, to taste

Chop the onion into fairly small pieces and the rest of the vegetables into hearty, bite-sized ones.

Melt the margarine in a large soup pot and cook the onion over low heat until transparent, about 10 minutes. Add the other chopped vegetables and continue cooking for 10 minutes, stirring occasionally. Add the water and bouillon, cover partially, and simmer for 30 minutes or until the vegetables are tender. (This soup can be cooled to this point and stored, covered, in the refrigerator for a few days.) Just before serving, season to taste and add a pinch of parsley to each bowl.

Serves 4–6

Stuffed Sole for Passover

   Melinda Strauss

This stuffed sole can be prepared in advance and baked right before serving.

8 sole fillets
Salt and pepper, to taste
³/₄ cup butter or pareve
　margarine
¹/₂ cup shallots, minced
¹/₂ cup mushrooms, chopped

2 egg matzohs
¹/₂ cup scallions, finely chopped
2 egg yolks, slightly beaten
¹/₂ teaspoon salt
Parsley and lemon slices for
　garnish

Preheat oven to 375°.

Rinse and wipe sole. Sprinkle with salt and pepper and set aside.

Melt 4 tablespoons butter in small pan over medium heat and sauté shallots for 2 minutes. Add mushrooms and sauté 5 minutes, stirring occasionally. Cool.

Break or chop matzoh into very small pieces in a large bowl. Add shallot mixture, scallions, 4 tablespoons melted butter, egg yolks and salt. Toss well.

Arrange four fillets skin side down in shallow buttered jelly-roll pan. Spread each fillet with ¹/₄ of the stuffing. Cover with remaining fillets, whiter sides up. Dot with 4 tablespoons butter. Fish can be covered and refrigerated at this point, and brought to room temperature before baking.

Bake for about 20 minutes, basting twice with the butter drippings in the pan.

Garnish and serve.

Serves 4 generously

Grandma's Apple Kugel

  Heni Koenig-Plonskier

Grandma Ethel's five grandchildren adore this quick and easy recipe, as do the rest of the gang.

3 pounds apples, peeled, cored and cut into ¼-inch slices

3 eggs

½ cup vegetable oil

¾ cup sugar or sucanat (available at natural food stores)

½ cup orange juice

Pinch of salt

1 cup unbleached white flour (substitute ¼ cup potato starch and ½ cup cake meal for Pesach)

½ cup crushed, pareve graham crackers (ground nuts for Pesach)

1 teaspoon cinnamon

Preheat oven to 350° and grease a 9 x 13-inch pan.

Place apples in a large bowl. In another bowl, beat eggs until frothy. Add oil, sugar, juice, salt, and flour to the eggs, then add the mixture to the apples, and toss until everything is combined. Spread evenly in the pan.

In a small bowl, combine graham crackers and cinnamon, and sprinkle over apple mixture. Bake for one hour or until a toothpick inserted into the center comes out clean.

This recipe can be made the day before and reheated at 350°.

Serves 10–12

Grape Freeze

   Jonah Strauss

1 medium-large bunch of red
  grapes
1 tablespoon sugar, or more
  to taste

¼ cup milk (optional)

Pick grapes off stem and wash thoroughly. Place in a bowl and freeze for 3 to 4 hours or until hard. Then chop grapes in a food processor until mushy. Mix in sugar and optional milk.

Return to bowl and freeze for 30 minutes to 1 hour until frozen to desired consistency.

Scoop into small bowls and serve.

Serves 14

PESACH FAMILY DINNER

Serves 16

Chopped Liver ✹ 132
Eggplant Salad ✹ 132
Orange Turkey Breast ✹ 133
Bubbie's Cauliflower Kugel ✹ 134
Boiled New Potatoes with Chopped Parsley
Chocolate Mousse Torte ✹ 135

Tuna-Horseradish Dip ✹ 136
Rolled Fish Fillets — double recipe ✹ 137
Potato Puff ✹ 137
Steamed Zucchini Rounds
Yali's Favorite Birthday Cake ✹ 138

Chopped Liver

  Arline Shapiro

1 pound calves liver
1/2 pound chicken livers
4 ounces mushrooms, sliced
Vegarine vegetable flavor spread (available in kosher food stores), or pareve margarine

1 hard-boiled egg
1 celery stalk, chopped
1 onion, chopped
Salt, to taste

Broil livers until pink in the middle only. In a skillet, sauté mushrooms over medium heat in vegetable spread until warmed through. Put all ingredients through a meat grinder or chop in a food processor. Add salt if desired.

Yields 6 cups

Eggplant Salad

  Miriam Hoffman

1 medium eggplant
5–6 cloves garlic, chopped
1 green pepper, finely chopped
1 red pepper, finely chopped

2–3 teaspoons parsley, chopped
1 teaspoon vegetable oil
1–1 1/2 tablespoons lemon juice
Salt, to taste

Prick eggplant with a fork and place in a microwavable dish. Bake in microwave for 12 to 14 minutes, or broil in a conventional oven until soft, about 20 minutes. Peel eggplant when cooled and chop finely. Place in a bowl and add all other ingredients. Mix well.

Serves 4

Variation: Broil the whole peppers with the eggplant, then peel, seed, and chop.

Orange Turkey Breast

   Ivy Feuerstadt

I usually marinate this turkey the night before I want to cook it.

1 5¹/₂-pound turkey breast, rinsed and dried well

Dash of garlic powder, or to taste

Dash of paprika, or to taste

Dash of pepper, or to taste

Dash of ground ginger, or to taste

1 cup unsweetened orange marmalade (regular, *kosher l'Pesach* orange marmalade for Pesach)

1 6-ounce can orange juice concentrate, defrosted

6 ounces dried apricots

¹/₂–³/₄ cup raisins (golden and dark mixed look pretty)

2 large onions, sliced

3 large carrots, sliced diagonally

1¹/₂ cups dry white wine

Kosher turkey breasts are usually sold frozen. Defrost and dry very well.

Preheat oven to 350°.

Place the turkey in a large roasting pan. Sprinkle the spices over the breast and rub the marmalade all over. Pour the orange juice concentrate over the turkey. Place the apricots, raisins, and vegetables around the turkey. Add the wine to the pan.

Roast the turkey for about 1¹/₂ hours, depending on weight until tender, basting every 30 minutes. (You can insert a roasting thermometer into the thickest part of the breast, and cook until it has an internal temperature of 185°.) If the top gets too brown before the rest has cooked, cover loosely with greased foil. Make sure there is liquid on the bottom of the pan. If not, add more wine.

Let the turkey sit for about 20 minutes before slicing. To serve, layer the meat over the vegetables and sauce, or pass the sauce separately.

Serves 6–8

Bubbie's Cauliflower Kugel

 Esther Kletter

1 onion
1 large head cauliflower
4 large eggs, beaten
2 tablespoons vegetable oil
$^1/_4$ teaspoon salt, or more to
taste

$^1/_4$ teaspoon pepper, or more to
taste
Paprika (optional)

Preheat oven to 375°.

Chop onion roughly and cut cauliflower into large pieces. Steam cauliflower and onion together until tender.

In a bowl, mash cauliflower and onion with a fork.

Pour oil to cover the bottom of a 9 x 13-inch pan, or 10-inch round casserole. Heat in the oven.

Meanwhile, add eggs to cauliflower and mix well. Mix in salt and pepper. Pour hot oil from pan into cauliflower mixture and stir. Pour all back into pan. Sprinkle with paprika if desired and bake about 35 to 45 minutes until firm and lightly browned on top.

Serve hot or at room temperature.

Serves 6–8

Chocolate Mousse Torte

    Varda E. Farber

This recipe originated at the Hyatt Regency's Trellis Garden Restaurant in Cambridge, Massachusetts. I discovered that by substituting margarine for butter it was a perfect pareve Pesach dessert. It takes some effort but is well worth it!

1½ cups pareve margarine
12 ounces pareve semisweet chocolate, cut in small pieces
12 extra-large eggs

1¾ cup sugar
Unsweetened cocoa powder
Confectioners sugar* (for Pesach see page 125)

Preheat oven to 325°. Cut a circle of waxed paper to fit a 10-inch springform pan and place paper in bottom of pan.

In a saucepan, melt margarine and remove from heat. Add chocolate and stir until melted, about 3 minutes. Let mixture cool slightly (2 to 3 minutes). Separate the eggs, keeping all the yolks and 7 of the whites. Place the yolks in a large bowl, add the sugar, and beat until the mixture forms pale yellow ribbons. Add the chocolate mixture, mix well and set aside.

Beat whites in another large bowl just beyond point where soft peaks form (do not beat until stiff). Fold whites into chocolate mixture gently but thoroughly. Reserving one cup at room temperature, pour batter into prepared pan.

Bake until tester inserted in center comes out clean, about 1½ hours. Let cake cool 10 minutes in the pan, then unlatch the tin and take off the ring.

Remove the top crust of the cake with a sharp serrated knife and reserve. Using a spatula (and your hands) press down around the sides of the cake to level the top. Let cool 10 minutes more. Invert cake onto platter. Let cool completely.

Frost top and sides of cake with reserved mixture. Crush reserved crust between two sheets of waxed paper using a rolling pin. Pat onto sides of cake. Dust the top with cocoa powder.

Serves 8–10

*If using confectioners sugar, place lace paper doily atop cocoa powder and sprinkle the sugar over it. Carefully remove to leave a decorative design. Don't fret: if it's not perfect, it's still delicious.

Tuna-Horseradish Dip

  Susan Sacks

1 6½-ounce can tuna,
  drained
8 ounces cream cheese,
  softened
3 tablespoons milk
2 tablespoons almonds,
  chopped, or more to taste

1 tablespoon onion, minced
1 tablespoon prepared white
  horseradish
¼ teaspoon garlic salt
Dash of pepper
Parsley for garnish, chopped

Preheat oven to 375°.

Mix all the ingredients, except parsley, together in an ovenproof dish and bake about 15 minutes, or until heated through.

Garnish with parsley.

Serve with matzoh crackers for Pesach or with chips the rest of the year.

Serves 8–10

Rolled Fish Fillets

 Faith Friedman

¹/₄ cup butter, melted
1 tablespoon lemon juice
¹/₄ teaspoon white pepper
¹/₄ teaspoon paprika
¹/₂ cup grated Cheddar cheese

¹/₄ pound broccoli florets,
  slightly steamed
1¹/₂ pounds flounder fillets
Lemon slices for garnish

Preheat oven to 375°.

In a small bowl, combine butter, lemon juice, and spices, and set aside. In another bowl, combine cheese and broccoli.

Lay out fillets. Place a couple of tablespoons of the broccoli and cheese mixture on each fillet and roll. Place seam side down in a baking dish. Pour butter sauce over fish and bake for 20 minutes, or until done.

Garnish with lemon slices.

Serves 4

Potato Puff

 Judy Adnepos

6 cups mashed potatoes
1 cup light sour cream
  (regular for Pesach)
1 cup lowfat cottage cheese
  (regular for Pesach)
1 tablespoon onion, minced

Salt and pepper, to taste
2 tablespoons butter, melted
2 teaspoons sesame seeds (omit
  for Pesach)

Preheat oven to 350° and grease a 2-quart casserole.

Combine the potatoes, sour cream, cottage cheese, onion, salt, and pepper and place into the casserole. Pour on melted butter and sprinkle with sesame seeds.

Bake 1 hour or until puffed and golden.

Serves 8

Yali's Favorite Birthday Cake

  Shula Reinharz

A recipe from my mother, Ilse Rothschild of River Edge, New Jersey. See below for Pesach variation.

2 cups broken cookies (plain, chocolate chip, butter, ginger; use *kosher l'Pesach* for Pesach)

2 tablespoons orange or coffee liqueur (optional; omit for Pesach)

10 ounces semi-sweet chocolate chips

1 ½ cups kosher marshmallows

½ cup milk

1 cup heavy cream, whipped

Jimmies, also known as sprinkles (optional; omit for Pesach)

Break the cookies into pieces and place in a 9-inch pie plate. Sprinkle with liqueur, if using.

In a double boiler, melt chocolate chips and marshmallows. Stir in milk, remove from heat and cool.

Stir in whipped cream.

Pour mixture over cookies in pie plate.

Freeze until ready to serve, sprinkled with jimmies.

Serves 6–8

PESACH SHABBAT LUNCH

Serves 8

Kiddush Wine
Sue's Salmon Roll ∾ 140
Salat Hatzilim — double recipe (*see Chanukah Dinners* ∾ 71)
Passover Spinach Muffins ∾ 141
Cold Steamed Broccoli and Cauliflower, Marinated in Salad Dressing
Bible Fruit Salad ∾ 142
Passover Fruit Kugel ∾ 144
Carrot Cake for Pesach ∾ 145

Sue's Salmon Roll

  Lisa Rosenfeld

This recipe was such a hit at our office party that Sue made copies for everyone. Her secret was out. Beacuse the dish looked elegant, we thought it would be complicated. In fact, it is really a quickie, with a high "ah" quotient.

½ small onion
8 ounces Neufchâtel cheese
(use regular cream cheese
for Pesach)

1 14¾-ounce can red salmon
1 cup fresh parsley, finely
chopped

Chop onion in food processor. Add cheese and salmon (without skin and bones). Mix in processor with short pulses just until ingredients start to look blended.

Place a piece of waxed paper about 18 inches long on your work surface. Sprinkle the parsley to cover the paper. Form the salmon into a log shape about 14 inches long on the parsleyed paper. Using the paper, roll the log up and over until it is covered with parsley. Transfer to a serving dish with a spatula. Cover and refrigerate until ready to serve.

Serve with vegetables or as a spread with crackers — use matzoh crackers for Pesach.

Serves 10–12

Passover Spinach Muffins

   Marlene Leffell

2 medium onions, chopped
1/2 cup celery, chopped
1 1/2 cups grated carrots
6 tablespoons pareve
   margarine or 3–4
   tablespoons vegetable oil
1 10-ounce box frozen
   spinach, defrosted and
   drained well

3 eggs, beaten, or 3 egg whites
   and 2 tablespoons vegetable
   oil
3/4 cup matzoh meal
1 1/2 teaspoons salt
1/4 teaspoon pepper

Preheat oven to 350° and grease a 12-cup muffin tin.

In a skillet over medium heat, sauté onions, celery, and carrots in pareve margarine until almost tender. Add spinach during last two minutes of cooking.

Transfer to a bowl, add eggs, matzoh meal, and seasonings. Spoon into the muffin tin. Bake for 45 minutes. If planning to reheat before serving, decrease baking time by 5 minutes.

Yields 12 muffins

Bible Fruit Salad

  Julie Arnow

The idea for this recipe came from Lillian Fink, publisher of the family cook-book Fink Family Favorites, *1979. It came to her one day during Sabbath services and took about one year of research to put together. It was Lillian's idea that by using fruits from the various chapters of the Bible, you could create a Bible fruit salad. The fruits that she chose are:*

Grapes (Isaiah 5:2)
Figs (Proverbs 27:18)
Dates (Joel 1:12)
Pomegranates (Deuteronomy 8:8)
Apples (Song of Solomon 2:3)
Apricots (called apples, Joel 1:12)
Almonds (Ecclesiastes 12:5)
Peanuts (Genesis 43:11)
Walnuts (Song of Solomon 6:11)

Sycamore figs (Amos 7:14)
Citrus (Leviticus 23:40)
Mulberries (II Samuel 5:23)
Melons (Numbers 11:5)
Oranges (Proverbs 17:29)
Honey (II Samuel 17:29)
Cream (Judges 4:19)
Cinnamon (Proverbs 7:17)

Using Lillian's ideas, I put together the following fruit salad.

4 oranges
3 apples
2 cups seedless grapes
1 small canteloupe
4 apricots
1 cup mulberries, or other berry
4 figs, chopped
4 dates, chopped
½ cup slivered or chopped almonds

¼ cup unsalted peanuts (omit for Pesach)
½ cup walnuts, chopped
Seeds of 1 pomegranate

Milk and Honey Dressing:
½ cup cream, half-and-half, or plain or vanilla yogurt
¼ teaspoon cinnamon
½ teaspoon honey, or more to taste

Always begin filling your bowl for fruit salad with the oranges. They are the foundation of the salad, and will keep other fruits from browning. Peel, then cut into slices. Break each round into triangles. Carefully remove all the seeds. Always try to capture all the juice and add it to the bowl.

Slice the apples, leaving the peel on, any way that pleases you. Add to the bowl.

For the grapes, a mixture of red and green is pretty. (If you have patience, concord grapes, which must be individually pitted, add a wonderful, tart flavor.) A very decorative way to add grapes to the fruit salad is to slice them, either by hand or by using the slicing blade of your food processor.

The nicest way to add melon is with a melon baller. If this is not available, cut the melon into wedges and discard the rind. Cut each wedge into triangles.

If apricots are available, they are a great treat. Slice, with the skin on, as they grew on the tree.

I sometimes add $1/2$ cup whole mulberries, then take the remaining $1/2$ cup and gently crush them to bring out the juices. Another alternative is to divide the berries into thirds: some whole, some crushed, and some for garnish.

The basis of the fruit salad is complete. In another bowl mix together the figs, dates, almonds, peanuts, and walnuts, and add it to the fruit. Add pomegranate seeds.

Mix dressing ingredients together in a bowl and toss.

I strongly suggest chilling the fruit salad with the dressing for at least several hours in a covered bowl.

Serves 10–12

Passover Fruit Kugel

   Melinda Strauss

1 cup boiling water
1³/₄ cups matzoh farfel
¹/₃ cup finely ground whole
  wheat matzoh
3 large eggs
¹/₄ cup melted butter
¹/₄ cup light cream

¹/₃ cup sugar
Dash of cinnamon
Dash of salt
1¹/₂ apples, chopped
1¹/₂ ripe bananas, mashed
¹/₄ cup raisins (optional)
¹/₃ cup nuts, chopped (optional)

Preheat oven to 350° and grease an 8 x 8-inch pan.

In a bowl, pour boiling water onto farfel and ground matzoh and leave to cool.

Add eggs one at a time and beat well after each addition. Mix in remaining ingredients.

Place in pan and bake for 1 hour. This recipe can be doubled to fill a 9 x 13-inch pan.

Serves 9

Carrot Cake for Pesach

  Judy Zomer

6 eggs, separated
1 cup sugar
1¼ cups grated carrots

1 cup almonds, finely ground
1 teaspoon lemon juice
1 teaspoon cinnamon

Preheat oven to 350° and grease an 8 x 12-inch glass baking dish or a 9-inch springform pan.

In a large bowl, beat egg whites with ½ cup sugar until peaks form, but do not overbeat.

In a separate bowl, beat yolks with the remaining sugar. Add the carrots, almonds, lemon juice, and cinnamon. Mix well. Fold in egg whites. Pour into baking dish.

Bake for 45 to 60 minutes, until lightly browned and a tester inserted in the center comes out clean.

Serves 8–10

Jewish Haute Cuisine, or,
Kosher in the Clouds

F rankly, keeping kosher can be a pain in the neck. Every time I have a bite to eat, I have to worry about an incredible number of seemingly arbitrary rules.

Meat and milk products at the same meal are a no-no and there have to be separate dishes for each. The only four-legged animals I can eat have to have split hooves and chew their cud. Most conventional fowl are all right but they can't have been killed in the hunt. They, as well as the other animals, have to be slaughtered according to very precise regulations which minimize the animal's pain. Having been slaughtered, they must be inspected. Permissible fish must have fins and scales. Nothing like eels or crabs that creep or slither along the floor of the ocean will do. During the week of Passover there are additional prohibitions. No food made with leaven is allowed. And this is just the beginning.

Some of these regulations are edifying enough or at least have edifying implications, but a lot of them, on the face of it, at least, seem rather silly. But as the French say, God is to be found in the details. It turns out that these laws make a very important contribution to my Jewish religious consciousness. Nowhere is this clearer than when trying to keep kosher on airplanes, since regular airline food won't do.

When I started observing the kosher food rules, I viewed my decision to do so as a very private one, something between me and the good Lord. It did not occur to me that if you want to keep kosher at 30,000 feet, a lot of other people are involved as well.

I ordered my first kosher airline meal through my travel agent when I purchased my ticket and then promptly forgot about it. It was a startling reminder of my obligations to several thousand years of Jewish tradition when a voice came over the airplane loud speaker: "Would passenger Israel with the kosher meal please identify himself?" After I timidly raised my hand, I waited for the stewardess to come over and pin on my big yellow star. What I discovered at that moment was that keeping kosher is a public Jewish declaration that carries with it a series of heavy responsibilities.

(There are Jews who keep kosher at home, but not when eating out. They often explain themselves saying that though they are not really religious, they want to make a statement about Jewish community values with their kosher homes. They have it backwards. The place you make a community statement is when you keep kosher out.)

At the airport ticket counter, I ask the clerk if my kosher meal has been put aboard. (It has been forgotten or sent to the wrong flight more than once.) The clerk consults the computer and assures me that everything is fine. I then remember that I need some money and ask if I can cash a check. "No, it is contrary to airline policy. But wait, you just ordered a kosher meal. I can certainly trust you. Don't make it too large a check though. I'll get into trouble."

I had labeled myself someone who is committed to religious ritual and whether I liked it or not, I now had to be committed to religious ethics as well. That airline clerk was betting her job on my religious rectitude. My tradition and I were both on the line. I guess that is exactly what is supposed to happen to me and this is what it means: I am obligated to sanctify God's name with my life. Both my own and my God's reputation were at stake. I didn't realize I was getting into all that by ordering some overcooked chicken. I hoped the check wouldn't bounce.

The plane was late in taking off. As a consolation prize, the stewardess came by with free drinks. She noticed my kosher meal. "I guess you won't be having an alcoholic beverage."

Wait a minute. That was good Scotch that was receding down the aisle. As far as she was concerned, if you eat "religious food" you don't drink alcohol. But she's wrong. Scotch has nothing to do with keeping kosher. In my books, Scotch is a lot less menacing than the pork or lobster on the menu, which is really dangerous. She wants to turn me into a kosher Southern Baptist. There is hardly time to discuss the theology of it all as she rolls by with her little cart. Do I stop her and tell her I want the drink, thereby forcing her to reconsider her religious categories and think about mine? Do I pass it up so that I not appear in her eyes as a hypocrite? What I discover is that the act of keeping kosher demands far more religious engagement than I ever could have anticipated.

Few matters test my religious sensibilities and my patience more than the other passengers who steal my meals. If the stewardess doesn't know who ordered the kosher meals and asks over the intercom, almost invariably a passenger who wanted a kosher meal but forgot to order it, who used to eat kosher meals twenty years ago and has decided to try again (just this once), or who has heard that kosher meals are better than the regular ones, raises his hand. And I am left without breakfast. As he munches away happily, I wait for my food. I wait and wait and wait. After a while, the stewardess discovers that there aren't any more kosher meals since someone else has taken my meal "by mistake." The stewardess reassures me if I would like the bacon and eggs instead, she would be happy to bring them. I am not reassured.

I glare at my seat-mate. He smiles back at me. "I grew up in an Orthodox home," he says. "Haven't had a kosher meal in a long time. Didn't know you could get them on airplanes. It sure is a new world. My mother would never have believed it. This is terrific. I should get one more often. Have you ever tried one? Oh, you keep kosher, too? You really do it all the time? Tell me why. It is a shame they don't have a meal for you." I mumble to myself, "Just my luck. Today you have to decide to keep kosher, on my breakfast, when I am starved!"

We talk. He really wants to have a serious conversation. We discuss what it means to try to turn eating into a religious act. What is my responsibility to the calf that I eat or to the potato? Can I do what I will with the produce of the earth? Does God really care how many hours I wait between eating milk and eating meat? I can't even figure out a decent way to make him feel guilty.

Now I carry a little bag of granola with me whenever I take a flight, just in case.

Kosher meals used to be a lot better than the regular airline meals. (On a few airlines, they still are.) The rumor among kosher eating passengers is that too many people began to eat them, including both Jewish and non-Jewish passengers who only ate kosher meals on airplanes. Since they cost more, the airlines wanted to discourage that practice so that only the passengers who had no alternative would order them. Now, you really have to have a religious mandate or a very specialized taste for bland brisket to enjoy kosher food on an airplane.

In hopes of having something a little more exciting, from time to time I have ordered a vegetarian meal instead of a kosher one. Since the kosher food rules mostly have to do with meat, there isn't much in a vegetable that isn't kosher. For a while that went well, but then airplane veggie dinners began turning out to be two apples and a carrot or a dish of celery sticks and a tomato. They drew no distinction between vegetarians and rabbits. The European and Asian airlines know what to do with a vegetable, but not the Americans. I went back to kosher.

A few years ago, I had occasion to be flying during the week of Passover. When my kosher meal arrived, I noticed that it contained food products like bread and noodles, which are permitted throughout the rest of the year but are prohibited during the Passover holiday. Closer inspection revealed that though it was indeed a kosher meal, it was not kosher for Passover.

"Stewardess," I announced, "I can't eat this meal. I ordered a kosher meal. This one isn't kosher."

"But sir," she said, "it says on the wrapper that it is kosher." Then I had my moment of secret revenge on that hapless stewardess for all those raw carrots, for those meals stolen by other passengers, for the Scotch that whizzed by me too quickly for debate.

"Last week this meal was kosher," I declared. "Next week it will be kosher. But this week, it isn't kosher."

Then I went back to my newspaper. This time, let the stewardess do the theology.

Rabbi Richard J. Israel, published in
The Kosher Pig, *Alef Design Group, 1993*

MOTHER'S DAY BREAKFAST

Serves 4–6

Crispy Waffles with Maple Syrup ∿ 150
or Raspberry Sauce (*see New Year's Day Brunch Buffet* ∿ 90)
Pink Drink — double recipe ∿ 151
Banana Bread or Muffins ∿ 151
Sliced Fresh Fruit
Coffee or Tea
Brown Rice Pudding ∿ 152

Crispy Waffles

Peggy Glass, *Home Cooking Sampler: Family Favorites from A to Z*,
Prentice Hall Press, 1989

*This rich batter and a hot waffle iron make greasing the iron between waffles
rarely necessary. If you can't find your mother's old, seasoned-with-love, waffle
iron, check a good cookware store for one that's made of heavy cast iron. If
there are any extra waffles, cool them on a wire rack and freeze them in a plastic bag. They can be heated quickly in a toaster for early school breakfasts.*

1 cup all-purpose flour
1 cup quick or old-fashioned
   rolled oats
1/4 cup fine yellow corn meal
1/4 cup unprocessed wheat or
   oat bran
2 tablespoons sugar
1 tablespoon double-acting
   baking powder

1 teaspoon baking soda
1/2 teaspoon salt
2 eggs, at room temperature
8 tablespoons unsalted butter,
   melted
3 cups buttermilk
Maple syrup

In a bowl, combine the flour, oats, corn meal, bran, sugar, baking
powder, baking soda, and salt. In another bowl, whisk together the
eggs, butter, and buttermilk. Heat the waffle iron and use about
1/2 cup batter for each waffle. Cook to a golden crispness. The waffle
iron should stop steaming from the sides when the waffles are ready.
Let the iron get hot again before adding more batter. Serve with
maple syrup.

Yields 12 6-inch waffles

Pink Drink

 Nancy Gans

2 cups pineapple juice
1 banana

5 strawberries
Sugar, to taste (optional)

Combine all ingredients except sugar in blender or food processor. If the banana is ripe enough, you may not need the sugar.

Serves 1–2

Banana Bread or Muffins

  Linda Jason

This recipe is great for those weeks when the kids eat fewer bananas than usual. The bread and muffins are moist and sweet.

3 large or 4 small ripe
  bananas
$\frac{1}{2}$ cup granulated sugar
$\frac{1}{2}$ cup brown sugar
1 large egg
$1\frac{1}{2}$ cups flour (any
  combination of white and
  whole wheat pastry flour)

$\frac{1}{4}$ cup melted butter or pareve
  margarine
1 teaspoon baking soda
Dash of salt
$\frac{3}{4}$ cup raisins, mini-chocolate
  chips, or nuts (optional)

Preheat oven to 325° and grease and flour one loaf pan, 3 mini-loaf pans, or one 12-cup muffin tin.

Mash bananas with fork in a bowl or in a food processor. Stir in remaining ingredients in the order given. Pour into the pan and bake for 1 hour or until a tester inserted in the center comes out clean. For muffins, pour into muffin cups and bake about 30 minutes or until a tester inserted in the center comes out clean.

Yields 1 loaf, 3 mini-loaves, or 12 muffins

Brown Rice Pudding

 Melinda Strauss

This pudding has a bit more character than the smooth comfort food we are used to when white rice is used. It tastes rich although the ingredients are not heavy, and it is a filling, chewy snack or dessert.

1½ cups cooked long-grain
   brown rice
1½ cups skim milk
¼ cup honey
¼ teaspoon salt

1 large egg, beaten
⅓ cup currants (optional)
1 tablespoon butter
½ teaspoon vanilla extract
Dash of cinnamon

Combine cooked rice, 1 cup of the milk, honey, and salt in a 2-quart saucepan, and cook over medium heat for 15 minutes, stirring occasionally. In a bowl, beat egg with remaining milk and stir into rice mixture. Add currants, if desired, and cook over low heat for 3 to 4 more minutes, stirring occasionally. Stir in butter and vanilla until butter melts. Spoon into serving dishes, sprinkle lightly with cinnamon.

Leave to set and serve slightly warm or refrigerate and serve cold.

Serves 4–6

SHAVUOT LUNCH

Serves 10–12

Kiddush Wine

No-Knead Whole Wheat Challah *(see Erev Yom Kippur Dinner* ~ 20)

Summer Indian Soup — double recipe ~ 154

Fat Harry's Cottage Cheese Pie — double recipe ~ 155

Dear Friends Fallen Soufflé ~ 156

Spinach, Avocado, and Orange Salad — double recipe ~ 158

Potato Puff *(see Pesach Family Dinner* ~ 137)

Carrot Salad *(see Rosh Hashanah Dinner* ~ 16)

Filo Fruit Strudel *(see New Year's Day Brunch Buffet* ~ 92)

Summer Indian Soup

 Judy Adnepos

1½ teaspoons vegetable oil
3 teaspoons cumin seeds
3 teaspoons mustard seeds
2 quarts water
1 teaspoon ground ginger
1 teaspoon ground cumin
1 teaspoon salt
4 medium red potatoes,
  chopped (leave skins on)

1½ cups cut green beans
3 cups peas
3½ cups skimmed buttermilk
1½ cups light sour cream
2 teaspoons lemon juice
2 teaspoons salt
½ teaspoon white pepper, or
  more to taste

Heat oil, cumin and mustard seeds over medium heat in covered small saucepan. When seeds start to pop, shake pan above heat until popping stops. Uncover and remove from heat. Set aside.

In a medium pot, bring water, ginger, cumin, and salt to a boil. Add potatoes and simmer for about 8 to 10 minutes. Add beans, cook for 2 minutes, and add peas, cooking an additional 2 minutes. (All vegetables should be al dente.)

While vegetables are cooking, whisk together buttermilk, sour cream, and lemon juice in a large bowl. Add seeds with oil. Drain cooked vegetables, and immediately add them to buttermilk mixture. Add salt and pepper. Stir and refrigerate for several hours. This is best served the day it is made.

Serves 6–8 generously

Variation: Add 1 or 2 whole chiles to pan with seeds.

Fat Harry's Cottage Cheese Pie

 Judy Adnepos

This makes two pies. It freezes well, so you can always have an extra on hand.

2 handfuls sliced mushrooms
1 green pepper, chopped
1 medium zucchini, grated
3 tablespoons butter
1 package frozen chopped
   spinach, defrosted and
   squeezed dry
2 cups lowfat cottage cheese

1 cup grated part-skim
   mozzarella cheese
3 eggs, beaten
2 tablespoons olive oil
1 teaspoon dried dill
Salt and pepper, to taste
2 9-inch pie crusts, pre-baked
   for 10 minutes

Preheat oven to 350°.

In a medium skillet, sauté mushrooms, pepper and zucchini in butter until almost tender. Add spinach and heat through.

In a bowl, combine remaining ingredients. Add the cooked vegetables. Place in the pre-baked pie shells. Bake for about 45 minutes, or until the pies start to brown on top.

Serves 8–10

Dear Friends Fallen Soufflé

 Julie Arnow

I feel truly thankful for the extraordinary people I am privileged to call my friends. This recipe is dedicated to all of them, they who are wise, kind and giving — and often late. With this recipe, 6:30 can be 7:00, and all is forgiven.

This is a fallen, rectangular soufflé, stuffed with vegetables and cheese, rolled and served with a spicy tomato sauce. It looks quite grand, and is a very nice Shabbos dinner for company, served with a green salad and challah (a little carrot soup would be nice, too). At Chanukah, it is a wonderful companion for latkes. But beware — this is not sukkah food! No temporary structures for this dish — it needs to be handled carefully. I would say take out your grandmother's china, but if your grandmother was anything like mine, she was too busy trying to keep body and soul together (often with boiled tongue and overcooked brisket) to collect any heirlooms of a physical nature. She would never have understood that financially solvent people would choose to celebrate Shabbat with a dish whose principal ingredient was zucchini. But then again, neither do my children. But, ah, my dear friends do.

Souffle roll:
- ¹/₂ cup all-purpose flour
- 6 tablespoons margarine, melted
- 2 cups milk
- 4 eggs, separated
- ¹/₂ teaspoon salt
- Pepper, to taste
- 2 teaspoons chives, chopped
- ¹/₄ teaspoon cream of tartar
- ¹/₃ cup grated Parmesan cheese

Filling:
- 4 small or 2 large zucchini, grated, salted, rinsed, and squeezed dry
- 2 cups onions, chopped
- 1 carrot, grated
- 6 broccoli florets, chopped
- 1 red bell pepper, sliced very thinly
- 1 teaspoon garlic, crushed or chopped, or more to taste
- Salt and pepper, to taste
- 3 tablespoons dried basil
- 2 tablespoons parsley, chopped
- ¹/₄ cup sesame seeds
- 8 ounces cream cheese, or 4 ounces cream cheese with ¹/₄ cup plain yogurt, drained

Sauce:

1 15-ounce can chopped
tomatoes, with liquid

1 green pepper, chopped

1 small onion, chopped

¼ teaspoon garlic, crushed
or chopped, or more to
taste

Dash of Worcestershire sauce,
or more to taste

Pepper, to taste

Parsley for garnish, chopped

For the soufflé roll, preheat oven to 350°. Grease 2 cookie sheets
or jelly roll pans (15½ x 10½ x 1-inch), line with waxed paper, grease
again, and dust with flour.

In a saucepan, add flour to melted margarine and cook over low
heat, stirring constantly, until smooth and bubbly, about 2 minutes.
Remove from heat and stir in milk, egg yolks, salt, pepper, and chives.

In a bowl, whip the egg whites and cream of tartar until stiff. Fold
in the flour mixture, then fold in the Parmesan cheese. The mixture
will look like a bumpy yellow cloud.

Immediately spread evenly onto cookie sheets and bake until
lightly browned and firm, about 35 minutes. After baking, immediately take each fallen soufflé off of the cookie sheet by placing a large
piece of aluminum foil, backed by another cookie sheet, over the pan
and inverting. It may look a bit wet; that's okay. (The soufflés may be
frozen at this point. Cover with aluminum foil and freeze in cookie
sheet or jelly roll pan. When frozen solid, invert onto foil, wrap well
with more foil, and store flat in freezer.)

To make the filling, sauté all the vegetables, including the garlic,
in a skillet over medium heat — no oil is necessary as the water in
the vegetables is sufficient — until the vegetables are barely tender
and the broccoli is still bright green. Add the spices, herbs, and seeds,
and sauté a minute or two longer. Take off the heat and mix in the
cream cheese.

Preheat oven to 350°. Grease a cookie sheet, line with aluminum
foil, and grease again.

Spoon half the vegetable mixture onto the short end of a soufflé
roll, about 1 inch from the sides and the bottom. Using the aluminum
foil to assist you, roll the soufflé around the filling. If it tears slightly,
that's fine. You may need a blunt knife to tease the soufflé off the foil.

Place the roll on the cookie sheet. Two spatulas will help you lift
the rolls. Repeat the process with the second roll. Place next to the
first roll on the cookie sheet. (The rolls can be refrigerated for up to
24 hours, or frozen before thawing and baking.) Bake for 35 minutes

Continued on next page

or until heated through and slightly browned. If extra liquid comes out of the rolls during baking, drain.

Meanwhile, combine all the sauce ingredients except for parsley in a small saucepan, bring to a boil, and simmer for several minutes, so all the flavors mingle.

To serve, put a small amount of sauce on top of each roll and garnish with chopped parsley. Put the rest of the sauce in a dish with a big spoon for your guests to use as they see fit (no food fights please!). Slice the soufflé at the table.

Serves 10 generously

Spinach, Avocado, and Orange Salad

 Brenda Freishtat

Dressing:
½ teaspoon grated orange zest
¼ cup orange juice
½ cup vegetable oil
2 tablespoons sugar
2 tablespoons wine vinegar
¼ teaspoon salt, optional

Salad:
2 pounds fresh spinach leaves, torn or cut into bite-sized pieces
1 small cucumber, sliced
1 avocado, peeled and sliced
2 tablespoons sliced scallions
¼–½ cup pecans or walnuts, chopped
1 11-ounce can mandarin oranges, drained

Combine the dressing ingredients in a jar. Shake well and refrigerate. This dressing will keep for several days.

Place vegetables, nuts, and oranges in a bowl. Pour dressing over all and toss to serve.

Serves 6–8

YOM HA'ATZMA'UT BRUNCH

Serves 12

Orange Juice
Bible Fruit Salad *(see Pesach Shabbat Lunch* ~ *144)*
Rich Almond Kugel ~ 160
Cottage Cheese Pie — double recipe ~ 161
Pita Bread
Cucumber Feta Cheese Salad — double recipe ~ 162
Abigail's Eggplant Salad from Israel ~ 163
Middle East Cabbage Salad ~ 164
Yogurt Coffee Cake ~ 165
Nana's Coffee Rolls ~ 166
Fresh Fruit Cream Cheese Tarts ~ 167

Rich Almond Kugel

Ivy Feuerstadt

1¹/₂ cups sugar
1 pound cream cheese,
  softened
1 cup butter, softened
6 eggs

2 teaspoons vanilla extract
1 teaspoon almond extract
12-ounces wide egg noodles,
  cooked al dente
1 quart nonfat milk, warmed

Preheat oven to 350°.

Place aluminum foil on bottom of oven to catch the drips. Grease a 9 x 13-inch baking dish.

In a mixer or food processor, combine everything except the noodles and milk.

Transfer to a large bowl and add milk and noodles. Mix well.

Place in the baking dish and bake for about 60 minutes, or until kugel is firm in the middle and slightly browned.

Serve either warm or at room temperature. Freezes well.

Serves 12

Cottage Cheese Pie

 Judy Adnepos

Although the recipe calls for a pie shell, it's good without it, too. And you can substitute any combination of hard cheeses for the Swiss. Leftover veggies also make a nice addition.

2 cups lowfat cottage cheese
1–1¹/₂ cups grated Swiss
  cheese
2 eggs, beaten
1 small onion, minced or
  grated

2 cups fried onion rings,
  crumbled, or 2 8-ounce cans
1 9-inch pie crust, pre-baked
  about 10–15 minutes

Preheat oven to 350°.

In a bowl, combine cheeses, eggs, and onion. Pour into the pre-baked pie crust. Top with crumbled onions. Bake for 40 minutes, or until the onions turn brown. Let stand 5 minutes before slicing

Serves 4–6

Variations: Substitute any other cheeses of your choice in place of the Swiss cheese. Add any leftover vegetables to the mixture when combining cheeses, eggs, and onions.

Cucumber Feta Cheese Salad

 Ivy Feuerstadt

2 large cucumbers, peeled,
  halved lengthwise, seeds
  removed, and sliced
Kosher salt
$^1/_2$ pound feta cheese
$^1/_4$ cup fresh lemon juice

$^1/_4$ cup olive oil
Freshly ground pepper
3 tablespoons dried mint, or to
  taste
Fresh mint for garnish

Place cucumber in colander and sprinkle with a few teaspoons of salt. Let stand in the sink or over a plate for 20 minutes to drain.

In a bowl, crush cheese with fork and mix with lemon juice and oil. Season with pepper.

Rinse and dry cucumbers. Combine with cheese mixture. Add dried mint. Place in shallow dish and decorate with fresh mint.

Chill about 1 hour.

Serves 4

Abigail's Eggplant Salad from Israel

    Miriam Hoffman

1 medium eggplant
Salt, to taste
Vegetable oil for frying
Juice of 2 lemons
5 cloves garlic, chopped or
  crushed

1 teaspoon vinegar of your
  choice
2 teaspoons fresh dill, chopped,
  or more to taste

Cut eggplant into ½-inch thick slices, place in a colander and sprinkle with salt. Let stand in the sink or over a plate for 20 to 30 minutes.

Wipe slices well, and fry in oil until tender but not mushy. Place fried eggplant in dish.

Combine remaining ingredients in a small bowl and pour over slices.

Refrigerate and serve as a cold side dish or salad.

Serves 4

Middle East Cabbage Salad

 Michael Haselkorn

A tabouli salad for garlic lovers, made with cabbage.

$1/2$ cup boiling water
$1/2$ cup raw cracked bulgar wheat
$1/4$ cup fresh lemon juice
$1/4$ cup olive oil
1 teaspoon garlic, minced (about 2 large cloves)
$1/2$ teaspoon dried oregano

$1/4$ teaspoon pepper
1 teaspoon salt (optional)
2 cups finely grated cabbage
$1/2$ cup parsley, finely chopped
1 cup canned chickpeas, rinsed and drained
1 cup carrots, thinly sliced
2 tablespoons scallions, minced

Pour water onto bulgar in a large serving bowl. Let stand 10 minutes, or until liquid is absorbed.

Combine lemon juice, oil, garlic, oregano, pepper, and salt in a jar and pour over bulgar. Mix well.

Add the remaining ingredients and toss thoroughly.

Chill for several hours and serve cold.

Serves 6–8

Yogurt Coffee Cake

 Melinda Strauss

This is a somewhat healthier version of the popular sour cream coffee cakes — a bit leaner, although just as sweet. It is a good recipe to try if you have considered adding whole wheat flour to your family's diet but are reluctant to give up familiar tastes in baked goods. Whole wheat (sometimes called whole grain) pastry flour is made from a softer wheat than regular whole wheat flour, and its texture is closer to that of white flour.

10 tablespoons margarine or butter
1 cup sugar
2 large eggs
2 cups whole wheat pastry flour
1 teaspoon baking powder
¼ teaspoon salt

1½ cups plain nonfat yogurt
1½ teaspoons vanilla extract
1 teaspoon baking soda
1½ cups walnuts, chopped
2 teaspoons cinnamon
2 tablespoons sugar
1 tablespoon sweetened cocoa (optional)

Preheat oven to 350°. Grease and flour a tube pan.

Cream margarine and sugar in food processor or bowl until fluffy. Add eggs and mix well and set aside.

Mix together flour, baking powder, and salt in a bowl and set aside.

Mix yogurt, vanilla, and baking soda together in another bowl.

Add the flour and yogurt mixtures alternately to the margarine mixture, blending well after each addition.

In a separate bowl, combine walnuts, cinnamon, sugar, and cocoa, if using.

Spoon half the batter into prepared pan, spreading it evenly, then sprinkle on half the nut mixture. Repeat with remaining batter and nuts. Using a knife, cut in and out of batter all around the pan so that the nut mixture swirls through but does not completely combine with the batter.

Bake for 60 to 65 minutes, or until a toothpick comes out clean and the top has started to brown slightly.

Cool on rack for 10 to 15 minutes and remove tube from outer pan. Allow cake to cool at least 20 minutes before lifting cake out of the tube.

Serves 10–12

Nana's Coffee Rolls

 P   Marjorie Perlman

1¹/₂ tablespoons dry yeast
(2 cakes compressed yeast
or about 2 packages dry
yeast)
¹/₂ cup warm water
3 eggs, or 6 egg whites
³/₄ cup granulated sugar
4 cups all-purpose flour,
sifted

1 cup plus additional unsalted
pareve margarine, melted
1 teaspoon cinnamon
¹/₄ cup sugar
1–2 cups golden raisins
¹/₂ cup brown sugar
24 whole pecans

Dissolve yeast in warm water in a small bowl.

Beat eggs and sugar together in a bowl until golden. Add yeast mixture to eggs alternately with flour and 1 cup of the melted margarine, mix well. Transfer to a large greased bowl, cover, and refrigerate overnight.

Mix cinnamon and sugar in a small bowl.

Roll out half the dough in a rectangle ¹/₄-inch thick. Spread generously with additional melted margarine and sprinkle with cinnamon-sugar mixture, and raisins. Roll up like a jelly roll, and repeat with remaining dough. Cut each roll into 12 pieces, each about 1¹/₂-inches thick.

Prepare 2 muffin tins of 12 cups each by putting 2 teaspoon melted margarine, 1 teaspoon brown sugar and 1 pecan into each muffin cup. Place one slice of dough in each cup. Let rise, covered with a tea towel, in a warm place until puffy and soft, about 2 hours.

Preheat oven to 350°.

Brush each slice with melted margarine. Bake on the middle rack for 15 to 20 minutes, until golden brown.

Remove rolls from pans while warm so they won't stick. Turn upside down to cool on racks.

Serve warm and enjoy. These rolls freeze well.

Yields 24 rolls

Fresh Fruit Cream Cheese Tarts

 Anne Waldoks

Attractive, delicious, and very easy to make! Great to serve for an after-dinner get-together, a Shabbat lunch dessert, or for Sunday brunch.

8 ounces cream cheese or
   Neufchâtel, softened
1 egg
¹/₄ cup sugar
¹/₄ teaspoon vanilla extract

2 tablespoons light sour cream
20 round vanilla wafer cookies
Sliced fresh fruit (kiwi, starfruit, grapes, or berries)

Preheat oven to 375°.

In a bowl, beat all the ingredients, except cookies and fruit, until creamy. Place vanilla wafers, flat side down, into 2-inch diameter "midget" foil baking cups. (This size is hard to find — the 2¹/₂-inch cups are more common in stores — but don't settle! Using the larger baking cups will cause the tarts to flatten out and this will dry out the the filling.) Top with creamed mixture.

Place foil cups on a cookie sheet and bake for 10 to 12 minutes. Do not overbake. They will still feel soft when done, but they'll harden as they cool. Garnish with fresh fruit.

Yields 20 tarts

FATHER'S DAY DINNER

Serves 4–6

Barbecued Beef Brisket ～ 170
Couscous Pilaf ～ 171
Spinach Salad with Mushrooms, Chopped Egg, and
Sliced Hearts of Palm
Fudgy Chocolate Torte ～ 172

Mollie Katzen's Spaghetti Puttanesca ～ 173
Eggplant Parmigiana ～ 174
Mixed Green Salad
Lemon Ices

Barbecued Beef Brisket

 Debby Zigun

This recipe was given to me by my friend Ellen Katz of Bedford, Massachusetts. It is one of her family's favorites. It needs to marinate overnight.

1 cup ketchup
1 cup water
1 tablespoon instant minced onion
2 tablespoons cider vinegar
1 tablespoon white horseradish
1 tablespoon prepared mustard

$^1/_2$ teaspoon pepper
$2^1/_2$–4 pounds brisket
2 large onions, sliced
4–5 carrots, sliced in 2-inch chunks
5 medium potatoes, quartered

In a bowl, combine ketchup, water, instant onion, vinegar, horseradish, mustard, and pepper. Place brisket in a nonaluminum covered casserole, fat side up. Pour mixture over brisket, marinate overnight.

Preheat oven to 350°.

Place onions on top of brisket. Cook covered for $2^1/_2$ to 3 hours. Add carrots and potatoes. Continue cooking, covered, 1 to $1^1/_2$ hours more.

Slice the meat and serve it with vegetables, using the pan juices as gravy.

Serves 6–8

Couscous Pilaf

 Chana Mayer

*This is a very versatile dish. You can use any vegetables you may have handy.
Add seasonings of your choice (basil, thyme, Tabasco). You could also add leftover
chicken or roast beef.*

2 cups boiling water or
  vegetable stock
$\frac{1}{2}$ teaspoon salt
1 cup couscous
2 tablespoons olive oil or
  pareve margarine
1 large onion, chopped into
  $\frac{1}{2}$-inch pieces
2 scallions, chopped into
  $\frac{1}{2}$-inch pieces
1 red pepper, chopped into
  $\frac{1}{2}$-inch pieces

1 zucchini, chopped into
  $\frac{1}{2}$-inch pieces
$\frac{1}{2}$ cup cooked or canned
  chickpeas
$\frac{1}{2}$ cup golden raisins
$\frac{1}{4}$ cup parsley, chopped
Crushed red pepper, to taste
  (optional)
Pareve margarine

Preheat oven to 350°.

In a large bowl, add water and salt to couscous. Cover and set aside
until all liquid is absorbed, about 5 minutes.

In large skillet, heat oil. Add onion, scallions, pepper, and zucchini
and cook over medium heat until soft. Place in an ovenproof casserole
dish and add chickpeas, raisins, parsley, optional crushed red pepper,
and couscous. Mix thoroughly. Dot with margarine.

Bake for 20 minutes.

Serves 6–8 as a side dish

Fudgy Chocolate Torte

 Janice Goldstein

³/₄ cup pareve margarine

6 tablespoons unsweetened
cocoa

1 cup sugar

²/₃ cup ground blanched
almonds

2 tablespoons all-purpose
flour

3 eggs, separated

2 tablespoons water

Chocolate Glaze:

2 tablespoons pareve margarine

2 tablespoons unsweetened cocoa

2 tablespoons water

1¹/₂ teaspoons vanilla extract

1 cup confectioners sugar

Preheat oven to 350° and grease and flour a 9-inch cake pan (do not use a vegetable oil spray on the pan; the cake won't come out).

Melt margarine in medium saucepan over low heat. Stir in cocoa and ³/₄ cup sugar. Blend until smooth and the sugar has melted. Remove from heat, cool 5 minutes, then transfer to a bowl.

Blend in almonds and flour. Beat in egg yolks, one at a time. Stir in water.

In another bowl, beat egg whites until foamy. Gradually add remaining sugar to egg whites, beating just until soft peaks form. Gently fold flour mixture into egg white mixture, blending thoroughly.

Pour into the cake pan and bake for 25 to 30 minutes or until a tester inserted in the center comes out clean. Cake will settle slightly.

Remove from pan onto wire rack and leave to cool completely.

Meanwhile, prepare the chocolate glaze. Melt margarine in small saucepan over low heat. Add cocoa and water, stirring constantly until mixture thickens. Do not boil. Remove from heat, and add vanilla. Gradually add confectioners sugar, beating with whisk until smooth.

Invert cake onto serving plate and spread the top and sides with chocolate glaze.

Serves 8

Mollie Katzen's Spaghetti Puttanesca

 Mollie Katzen

This is an intensely seasoned, substantial tomato sauce for spaghetti that you can whip up in just 15 minutes. Serve with green salad and crusty fresh bread.

Note: the anchovies blend in well. If you are hesitant, but curious, give them a chance. If you are adamantly opposed, you can leave them out and it will taste fine. (We tested this recipe "as is" on an avowed anchovy-hater, without his knowledge, and he thought the sauce was delicious.) Also, the amount of anchovies and olives can be adjusted to suit your taste.

³/₄–1 pound spaghetti
1 20-ounce can whole
   tomatoes
1 6-ounce can tomato paste
6–8 medium cloves garlic,
   sliced thin
8–10 Kalamata olives, pitted
   and sliced

3–4 anchovies, finely minced
   (optional)
Black pepper, to taste
¹/₄ cup parsley, finely minced (this
   can be done in a few quick
   spurts in the processor)
Parmesan cheese, freshly grated

Put up spaghetti water to boil.

Meanwhile, for a smooth sauce, purée the tomatoes in their juice in the food processor. For a chunkier sauce, chop the tomatoes with a knife (save the juice). Combine tomatoes and juice, tomato paste, garlic, olives, and anchovies in a saucepan, and heat gently to a boil. Reduce heat and simmer while spaghetti cooks. Add black pepper to taste. Drain spaghetti well, and combine with sauce.

Serve immediately, topped with parsley and Parmesan.

Serves 4–6

Eggplant Parmigiana

 Anne Waldoks

I found this recipe when I was 14 years old, and loved to cook "fancy" things. My family loved the dish, and so has everyone else who's had it over the years since then. In 1968, it seemed quite exotic to us. Now eggplant parmigiana sounds as exotic as tuna casserole!

1 1-pound can Italian-style tomatoes, undrained
1 6-ounce can tomato paste
1 teaspoon salt
1 tablespoon brown sugar
1/2 cup onion, chopped
2 tablespoons margarine
1 cup water
1 eggplant, approximately 1 1/2 pounds

2 eggs, slightly beaten, or 4 egg whites
1 tablespoon water
1/2 cup bread crumbs
1 1/4 cups Parmesan cheese, freshly grated
Vegetable oil, as needed
8 ounces part-skim mozzarella cheese, sliced

Preheat oven to 350°.

In a saucepan, combine tomatoes, tomato paste, salt, sugar, onion, margarine, and water. Bring to boil, then simmer for 20 minutes, and set aside.

Wash, peel, and cut eggplant into thin round slices. (No need to salt the eggplant — for some reason, it is not bitter at the end of the recipe.)

Combine eggs and 1 tablespoon of water in a pie plate.

On a sheet of waxed paper, combine bread crumbs with 1/2 cup Parmesan cheese.

Dip eggplant into egg mixture, then into crumb mixture. Sauté over medium-high heat in hot oil on each side and drain on paper towels.

Arrange 1/2 the eggplant in the bottom of a casserole (I use a rectangular 9 x 12-inch). Sprinkle with 1/2 the remaining Parmesan cheese and 1/2 the mozzarella, and cover with 1/2 of the tomato sauce. Repeat for the second layer, but omit the mozzarella.

Bake uncovered for 20 minutes. Arrange remaining mozzarella over top and bake 20 minutes more.

Serves 6–8

JULY 4TH BARBECUE

Serves 12–14

Coleslaw for H. ~ 176
Herbed Rice Salad — double recipe ~ 177
Barbecued Chicken ~ 178
Grilled Chicken Caribbean — double or triple recipe ~ 179
Cucumbers Vinaigrette ~ 180
Sesame Broccoli ~ 180
Grilled Baby Eggplant ~ 181
Summertime Blueberry Tart ~ 182
Lemon Meringue Pie ~ 183
Pareve "Ice Cream" Sundaes

Peanut Coleslaw — double recipe ~ 184
Cookie's Special Cold Rice Salad — double recipe ~ 185
Grilled Fish Steaks ~ 186
Grilled Halibut Kabobs — double recipe, if necessary ~ 187
Cucumbers Vinaigrette ~ 180
Chinese Fresh Broccoli Salad — double recipe ~ 188
Grilled Baby Eggplant ~ 181
Summer Berry Pie ~ 188
Lemon Meringue Pie ~ 183
Ice Cream Sundaes

Coleslaw for H.

 P Alisa Israel Goldberg

This coleslaw should marinate for several hours in the refrigerator before serving.

1 medium-large head green cabbage, sliced thinly or grated

4 large carrots, grated

1 medium red onion, chopped

Dressing:

¹/₃ cup white vinegar

2 tablespoons sugar

2 tablespoons vegetable oil

¹/₂ teaspoon dry mustard

1 teaspoon salt

Dash of Worcestershire sauce, or to taste

2 teaspoons caraway seeds

In a large bowl, toss together the cabbage, carrots, and onion.

In a small bowl, whisk together the dressing. Pour over the cabbage mixture and toss well to mix.

Refrigerate for several hours.

Serves 6–8

Herbed Rice Salad

 Ellie Shrage

This is a good summer salad that is easy to make and lasts up to 3 days in the refrigerator.

Dressing:
2 tablespoons Dijon mustard
1/2 cup red wine vinegar
3 teaspoons sugar
1 cup corn oil
Salt and pepper, to taste

3 cups white or brown rice, cooked in vegetable stock or boullion (I prefer to use 1 box Near East Rice Pilaf®, if available*)
Handful fresh pea pods, sliced down the middle
1 cup frozen peas, defrosted
1/4 cup currants
1/4 cup fresh dill, chopped, or more to taste
1/4 cup fresh parsley, chopped, or more to taste

Combine dressing ingredients in a jar and shake well.

Place the cooked rice in a bowl and add 1/2 cup dressing to warm rice. Mix well.

When rice is cooled, add remaining ingredients, and more dressing to taste. Best served at room temperature.

Serves 6

*If using Near East Rice Pilaf®, omit the butter or margarine they suggest.

Barbecued Chicken

 Ivy Feuerstadt

Best to marinate overnight. I do this in ziplock bags, which are great for making sure all the chicken is getting coated with marinade — and they leave one less dish to clean!

Marinade:
2 cups fresh orange juice
Zest of 2 oranges
¹/₂ cup balsamic vinegar
¹/₄ cup olive oil

2–3 cloves garlic, peeled and crushed

3 3-pound chickens, jointed

Combine marinade ingredients in a glass jar with a tight-fitting lid and shake well. Pour over chicken. Cover and refrigerate in bags or a nonaluminum pan, at least 2 hours, or overnight.

Bring the chicken back to room temperature and prepare the coals. Grill the chicken until cooked through, basting faithfully with the marinade.

Serves 12

Grilled Chicken Caribbean

 Chana Meyer

The marinade has a bite, but the chicken stands up well to its spiciness.
It should be refrigerated at least 2 hours, or overnight.

Marinade:

2 tablespoons grated fresh
  ginger
3 tablespoons chives,
  minced
¼ cup fresh lime juice
1 teaspoon grated lime zest

½ teaspoon dried rosemary,
  crushed
¼ cup fresh coriander, minced
2 tablespoons vegetable oil

1 chicken, cut into eighths

Blend all marinade ingredients in a food processor. Pour evenly over chicken in a nonaluminum pan. Allow to marinate refrigerated at least 2 hours, or even overnight.

Bring the chicken back to room temperature and prepare the coals. Grill the chicken until cooked through, basting faithfully with the marinade.

Serves 3–4

Cucumbers Vinaigrette

  Roberta Hoffman

This is a very popular side dish — easy to make, and easily halved or doubled. It stores in the refrigerator for many days and is great with meat, poultry, or dairy dishes.

1 ⅓ cups wine vinegar or cider vinegar (use red wine vinegar for Pesach)
1 ⅓ cups water
½ cup sugar, or more to taste

Salt and pepper, to taste
½ cup fresh chives, chopped
5 cucumbers, peeled and thinly sliced

In a shallow bowl, mix together everything except the cucumbers. Put the cucumbers in a separate bowl and pour dressing over all.

Refrigerate several hours or overnight, turning cucumbers occasionally to mix well.

Serves 12 generously

Sesame Broccoli

 Marlene Leffell

Tastes great hot or at room temperature, and can be made ahead.

1 large bunch broccoli, trimmed and broken into florets
½ cup sesame seeds, toasted

¼ cup Sake or Chinese wine
½ tablespoon soy or tamari sauce
2 teaspoons honey

Steam broccoli until crisp-tender. Drain thoroughly. (Cool to room temperature if desired.)

Combine sauce ingredients in a bowl. Shortly before serving, add to the broccoli and toss to mix well.

Serves 6

Grilled Baby Eggplant

 Hilary Greenberg

A summertime favorite that goes well with fish and chicken.

6 small eggplants or about 3
   regular eggplants, sliced
Olive oil, as needed

Dressing:
2 tablespoons red wine vinegar
1 teaspoon Dijon mustard
Pepper, to taste
1/4 cup olive oil
2 tablespoons red onion, finely
   chopped
Dried rosemary or marjoram
   (optional)

Wash eggplant and halve lengthwise, leaving stems intact. Cut shallow crosshatch pattern on cut side, brush with oil and grill, turning frequently until soft, about 15 to 20 minutes.

    Whisk together the vinegar, mustard, and pepper. Gradually, add the oil. Add the red onion and rosemary, and sprinkle over cooked eggplant. Serve at once.

Serves 6

Summertime Blueberry Tart

  Sharon Jacobs

*This is a "cool" pie to make in the summer heat since only the shell is baked
and the filling is quickly cooked on top of the stove. This recipe works well with
strawberries, raspberries, and blackberries.*

³/4 cup sugar
3 tablespoons cornstarch
Dash of salt
¹/4 cup water
4 cups fresh blueberries, plus
    extra for garnish

1 tablespoon butter or pareve
    margarine
1 tablespoon lemon juice
1 9-inch pie shell, pre-baked

Combine sugar, cornstarch, and salt in a medium saucepan. Add
water and 2 cups of the blueberries. Cook over medium heat, stirring
constantly, until mixture comes to a boil and is thickened and clear
(mixture will be quite thick). Remove from heat and stir in butter or
margarine and lemon juice. Cool.

    Place remaining 2 cups blueberries into the baked pie shell.
Top with cooked berry mixture. Chill for at least one hour. Serve
garnished with extra fresh berries.

Serves 6

Lemon Meringue Pie

 Hilary Greenberg

This is a great dessert — tart, light, and wows them every time! I use home-made pie crust only. It's definitely worth the effort. Although the pie tastes best the day you make it, the crust can be made ahead and frozen.

1/4 cup cornstarch
3 tablespoons all-purpose
   flour
1 3/4 cups sugar
1/4 teaspoon salt
2 cups hot water
4 egg yolks, slightly beaten

Juice of 1 1/2 lemons
1 tablespoon grated lemon zest
4 egg whites
1/4 teaspoon cream of tartar
1/2 cup superfine sugar
1 9-inch pie crust, pre-baked
   for 8–10 minutes

Preheat oven to 400°.

In a medium saucepan, combine cornstarch, flour, sugar, and salt, mixing well. Gradually add hot water to saucepan, cooking over medium heat, and stir until smooth. Bring to a boil, stirring as needed so that the bottom does not burn. Boil for 1 minute until mixture is shiny and translucent. Remove pan from heat.

Slowly stir some of the mixture into the egg yolks. When thoroughly mixed, pour back into the saucepan and stir to blend. Return pan to low heat and cook for 5 minutes, stirring occasionally. Remove from heat and stir in lemon juice and peel. Set aside to cool.

In a large bowl, beat egg whites with cream of tartar until frothy. Gradually add sugar, 2 tablespoons at a time, beating after each addition, until stiff peaks form.

Pour lemon filling into pie shell. Spread meringue on top, being carefully to take it right up to the crust to seal in the filling. Swirl top decoratively. Bake for 5 to 7 minutes, until meringue is golden.

Cool on rack for 2 1/2 to 3 hours and cut with a wet pie knife.

Serves 6

Peanut Coleslaw

 P   Phyllis Santis Stewart

1 small, head red cabbage	$^{1}/_{3}$ cup peanut butter
Sea salt	$^{1}/_{4}$ cup cider vinegar
3 scallions, green parts only, sliced	$^{1}/_{3}$ cup peanut oil
	Salt, to taste
$^{3}/_{4}$ cup dry roasted peanuts	

Slice cabbage thinly, place in a colander and sprinkle with sea salt. When cabbage is wilted, about 20 minutes, rinse and pat dry. Mix with scallions and peanuts.

Blend peanut butter and vinegar in a bowl. Mix in oil and add salt to taste. (At this point it should be a bit salty, but it will diffuse when mixed into the salad.) Blend peanut mixture into coleslaw. Chill or serve immediately at room temperature.

Serves 6–8

Cookie's Special Cold Rice Salad

 Judy Gray

5 tablespoons mayonnaise,
  or to taste
1 teaspoon curry powder, or
  to taste
1 clove garlic, halved
4 cups cooked rice, cooled
1 green pepper, chopped

1 red pepper, chopped
3 scallions, chopped
$1/2$ cup raisins
5 tablespoons chutney,
  chopped, or to taste
$1/2$ cup shelled peanuts

In a bowl, mix mayonnaise and curry powder and set aside.

Rub salad bowl with garlic and discard. Put rice in salad bowl. Add peppers, scallions, and raisins. Mix in mayonnaise and curry mixture.

Immediately before serving, add the chutney and peanuts.

This dish may be prepared a day ahead except for adding the peanuts and chutney (if the peanuts are added too much in advance they will get soggy).

Serves 6–8

Grilled Fish Steaks

 P   Michael Babchuck

Firm-fleshed fish, when grilled on a barbecue, provides a low-cholesterol alternative to red meat. Salmon, tuna, and swordfish are especially successful on the grill.

12–14 ½-inch fish steaks
¾ cups fresh lime juice

1 tablespoon cajun seasonings, or to taste (available at supermarkets)

Rinse fish in cold water. Pat dry and place in a nonaluminum dish. Pour lime juice over the steaks and sprinkle with cajun seasoning. Turn steaks over and sprinkle with more seasoning. Let the fish marinate in the refrigerator for 15 to 20 minutes. (Any longer will tend to make the fish too pungent, overpowering the naturally delicate flavor.)

Prepare the coals, and grill the fish with cover closed for 4 to 5 minutes on each side, or until done, basting with marinade. (Allow more time for thicker steaks.) Steaks should be firm, but still juicy when lightly pressed.

Serves 12–14

Grilled Halibut Kabobs

 Alisa Israel Goldberg

³/₄ cup fresh lemon juice
¹/₂ cup olive oil
2 cloves garlic, crushed
Salt and pepper, to taste
3 pounds halibut, cut into
   1-inch chunks
1 medium red onion, cut
   into thin rings

Bay leaves (as many as there
   are fish chunks, or about 36),
   soaked in boiling water for
   10 minutes
2 large yellow peppers, seeded
   and cut into ³/₄-inch chunks
   (also as many as there are
   fish chunks)

In a bowl, whisk lemon juice and oil together, add garlic and season with salt and pepper.

Place fish chunks in a shallow nonaluminum dish. Cover with onion rings. Pour oil and lemon juice mixture over the top. Cover and marinate, tossing occasionally, in the refrigerator for up to 6 hours.

Thread fish onto skewers, interspersing with bay leaves, yellow peppers, and red onion rings twisted into "figure eight" shapes around the skewer.

Prepare the coals and grill, turning skewers every 5 minutes or so until done, about 15 minutes.

Serves 6

Chinese Fresh Broccoli Salad

 Ruth Spack

1 1/2 pounds fresh broccoli
2 tablespoons tamari or soy sauce
1 tablespoon wine vinegar
3 tablespoons peanut oil

2 cloves garlic, crushed
1 teaspoon sugar
Pepper, to taste
1/3 cup pine nuts, almonds or walnuts, chopped

Trim broccoli, cut into florets, and slice stalks. Parboil in a little salted boiling water until just tender (less than 6 minutes), rinse quickly with cold water, drain and cool. Spoon into a nonaluminum bowl.

Combine remaining ingredients except nuts in a small bowl, pour over broccoli, and mix.

Serve sprinkled with nuts.

Serves 4 generously

Summer Berry Pie

 Cathy Felix

Our favorite summer pie. Use any summer berry or combination of them.

1 9-inch pie crust, pre-baked
1 cup berries, or enough to cover bottom of crust
8 ounces Neufchâtel cheese
1/2 cup nonfat plain yogurt

1/4 cup honey
1 1/2 teaspoon vanilla extract
Grated zest of 1/2 lemon or orange

Cover bottom of crust with berries. Combine remaining ingredients in a food processor or bowl until smooth. Pour over berries.

Chill at least 4 hours and serve cold.

Serves 6

VEGETARIAN BARBECUE

Serves 8

Ginger Cucumber Salad

    Marsha Slotnick

3 large cucumbers, peeled,
  halved lengthwise, seeds
  removed, and sliced
1/2 cup white vinegar
1/3 cup sugar

2 tablespoons sesame seeds,
  toasted (omit for Pesach)
1–2 tablespoons fresh ginger,
  finely chopped

Rinse cucumbers and pat dry.

In a small stainless steel or enamel pot, bring the vinegar and
sugar to a boil. Place cucumbers in a nonaluminum bowl and add the
vinegar and sugar mixture. Make sure you get all the sugar out of the
pot. Add sesame seeds and ginger. Mix and chill thoroughly.

Serves 6

*Variations: You could use cider vinegar or Chinese rice vinegar or substitute
1 cup chopped fresh coriander (cilantro) for the ginger.*

Mediterranean Rice Salad

   Phyllis Santis Stewart

2 large green peppers, finely
  chopped
2 large tomatoes, seeded and
  finely chopped
1/2 red onion, finely chopped
6–8 cloves garlic, crushed
4 celery stalks, finely chopped

1/2–1 cup fresh basil, chopped
1/2–1 cup fresh oregano, chopped
Salt, to taste
1/2 cup balsamic vinegar
2/3 cup olive oil, or more to taste
8 cups cooked brown rice,
  firmly packed and cooled

Mix vegetables and herbs together in a large nonaluminum bowl.
Season with salt, most of the vinegar and some oil. Add cooked rice,
and mix. Add remaining vinegar and oil and any other seasonings
to taste.

Serves 12–14

Savory Soy Burgers

    Rhonda Books

We never stop enjoying these healthy barbecued burgers. The beans need to soak overnight.

2 cups soybeans
3 cups water
$^{1}/_{2}$ teaspoon sea salt
2 tablespoons tamari or soy sauce
1 cup cooked brown rice
$^{1}/_{2}$ cup grated cheese (optional)
1 cup toasted sesame seeds
$^{1}/_{3}$ cup whole wheat flour

2 eggs, beaten
$^{1}/_{2}$ teaspoon dried basil
2 tablespoons scallions, chopped
4 tablespoons corn oil
$^{1}/_{2}$ teaspoon toasted sesame oil
8 hamburger buns spread with butter or pareve margarine
Tomato and cucumber slices

Cover beans with water in a bowl and refrigerate overnight.

Drain beans into a pot, add 3 cups of water and the salt, and bring to a boil. Simmer covered for about 2 hours or until beans are tender, adding 4 teaspoons tamari sauce during last 30 minutes of cooking. Skim off skins and foam from top, and drain.

Chop beans coarsely and combine in a large bowl with rice, optional cheese, sesame seeds, flour, eggs, remaining tamari sauce, and basil.

Sauté onions in 2 tablespoons of corn oil until translucent and add to mixture.

In a small bowl, mix together remaining corn oil and sesame oil. Shape the mixture into 8 patties and brush top and sides with oils. Grill patties, oiled sides down to start, 4 inches from coals, 6 to 7 minutes on each side.

Serve on buns with tomato and cucumber slices.

Yields 8 burgers

Curried Tofu Pasta Salad

 Debby Abel-Millman

Originally, this recipe came from my mother-in-law. It called for chopped cooked chicken. I needed a pareve dish that was different for a Yom Kippur potluck break fast. Tofu was substituted for chicken, and the recipe has proven to be a good variation on more traditional pasta salads.

Dressing:
²/₃ cup Italian-style salad
   dressing
2 teaspoons curry powder
Dash of ground black pepper
1 teaspoon salt (optional)
¹/₂ cup chutney, chopped

2 cups uncooked rotini
1 pound firm tofu, cut into
   small cubes
¹/₃ cup celery, chopped
2 scallions, chopped
¹/₃ cup raisins
Slivered almonds (optional)

In a small bowl, combine Italian dressing with curry powder, pepper, salt, and chutney. (To give the tofu and salad a stronger flavor, double the amount of dressing and marinate the tofu in it for several hours before assembling the salad.)

Cook rotini in plenty of boiling water until al dente.

In a large bowl, combine dressing, tofu, pasta, and remaining ingredients, except for almonds. Chill 2 to 3 hours.

Sprinkle with almonds before serving.

Serves 4–6

Pareve Carrot Cake

 Marlene Leffell

4 eggs
1 cup vegetable oil
1 navel orange, peeled and puréed (about 4 tablespoons)
2 cups all-purpose flour
2 cups granulated sugar
2 teaspoons baking powder
2 teaspoons cinnamon
2 teaspoons nutmeg

1 teaspoon salt
2 cups grated carrots
1/2 cup nuts or raisins, chopped

Lemon frosting:
1/2 cup pareve margarine
3 tablespoons lemon juice
3 cups confectioners sugar
1/2 tablespoon grated lemon rind

Preheat oven to 350° and grease a 9 x 13-inch dish or 2 9 x 5-inch loaf pans.

Beat eggs well in a large bowl. Add oil and orange purée and beat together.

Combine dry ingredients in a separate bowl. Add to egg mixture and mix well. Add grated carrots and nuts or raisins. Continue beating until everything is combined.

Pour the batter into the pan. Bake for 50 minutes or until a tester inserted in the middle comes out clean. Cool for 10 minutes in the pan and then remove to a rack.

To make frosting, cream the margarine in a bowl. Add the remaining ingredients and blend until fluffy. Frost cake when cool.

Yields 1 large cake or 2 loaves

SHABBAT MEALS
FOR ALL SEASONS

Appetizers

Ceviche ～ 228
Spinach Cheese Pie ～ 89

Bread

Challah ～ 5
No Knead to Stay around the House
    Challah ～ 25
No-Knead Whole Wheat
    Challah ～ 20

Salads

Curried Tuna Salad ～ 234
Ginger Cucumber Salad ～ 190
Greek-Israeli Eggplant Salad ～ 201
Herbed Rice Salad ～ 177
Italian Lentil Salad ～ 235
Molded Rice Salad ～ 233
Wheat Berry Waldorf Salad ～ 229

Soups

Chicken Soup ～ 7
Cucumber Yogurt Soup ～ 227
Mushroom Barley Soup ～ 22
Simple Vegetable Soup ～ 126
Winter Vegetable and Kasha
    Soup ～ 212

Main Dishes — Meat

Bourbon Chicken ～ 199
Chicken Verdicelieo ～ 218
Mother's Glorified Veal Chops ～ 219
No-Fail Chicken ～ 208
Polynesian Chicken ～ 209
Cold Sesame Stick Chicken
    Sandwiches ～ 232
Stuffed Cabbage ～ 207

Main Dishes — Dairy

Pasta with Pesto ～ 13
Salmon Dijon ～ 223
Spinach Cheese Pie ～ 89
Vegetable Pie ～ 231
Very Easy Pasta ～ 213

Main Dishes — Pareve

Company Fish ～ 211
Fish Soup St. Tropez ～ 203
Fish Stew ～ 222
Millet Vegetable Stew ～ 202

Vegetables

California Sweet Potato Bake ～ 199
Eggplant with Red Bell Peppers ～ 220
Fried Rice ～ 210
Gingered Pear and Cranberry
    Sauce ～ 64
Orange Brown Rice ～ 48
Orange Bulgar Pilaf Salad ～ 16

Desserts

Chocolate Crunchies ～ 40
Chocolate Chip Mandelbrot ～ 110
Coconut Balls ～ 109
Cran-apple Crisp ～ 50
Fresh Fruit Cream Cheese
    Tarts ～ 167
Italian Plum Cake ～ 200
Shabbat Chocolate Cake ～ 221
Sheets of Chocolate ～ 230
Tarts ～ 167
Yali's Favorite Birthday Cake ～ 138
Zucchini Bread ～ 24

AUTUMN SHABBAT DINNER

Serves 4–6

Kiddush Wine
Challah (*see Rosh Hashanah Dinner* ～ 5)
Chicken Soup (*see Rosh Hashanah Dinner* ～ 7)
Bourbon Chicken — double recipe if necessary ～ 199
California Sweet Potato Bake ～ 199
Gingered Pear and Cranberry Sauce (*see Thanksgiving Dinner* ～ 64)
Steamed Green Beans
Italian Plum Cake ～ 200

Kiddush Wine
Challah (*see Rosh Hashanah Dinner* ～ 5)
Greek-Israeli Eggplant Salad ～ 201
Millet Vegetable Stew ～ 202
Mixed Green Salad
Italian Plum Cake ～ 200

Kiddush Wine
Challah (*see Rosh Hashanah Dinner* ～ 5)
Pasta with Pesto ～ (*see Rosh Hashanah Dinner* ～ 13)
Fish Soup St. Tropez ～ 203
Endive, Radicchio, and Arugula Salad
Italian Plum Cake ～ 200

My Mother's Shabbat

My mother was a wonderful *baaleboste*. Her cooking and baking were outstanding, and she made everything herself. She baked beautiful challahs for Shabbat and Yom Tov, she made her own noodles, and her chicken soup was, in the words of Heinrich Heine, "heavenly ambrosia." Her chocolate cake was soft and delicious, her cookies were crispy and melted in your mouth. Our son, Hillel, once tried to replicate her cookies because he loved them so much. Even though she gave him the recipe, she was unable to give him precise ingredients. As a result, the cookies were good, but they were not quite the real thing. The moral of the story is: a son is not a mother.

On Shabbat evenings, when I used to go to Shul with my father, who was a cantor with a great tenor voice, I found it difficult to concentrate on the davening. I kept thinking of the gefilte fish, the chicken soup, the chicken and kugel, and the cookies and tea that followed. Who knows? Perhaps if my mother had not been such a good *baaleboste,* I might have davened with greater *kavanah.*

There was one more dimension to our meals on Shabbat and for that matter, on weekdays as well. We always had *Oreach,* a guest at our table. Itinerant Jews who were *Meshulachim* agents for various Yeshivot and other Jewish institutions would always be invited to our home by my father for a meal or to stay over for Shabbat. My mother never remonstrated. She knew the importance of the Mitzvah of *Hachnasat Orchim,* or welcoming the stranger, and she fulfilled that Mitzvah all the years of her married life.

My mother's delicious food was a symbol of the love and joy which she brought to our family and to all who came to our home. We always said a blessing over her food. We should have said a blessing over her.

Rabbi Samuel Chiel

Bourbon Chicken

 Nancy Gans

My mother makes this for a very easy company dinner. The marinade is also good with steak, especially if it's grilled. This recipe can be doubled or tripled.

⅓ cup bourbon	⅓ cup tamari or soy sauce
⅓ cup honey	1 chicken, cut into eighths

Combine bourbon, honey, and tamari sauce in a small bowl. Pour over chicken in a nonaluminum pan. Marinate 3 to 4 hours (or overnight if you like a stronger flavor).
Preheat oven to 350°.
Bake for 45 to 50 minutes, or grill for approximately 18 minutes.

Serves 3–4

California Sweet Potato Bake

  Esther White

4 medium sweet potatoes	¼ cup butter or pareve margarine
½ cup brown sugar	3 tablespoons cooking sherry
1 tablespoon cornstarch	2 tablespoons chopped walnuts
¼ teaspoon salt	½ teaspoon dried orange zest
1 cup orange juice	
¼ cup seedless raisins	

Cook potatoes in boiling salted water until tender. Drain, peel, and halve lengthwise. Arrange in a shallow baking dish.
Preheat oven to 350°.
In small saucepan, mix sugar, cornstarch, and salt. Blend in juice and raisins. Stir while bringing to a quick boil. Add remaining ingredients. Blend well. Pour over potatoes and bake uncovered for 20 minutes.

Serves 4–6

Italian Plum Cake

   Fran Morrill Schlitt

This is a foolproof recipe for non-bakers. Use only Italian purple plums. It's perfect for the High Holidays. I make several at a time and freeze the cakes for use all winter. Serve warm and top with pareve or dairy vanilla ice cream.

52 Italian plums, pitted and quartered
6 tablespoons all-purpose flour
1/2 cup brown sugar
1 teaspoon cinnamon

Streusel topping:
2 cups granulated sugar
2 teaspoons baking powder
2 cups all-purpose flour
1/2 teaspoon salt
2 eggs, well beaten
1 cup butter or pareve margarine, melted

Preheat oven to 375°. Place a large piece of aluminum foil on the bottom of the oven to catch the drips.

Place the plums in the bottom of a 9 x 13-inch (or larger) glass baking dish.

In a small bowl, combine the flour, sugar, and cinnamon. Sprinkle this mixture over the plums.

In a medium bowl, mix together the topping ingredients (except butter or margarine). Sprinkle it evenly over the plums. Pour the melted butter over all.

Bake for 45 minutes or until the topping starts to brown.

This cake freezes well.

Serves 12

Variations: You can cut back on the sugar in the streusel topping and use less butter. You can also substitute half of the flour with whole wheat pastry flour.

Greek-Israeli Eggplant Salad

    Miriam Hoffman

1 medium eggplant
Salt and pepper, to taste
5–7 cloves garlic, chopped
Fresh parsley, chopped, to
   taste
1/2 green pepper, chopped
1 small onion, finely
   chopped

1 pickle, cubed
Juice of 1 lemon

Garnishes:
Sliced green olives (optional)
Sliced radishes (optional)
Tomato slices, cut in half
   (optional)

Prick skin of eggplant with a fork and cook in a microwavable dish in the microwave oven for 12 to 14 minutes, or use a regular 350° oven for about 40 minutes, until soft. When eggplant has cooled, peel off the skin. Chop finely, and add rest of ingredients in a large bowl, one at a time, mixing gently.

Chill, garnish, and serve as an appetizer or side dish.

Serves 4–5

Millet Vegetable Stew

 Joni Schockett

Millet is a fast-cooking, easy-to-use grain. It has a mild flavor which takes on seasonings very well. My family prefers this stew with lots of vegetables, but you can adjust to your own tastes. Be creative. Any firm vegetable such as broccoli or cauliflower, chopped red pepper for color, sunflower seeds, or chopped tomatoes can be added.

1 1/2 cups millet
8 cups water
1/3 cup canola oil
1/3 cup tamari sauce, or more to taste
3 large cloves garlic, crushed, or more to taste
3–4 large carrots, sliced

2–3 celery stalks, sliced
8 small red potatoes, washed and cut into chunks
1 medium or large onion, coarsely chopped
1 1/2 cups fresh shelled peas, or 1 10-ounce package frozen baby peas, defrosted

Rinse millet by placing in a large measuring cup, fill with cold water, stir, and pour off water. Repeat.

Place millet in a large pot with 5 cups of water. Bring to a boil. Reduce heat to a simmer and add the oil, tamari, garlic, carrots, celery, potatoes, and onions. Cover and cook for 30 to 40 minutes, until carrots and potatoes are just tender. You may need to add more water, up to 8 cups, as water is absorbed by the millet. Stir frequently as millet has a tendency to stick. Add the peas and heat through.

Serves 4–6

Fish Soup St. Tropez

 Arlene R. Remz

Every winter I make an enormous batch of the vegetable stock for this soup and freeze it. It becomes one of my "quick and easy" dinners: with some fish and a loaf of bread, I have a well balanced meal in 5 minutes.

1 tablespoon olive oil
2 onions, chopped
2 carrots, sliced
1 green pepper, chopped
1 red pepper, chopped
2 cloves garlic, minced
1 28-ounce can whole peeled tomatoes
1 bay leaf
1/2 teaspoon crushed red pepper
3 strips orange zest (1/2-inch by 3-inches)

1/2 teaspoon fennel seeds
1/2 teaspoon dried thyme
3 medium potatoes, peeled and cut in 1/2-inch cubes
2 cups water
1 cup white wine
2 pounds white, firm-fleshed fish, cut in chunks
Parsley, chopped, to taste (optional)
Salt and pepper, to taste

Heat oil in large pot over medium heat. Sauté onions, carrots, peppers, and garlic in oil until tender. Add tomatoes, bay leaf, crushed red pepper, orange peel, fennel seeds, and thyme. Raise heat and bring to a boil. Add potatoes, cover, and simmer 15 minutes. Add water and wine, raise heat, and bring to a boil again. Reduce heat and simmer uncovered for 15 to 20 minutes, until potatoes are tender. Remove orange zest and bay leaf. (At this point, the soup can be frozen. Defrost before returning to a boil.)

Add fish and optional parsley, and cook 2 to 5 minutes until fish flakes easily (don't overcook). Season to taste with salt and pepper.

Serves 5 generously

WINTER SHABBAT DINNER

Serves 4–6

Kiddush Wine
No-Knead Whole Wheat Challah (*see Erev Yom Kippur Dinner* ~ 20)
Stuffed Cabbage ~ 207
Simple Vegetable Soup (*see Pesach Seder* ~ 126)
Mixed Green Salad
Lemon Ices

Kiddush Wine
No-Knead Whole Wheat Challah (*see Erev Yom Kippur Dinner* ~ 20)
Chicken Soup (*see Rosh Hashanah Dinner* ~ 7)
No-Fail Chicken ~ 208
or
Polynesian Chicken ~ 209
Fried Rice — halve recipe ~ 210
Steamed Carrots
Cran-apple Crisp (*see Dinner in the Sukkah* ~ 50)

Kiddush Wine
No-Knead Whole Wheat Challah (*see Erev Yom Kippur Dinner ~ 20*)
Simple Vegetable Soup (*see Pesach Seder ~ 126*)
Company Fish — half recipe ~ 211
Wild Rice
Sauté of Pea Pods
Zucchini Bread (*see Erev Yom Kippur Dinner ~ 24*)
Lemon Ices

Kiddush Wine
No-Knead Whole Wheat Challah (*see Erev Yom Kippur Dinner ~ 20*)
Hummus
Winter Vegetable and Kasha Soup ~ 212
Mixed Green Salad
Chocolate Chip Mandelbrot (*see A Mishloach Manot Basket for Purim ~ 110*)

Kiddush Wine
No-Knead Whole Wheat Challah (*see Erev Yom Kippur Dinner ~ 20*)
Spinach Cheese Pie (*see New Year's Day Brunch Buffet ~ 89*)
Very Easy Pasta ~ 213
Salad of Romaine Lettuce, Mandarin Oranges, and Slivered Almonds
Chocolate Crunchies (*see Break Fast Buffet ~ 40*)

Stuffed Cabbage

  Rita Feuerstadt

Sauce:
3 28-ounce cans crushed
  tomatoes
1 12-ounce can tomato paste
1½ cups brown sugar
Juice of 3 lemons
1 cup golden raisins
1½ Granny Smith apples,
  peeled and thinly sliced

1 teaspoon salt, or more to taste
½ teaspoon pepper, or more to
  taste

3 pounds ground beef
2 potatoes, peeled and grated
1½ onions, minced or grated
2 large eggs, separated
3 heads Savoy cabbage, cored

To prepare the sauce, combine all the sauce ingredients in a large pot. Bring to a boil and simmer while preparing the cabbage rolls. (This makes a very large amount, and some of it can be used to baste the rolls. It also tastes great by itself over rice or barley.)

In a large bowl, combine ground beef, potatoes, onions, and egg yolks, and blend well. Season to taste with salt and pepper, and set aside.

Beat egg whites in a separate bowl, until stiff. Fold them gently into meat mixture.

In a large pot, cook each cabbage in simmering water until soft enough to remove the leaves without breaking. Remove cabbage and drain. Gentle separate the leaves from the head. Using the larger leaves, place one on a flat surface, and place two tablespoons of filling at the core end of the leaf. Roll the end over to just cover the filling. Tuck in the sides, and then finish rolling up completely. Continue making rolls until all the filling is used up. (There may be some left-over meat; roll into small meatballs.

Preheat oven to 350°.

Chop the remaining small cabbage leaves and put half in the bottom of a roasting pan. Add sauce to cover, and add rest of chopped cabbage. Place rolls, seam side down, layering if necessary. Pour sauce over the rolls and reserve extra sauce for basting during baking. (If there are extra meatballs, add them to the pan.) Bake covered for two hours, basting occasionally.

Yields about 3 dozen rolls

ail Chicken

 Marsha Slotnick

This chicken recipe is easy to make and has been given to many people who have enjoyed it. Stuffed boneless chicken breasts are also delicious prepared this way.

2 chickens, cut in eighths
Paprika, to taste
Garlic powder, to taste
3 onions, sliced
6 tablespoons pareve margarine

2 cups light brown sugar
2 tablespoons soy sauce, or more to taste
Blanched almonds sautéed in pareve margarine (optional)

Sprinkle chicken with paprika and garlic powder and broil on skin side only until browned, about 7 minutes. Place in an ovenproof serving dish.

Preheat oven to 350°.

Sauté onion slices over medium heat in margarine until translucent, about 10 minutes. Add brown sugar and soy sauce and continue stirring over low heat until dissolved.

Spoon sauce over chicken. Cover with foil and bake for 1 hour. When ready to serve, top with almonds, if desired.

Serves 6–8

Polynesian Chicken

 Marsha Slotnick

A wonderful main course, this far-eastern dish can be made a day ahead and reheated. (Sometimes it tastes even better the next day!) Made with wings only, it's a delicious hors d'oeuvre.

2 small chickens, cut into eighths
Celery salt, to taste
Garlic powder, to taste
Salt and pepper, to taste
Few pinches of dried thyme
1/2 cup water plus 2 tablespoons
1 cup sugar

1/2 cup white vinegar
Paprika, to taste
1/2 onion, chopped
1/2 green pepper, chopped
4 tablespoons cornstarch mixed with 2 tablespoons water
1 1/2 cups pineapple chunks
1/2 cup mandarin oranges

Preheat oven to 300°.

Place chicken in a nonaluminum ovenproof pan and sprinkle with celery salt, garlic power, salt, pepper, and thyme.

Combine one-half cup water, sugar, vinegar, lots of paprika, onion, and green pepper in a saucepan and boil for 5 minutes.

Add one-half the cornstarch and water mixture to the saucepan, continue boiling until thick, and pour over chicken. Spread fruit with juices over chicken.

Cover with foil and bake for 2 hours.

Remove from oven, increase heat to 350°, and drain juices from pan into a saucepan. Add remaining cornstarch and water mixture. (Use more cornstarch for a thicker sauce.) Boil until thick and then pour back over chicken. Return chicken to oven and bake uncovered until brown, about 30 minutes more.

This chicken freezes well.

Serves 4–6

Fried Rice

 Marsha Slotnick

Everybody loves this rice. It makes a large amount, enough for a crowd, and freezes well.

4 cups long grain rice	1 ½ green peppers, sliced
2 medium onions, chopped	½ cup pareve margarine
2 celery stalks, sliced	3 eggs
8 ounces mushrooms, sliced	10 tablespoons soy sauce

Preheat oven to 350°.

Cook rice in a large pot until tender.

In a large skillet, sauté onions, celery, mushrooms, green peppers in pareve margarine, until tender, about 20 minutes. Add to the rice.

In the same skillet scramble the eggs, add to the rice, and mix thoroughly. Add soy sauce. Stir gently.

Place in large ovenproof casserole. Bake covered for 1 hour.

Serves 12–14

Company Fish

 P Sue Pucker

This recipe gets rave reviews every time I serve it!

Marinade:
1/3 cup soy or tamari sauce
1/2 teaspoon black pepper
1/4 cup fresh lime juice
2–4 cloves garlic, minced
1 tablespoon Dijon mustard

Grated zest of 2 limes
1/4 cup peanut oil
1/4–1/2 cup scallions, chopped
4 pounds ocean perch (skin removed) or salmon

Combine marinade ingredients in a small bowl. Place fish in a non-aluminum dish and cover with marinade. Refrigerate for 3 to 6 hours.

Preheat broiler. Broil fish 4 to 8 minutes until brown. (Cooking time depends upon thickness of fish and proximity to broiler.)

Transfer to platter and spoon the sauce over fish. Serve immediately.

Serves 8–10

Winter Vegetable and Kasha Soup

 Jan Pevar

I serve this to company and everyone always loves it! I would suggest doubling the recipe as it goes fast. Very filling, tasty, and the kasha gives it its unusual, nutty flavor.

$^1/_2$ cup uncooked coarse grain kasha (buckwheat groats)

1 egg, lightly beaten

4 teaspoons canola or olive oil

1 cup onions, chopped

1 cup red or green bell peppers, chopped

$^1/_2$ cup carrots, thinly sliced

$^1/_2$ cup celery stalk, thinly sliced

$1^1/_2$ quarts water or vegetable stock

1 cup canned Italian tomatoes, drained, chopped and seeded

2 cups broccoli florets

2 cups cauliflower florets

2 cups mushrooms, sliced

Salt and pepper, to taste

In a small bowl, combine kasha and egg. Set aside.

In a large saucepan, heat oil, and add onions, peppers, carrots, and celery. Cook over medium heat, stirring frequently until crisp-tender, about 2 minutes. Add kasha mixture and sauté, stirring constantly, until egg is cooked, about 1 minute. Add water and tomatoes, and continue to stir until mixture boils. Simmer for 15 minutes. Stir in remaining vegetables and cook until softened, about 15 minutes longer. Season with salt and pepper.

Serves 4

Very Easy Pasta

 Cathy Felix

³/₄ cup margarine or butter
1 pound mushrooms, sliced
2 cloves garlic, minced
2¹/₄ cups parsley, chopped
12 ounces narrow noodles

1 cup light sour cream, at room temperature
³/₄ cup freshly grated Parmesan cheese
Salt and pepper, to taste

In a skillet, melt margarine, add mushrooms, and cook over low heat for about 5 minutes. Add garlic and cook 1 minute more. Add 2 cups parsley and cook for 2 minutes. (These vegetables can be made ahead and added to the pasta later if the mushrooms are slightly under-cooked; re-heat the mixture before tossing with pasta.)

Cook noodles, drain, return to pan, and pour mushroom mixture over. Toss gently, add sour cream and ¹/₂ cup grated Parmesan. Add salt and pepper to taste. Spoon onto platter, surround with remaining parsley and sprinkle with remaining cheese. Serve immediately.

Serves 4

SPRING SHABBAT DINNER

Serves 4–6

Kiddush Wine
Challah (*see Rosh Hashanah Dinner* ～ 5)
Chicken Verdicelieo ～ 218
or
Mother's Glorified Veal Chops — double recipe ～ 219
Eggplant with Red Bell Peppers ～ 220
Orange Brown Rice (*see Dinner in the Sukkah* ～ 48)
Steamed Fiddlehead Ferns
Shabbat Chocolate Cake ～ 221
with Raspberry Sauce (*see New Year's Day Brunch Buffet* ～ 90)

Kiddush Wine
No-Knead Whole Wheat Challah (*see Erev Yom Kippur Dinner* ～ 20)
Spinach Salad (*see Chanukah Dinner* ～ 66)
Fish Stew ～ 222
Shabbat Chocolate Cake ～ 221
with Raspberry Sauce (*see New Year's Day Brunch Buffet* ～ 90)

Kiddush Wine

No Knead to Stay Around the House Challah
(*see Erev Yom Kippur Dinner* ～ 25)

Mushroom Barley Soup (*see Erev Yom Kippur Dinner* ～ 22)

Salmon Dijon — double recipe ～ 223

Steamed Fiddlehead Ferns

Orange Bulgar Pilaf Salad (*see Rosh Hashanah Dinne*r ～ 16)

Fresh Fruit Cream Cheese Tarts (*see Yom Ha'atzma'ut Brunch* ～ 167)

Belching and Benching

Shabbat dinners derive their intensity from the fact that we are not only filling our everyday selves, but also nourishing an extra soul, the *neshama yeteira*. This spiritual addition enters us as the Shabbat candles are lit and the sweet Shabbat Shalom kisses and hugs envelop us.

Perhaps this Shabbat stowaway accounts for the extra helpings I pile on my plate every Friday night. These helpings are aided in their descent into the inner recesses by gallons of seltzer, resulting in a cacophony of epiglottal eruptions that bring me relief and stern looks of disapproval from my 12-year-old daughter. But soon she will, too, succumb to the ubiquitous grepses and belches, evoking my 4-year-old daughter's response of "Happy Burpday," a favorite expression of her grandmother's.

Even though the menus of Shabbat dinners now enjoyed in my suburban home are more varied than the predictable Friday night fare of my Eastern European mother (chopped liver, chicken soup with lokshen, soup chicken that fell from the bone, overcooked vegetables — followed by compote concocted from sweetened and lemoned dried fruit), the seltzer remains prominent.

Even as it accompanies croutoned gazpacho, cajun chicken, hot and cold sesame noodles, marinated mushroom and spinach salad, and strawberry-peach diet mousse, the bottles of bubbly do their dirty work, evoking comfortable and familiar sounds that will lead from belching to benching. There is so much to be thankful for as we sing praises for our lot. As our children's voices chime with our own, we hear an occasional, nearly squelched belch, attesting to our hope that our bounty continue and be shared by our loved ones — in all its manifestations.

Moshe Waldoks, co-editor, The Big Book of Jewish Humor

Chicken Verdicelieo

 Carole Jabbawy

I learned about this recipe years ago in a Northern Italian cooking class. It's light and delicious.

3¹/₂ pounds boneless chicken breasts

1 teaspoon salt, or more to taste

¹/₄ teaspoon pepper, or more to taste

1 cup all-purpose flour for dredging

¹/₄ cup vegetable oil

4 tablespoons pareve margarine

1–1¹/₂ cups mushrooms, sliced (¹/₂ cup for each breast)

1 14-ounce can artichoke hearts in water, drained and sliced

³/₄–1 cup white wine

Juice of ¹/₂ lemon

2 cups chicken stock

Parsley for granish

Slice chicken breasts into 2-inch pieces. Combine salt, pepper, and flour. Dip the chicken pieces into flour mixture. Sauté chicken pieces in oil and margarine in a skillet over medium heat for 5 to 7 minutes on each side, or until lightly brown. Reserve on platter and keep warm.

Add mushrooms and artichoke hearts to drippings in pan. Cook 1 to 2 minutes. Add white wine. Add chicken and sauté briefly. Add lemon juice and chicken stock to make abundant sauce and cook to heat through. Season with salt and pepper to taste. Garnish with parsley.

Serves 4–6

Mother's Glorified Veal Chops

 Lois Nadel

For a family-style company dinner, bake and serve this mouthwatering dish in a pretty casserole.

4 veal chops, trimmed
³/₄ cup all-purpose flour for dredging
Coarse kosher salt and pepper, to taste
¹/₂ cup cornflake crumbs
¹/₂ cup bread crumbs
¹/₂ cup fried onion rings, crumbled, or ¹/₂ can (4 ounces)

¹/₄ teaspoon dried thyme
3 eggs, beaten
4 tablespoons olive or canola oil
1 clove garlic
8 ounces mushrooms, sliced
1 8-ounce can stewed tomatoes
¹/₂ cup white wine
1 small green pepper, julienned

Wipe veal chops with damp paper towel and pat dry. Dredge the chops in flour on both sides and sprinkle on kosher salt and pepper to taste. Rub into chops.

On a plate, mix together cornflake crumbs, bread crumbs, crumbled onions, and thyme. Dip chops in egg, then into crumb mixture, patting crumbs firmly onto chops. Let sit for at least 30 minutes. (Or you can bread them in the morning and keep them in the refrigerator until ready to sauté.)

Preheat oven to 325°.

In a large skillet over medium heat, sauté chops in oil, with the garlic, until browned. Transfer to a shallow pan or large casserole.

Skim off fat from the skillet, leaving the drippings. Add sliced mushrooms, stewed tomatoes, wine, and green pepper. Mix together briefly and spoon over and around the chops.

Cover and bake for 1¹/₂ to 2 hours, then uncover for 30 minutes or more, until most of the liquid is reduced. After baking, a gravy can be made from the liquid left on the bottom of the casserole by adding ¹/₈ cup hot water, wine, or stock.

Serves 4

Variation: This recipe can be made with four large chicken breast halves.

Eggplant with Red Bell Peppers

 Phyllis Santis Stewart

1 medium eggplant
Salt, to taste
2 tablespoons olive oil
1–2 red bell peppers,
 julienned
2–3 cloves garlic, crushed
1/2 teaspoon dried rosemary
1 teaspoon dried oregano
1/2 cup fresh basil leaves,
 chopped, or 1 1/2
 tablespoons dried

1 1/2 tablespoons tamari sauce
1/2 teaspoon Dijon mustard
Pinch of cayenne pepper or
 dash of Tabasco sauce
Black pepper, to taste
1 tablespoon balsamic vinegar

Cut eggplant into 1/2-inch slices, place on paper towels, and sprinkle with salt. Let stand for 20 minutes or until eggplant releases its bitter juices. Pat dry with paper towels. Cut into strips. Sauté eggplant in oil in a sauté pan over medium heat until it is limp (cover if necessary).

Add red pepper, garlic, rosemary, oregano, and basil. Gently toss in pan to cover with oil. Add tamari sauce and cover. Cook until all the vegetables are tender but not mushy or discolored; the pepper should remain bright red, the eggplant should be tender but not falling apart. Add mustard, cayenne or Tabasco, black pepper, and vinegar. Cook covered for 5 more minutes over gentle heat. Remove cover and cook until all liquid is absorbed but before the vegetables start sticking to the pan, about 5 to 7 minutes. Serve hot as a vegetable dish or cold as a salad.

Serves 6

Shabbat Chocolate Cake

 Ivy Feuerstadt

This is a revised and updated version of Roberta Hoffman's Black Magic Cake in Solomon Schechter's earlier book, From Soup to Nosh.

1 cup unbleached white flour
³/₄ cup whole wheat pastry
  flour
1 cup unsweetened cocoa
2¹/₄ cups sugar
1 teaspoon baking powder
2 teaspoons baking soda
³/₄ cup pareve margarine,
  melted and cooled

1 teaspoon vanilla extract
2 large eggs
1 cup espresso coffee (2
  teaspoons instant espresso
  dissolved in 1 cup hot water)
1 cup plain soy milk

Preheat oven to 350°. Grease and flour a bundt pan.

Combine flours, cocoa, sugar, baking powder, and soda in a large bowl. Add remaining ingredients and beat for about 2 minutes (batter will be thin).

Pour into bundt pan and bake for 40 to 45 minutes until a tester inserted in the center comes out clean. For a 9 x 13-inch pan, bake 50 minutes. Cool cake and serve with Raspberry Sauce, page 90.

Serves 10–12

Fish Stew

 Michael Babchuck

This recipe offers an alternative to its beefy cousins and is equally substantial. Fish markets most often offer chunky pieces of fish which may be used fresh or frozen. Haddock, cod, and scrod are best.

Fish stock:
3 pounds fish bones
2 tablespoons extra virgin olive oil or pareve margarine
4 quarts water
2 onions, coarsely chopped
2 carrots, coarsely chopped
2 celery stalks with leaves, chopped
3 cloves garlic, unpeeled
1 teaspoon dried thyme
3 bay leaves
10 peppercorns
2 teaspoons salt

Stew:
1 large onion, chopped
2 cloves garlic, minced
4 tablespoons green pepper, chopped
4 tablespoons olive oil
4 cups fish stock
2 cups tomatoes, chopped and peeled, or homemade tomato sauce
4 medium potatoes, finely chopped
2 celery stalks, chopped
1 tablespoon steak sauce
2 bay leaves
Salt and pepper, to taste
1 pound white, firm-fleshed fish, cut into chunks
1 tablespoon parsley, minced

To prepare the stock, wash bones in several changes of water. Heat oil in a large pot, add water and bones, bring to a boil and cook for 5 minutes, stirring often. Add rest of ingredients and simmer covered for 30 minutes. Strain. (This makes about 12 cups stock. At this point any extra may be cooled and refrigerated for up to one week, or frozen for later use.)

For the stew, sauté the onion, garlic, and pepper in oil in a large pot over medium heat until onion is transparent, about 15 minutes.

Add stock, tomatoes, potatoes, celery, steak sauce, bay leaves, salt, and pepper. Cook until the potatoes are tender, about 10 minutes. Add the fish and parsley. Break up fish into bite-sized pieces.

Simmer until the fish just begins to flake, which will only take a few minutes. Remove bay leaves and serve immediately.

Serves 8–10

Variation: For a thicker stew, add 1/3 cup of orzo with the potatoes.

Salmon Dijon

 Brenda Freishtat

This is easy and elegant and is a wonderful dish for company.

2 tablespoons olive oil
1/4 cup shallots, minced
1/2 cup clarified butter or margarine
1/2 cup dry white wine
4 6-ounce fillets salmon, skinned

1/4 cup heavy cream or half-and-half
1/4 cup Dijon mustard
2 tablespoons fresh parsley, minced
Salt and pepper, to taste
Parsley for garnish

In a large skillet, heat oil over medium heat and cook shallots until soft, about 5 minutes. Add butter and wine, and bring to simmer. Add salmon and cook until just done, about 7 minutes. Transfer salmon to a warm platter and cover loosely. Reduce liquid in the skillet over medium heat by a third. Whisk in cream, mustard, parsley, salt, and pepper. Simmer 2 minutes more. Serve over salmon and garnish with parsley.

Serves 4

SUMMER SEUDAH SHLISHIT

Serves 4–6

*It is a special mitzvah to eat three meals on Shabbat. Since one meal is on
Friday evening, the other two are eaten during the day. In communities
where Shabbat services last most of the morning, the second main Shabbat
meal is eaten at about noon or shortly thereafter. The third meal, known
as the seudah shlishit, is then eaten in the very late afternoon, before
sundown. This meal is usually simple, but on long summer days it can
be a light family dinner. There is no kiddush, but the blessings are recited
over bread or challah.*

No Knead to Stay around the House Challah
(*see Erev Yom Kippur Dinner* ᴗ 25)
Cucumber Yogurt Soup ᴗ 227
Ceviche ᴗ 228
Wheat Berry Waldorf Salad ᴗ 229
Sheets of Chocolate with Fresh Raspberries ᴗ 230

Challah (*see Rosh Hashanah Dinner* ᴗ 5)
Vegetable Pie ᴗ 231
Cold Steamed Green Bean, Carrot, and Cauliflower Crudités
Yali's Favorite Birthday Cake (*see Pesach Family Dinner* ᴗ 138)

No-Knead Whole Wheat Challah (*see Erev Yom Kippur Dinner* ⌇ 20)
Cold Sesame Stick Chicken Sandwiches ⌇ 232
Molded Rice Salad ⌇ 233
Ginger Cucumber Salad — use Coriander variation
(*see Vegetarian Barbecue* ⌇ 190)
Ices

Challah (*see Rosh Hashanah Dinner* ⌇ 5)
Curried Tuna Salad ⌇ 234
Herbed Rice Salad (*see July 4th Barbecue* ⌇ 177)
Italian Lentil Salad ⌇ 235
Coconut Balls (*see A Mishloach Manot Basket for Purim* ⌇ 109)

Cucumber Yogurt Soup

  Ivy Feuerstadt

This is nice to serve in a mug or glass, with a long scallion as a garnish.

¹/₂ cup golden raisins
4 cups plain nonfat yogurt
6 ice cubes
1 cup cold water
2 cucumbers, peeled, seeded, and chopped into small pieces

¹/₄ cup scallions, chopped
1 teaspoon salt (optional)
¹/₂ teaspoon white pepper
¹/₄ cup fresh parsley, chopped
2 tablespoons fresh dill, chopped, or more to taste

Soak raisins in enough warm water to cover for 5 minutes. Drain and pat dry.

Place yogurt in a large bowl and add ice cubes, water, cucumbers, scallions, raisins, salt, and pepper. Mix thoroughly. Mix in parsley and dill. Refrigerate. Serve cold (make sure ice cubes are melted).

Serves 6–8

Ceviche

 Jone Dalezman

This is a typical Peruvian appetizer of fish, marinated overnight. It's spicy, and great for the summer.

1 pound halibut, haddock, or any white, firm-fleshed fish
1 clove garlic, halved
Juice of 10 limes
2 tablespoons white vinegar
Salt and pepper, to taste
1 medium onion, julienned or finely sliced

1 hot pepper, chopped
1 large or 2 small sweet potatoes
2 ears corn
Crushed red pepper (optional)
Lettuce leaves, for serving

Dice the fish and put it in a glass dish that has been rubbed with half of the garlic clove. Cover with half of the lime juice and 1 tablespoon white vinegar. Season with salt and pepper.

Place onion strips in another glass dish that has been rubbed with the other half of the garlic clove. Add the hot pepper and cover with the rest of the lime juice and white vinegar. (Wash hands thoroughly after preparing hot pepper, and keep pepper juice away from eyes.)

Cover both dishes and refrigerate overnight.

The next day, bake the sweet potatoes until tender. Cool, peel, and cut into 5 or 6 pieces. Cut each ear of corn into 2 or 3 pieces and steam until tender. Two hours before serving, mix the fish with the onions and continue to marinate in the refrigerator. You can add crushed red pepper if you want it spicier.

To serve, line a platter with lettuce leaves. Put the fish and onion mixture in the middle of the platter and arrange the corn and sweet potatoes around it.

Serves 6

Wheat Berry Waldorf Salad

 Phyllis Strauss

½ cup raw wheat berries
   (found at natural food
   stores)
3½ cups water
½ cup vanilla yogurt
2 tablespoons mayonnaise

Dash of salt
½ cup celery, thinly sliced
2 medium apples, chopped
Lettuce leaves for serving

Combine wheat berries with water in a saucepan and bring to a boil.
Reduce heat and simmer covered for one hour. Drain.

Stir together yogurt, mayonnaise, and salt in a large bowl. Add
wheat berries and celery. Mix in apples, cover, and chill for one hour
or longer.

Line your prettiest bowl with lettuce. Add salad and enjoy.

Serves 4

Sheets of Chocolate

 Linda Bick-Helfgott

These are highly addictive, usually eaten with one utensil: a knife!

2 cups sugar
2 cups all-purpose flour
1 cup margarine
4 tablespoons cocoa
1 cup water
$^1/_2$ cup milk
1 tablespoon baking soda
2 eggs, slightly beaten
1 teaspoon cinnamon
1 teaspoon vanilla extract

Icing:
$^1/_2$ cup margarine
4 tablespoons cocoa
6 tablespoons milk
4 cups confectioners sugar
1 teaspoon vanilla extract

Preheat oven to 350°.

Sift sugar and flour together in a bowl.

Place margarine, cocoa, and water in a pan and bring to a rapid boil. Pour over sugar and flour mixture. Stir.

In a separate bowl, mix milk with baking soda, eggs, cinnamon, and vanilla. Combine with cocoa-flour mixture. Pour into an 11 x 15-inch jelly roll pan. Bake 20 to 25 minutes or until a tester inserted in the center comes out clean.

Five minutes before the cake is completely baked, prepare the icing. Melt margarine with cocoa and milk over a low flame. Remove from heat and add sugar and vanilla. Mix well. Pour icing over cake and let stand. Cool completely in the pan before slicing.

Serves 12–14

Variations: Add $^3/_4$ cup raisins and $^3/_4$ cup chocolate chips to batter. Add $^1/_2$ cup chopped walnuts to icing.

Vegetable Pie

 Lyn Kissoon

This pie is wonderful either as a vegetable side dish or a vegetarian main course.

½ cup white rice
12 ounces zucchini, chopped
½ cup combination parsley
  and scallions, chopped
½ red pepper, chopped
1 large onion, finely chopped
½ cup grated carrots
1 10-ounce package frozen
  chopped spinach, defrosted
  and squeezed dry
2 cups corn
3 cloves garlic, finely chopped

1½ cups grated Swiss cheese
¼ cup grated Parmesan cheese
1 egg, beaten
2 tablespoons olive oil
½ teaspoon crushed red pepper
1 teaspoon salt
13 tablespoons butter
⅓ cup cold water
2½ cups all-purpose flour
1 egg yolk
2 tablespoons water

Place rice in a small bowl and cover with warm water.

In a large bowl, combine the zucchini, parsley, scallions, chopped red pepper, onion, carrots, spinach, and corn. Add garlic, cheeses, egg, olive oil, salt, and pepper. Drain rice well and add to vegetable mixture.

Preheat oven to 400°.

To prepare pastry dough, melt butter in small saucepan over low heat. Remove from heat and stir in cold water and flour. Mix just until blended. Divide dough in half and make two balls. (The crust has the consistency of rubber before it is cooked.)

Place one ball between two sheets of waxed paper, lightly floured. Roll out to ⅛ inch and line a 10-inch pie plate or quiche dish. Trim, leaving a 1-inch overhang. Fill with vegetable mixture.

Roll out second ball of dough to cover filling. Trim, leaving a 1-inch overhang.

In a small bowl, beat together the egg yolk and water. Moisten pastry edges with this mixture, then seal and flute edge. Brush top of pie with egg-yolk mixture. Roll out extra dough and cut into shapes — flowers, leaves, butterflies — and decorate the top of the crust. Brush with egg mixture. Make slits for steam vents.

Bake for 1 hour. Cool on a rack. Serve warm or at room temperature.

Serves 8–10

Sesame Stick Chicken

 Arlene R. Remz

This chicken needs to marinate for several hours, or overnight. It's equally delicious served cold in sandwiches.

½ cup tamari or soy sauce

5 tablespoons dry sherry

4 tablespoons vegetable oil

4 tablespoons orange marmalade

2 tablespoons honey

3 cloves garlic, minced

3 teaspoons toasted sesame oil

½ teaspoon Tabasco sauce

4 whole boneless chicken breasts, cut in half

12 3½-inch pareve sesame breadsticks, crushed lightly

4 tablespoons pareve margarine

Combine tamari or soy sauce, sherry, vegetable oil, marmalade, honey, garlic, sesame oil, and Tabasco sauce in blender or food processor. Pour into 9 x 13-inch nonaluminum pan. Add chicken and turn several times to coat evenly. Cover and chill several hours or overnight, turning occasionally.

Preheat oven to 375°.

Remove chicken and reserve marinade. Arrange chicken breasts in a single layer, sprinkle with crushed breadsticks, and dot with margarine. Baste with the marinade, soaking breadstick crumbs. Bake, basting frequently, until chicken is tender, about 25 to 35 minutes.

Serves 6–8

Molded Rice Salad

 Ivy Feuerstadt

3 cups white rice, cooked in vegetable stock or boullion (I prefer to use 1 box Near East Rice Pilaf®*)

3 cups brown rice, cooked in vegetable stock or boullion (I prefer to use 1 box Near East Wheat Pilaf®)

³/₄ cup light mayonnaise

2¹/₂ tablespoons curry powder

¹/₂ cup chutney, chopped

3 ounces macadamia nuts, chopped

³/₄ cup golden raisins

¹/₂ cup water chestnuts, sliced

¹/₂ red pepper, chopped, for garnish

1 handful fresh peapods, sliced lengthwise, for garnish

Place cooked rice in a large bowl and let cool.

Combine the mayonnaise and curry powder in a small bowl and add to the rice mixture. Add remaining ingredients, except red pepper and peapods, and mix well. Place the rice mixture into a 8¹/₂ x 4¹/₂-inch loaf pan. Pack gently. Refrigerate.

When ready to serve, run a knife around the sides of the pan. Carefully invert onto a serving platter or dish. Place the chopped red peppers on top and the sliced peapods around the sides.

Serves 8–10

*If using Near East pilafs omit the butter or margarine they suggest.

Curried Tuna Salad

 Alisa Israel Goldberg

1 12½-ounce can tuna, drained
½ cup celery, chopped
½ cup scallions, chopped
½ cup blanched, slivered almonds (toasted, if desired)
⅓ cup currants
2 generous tablespoons curry powder

4–6 tablespoons chutney (any kind is fine; if it has any really big chunks of fruit or vegetables in it, cut them into bite-sized pieces.)
4–6 tablespoons light mayonnaise
Pepper, to taste

Mix all ingredients together in a large bowl. Add more curry powder, chutney, and/or mayonnaise to taste. Serve with crackers or use to make sandwiches.

Yields about 4 cups

Italian Lentil Salad

 P   Ivy Feuerstadt

This is a great salad for a buffet. It has a long refrigerator shelf-life, so you can enjoy it for many days. It is best made the day before you plan to serve it.

2 cups onion, minced
2 tablespoons corn oil
1 pound brown lentils, rinsed and picked over
1 36-ounce can tomatoes, puréed
1 cup olive oil
1 cup boiling water
2 tablespoons garlic, minced

1 teaspoon dried oregano, or more to taste
1 teaspoon dried basil, or more to taste
3 bay leaves
3 tablespoons lemon juice
Salt and pepper, to taste
Fresh parsley, minced, for garnish

In a large pot, cook onions in oil over moderate heat until soft, about 10 minutes. Add lentils, tomatoes, olive oil, and water, and mix. Add garlic, oregano, basil, and bay leaves. Bring to a boil. Cook the mixture covered, stirring occasionally, over low heat for about 1 hour, or until most of the liquid has evaporated and the lentils are tender. (Don't cook too long or they will be mushy.)

Transfer the lentils to a bowl. Stir in lemon juice, salt, and pepper. Remove the bay leaves. Cover and refrigerate. Bring to room temperature before serving, garnished with minced fresh parsley.

Serves 12–14

A TASTE OF SEPHARDIC TRADITION: A SHABBAT LUNCH BUFFET

Serves 12

Kiddush Wine

Pita Bread

Challah (*see Rosh Hashanah Dinner* ～ 5)

Sutlach — double recipe ～ 239

Hard-boiled eggs, served warm

Spinach Bolemas ～ 240

Potato Borrekitas ～ 241

My Grandma's Yaprakes ～ 242

Kippered Salmon

Greek Olives

Sliced Tomatoes

Fresh Fruit

A Taste of Sephardic Tradition

Until I met my wife and her family, who came to the United States from Turkey and Rhodes in the early part of the century and finally settled in Seattle, the only contact I'd had with Sephardic food was an occasional meal at a restaurant in Israel. I was as immediately captivated by their foods as by their other charms, and proceeded to eat enormous quantities of bolemas, borekas, and yaprakes during each visit West.

As I have tried to come to terms with my Ashkenazic identity amidst my numerous Sephardic relatives, I have come to the conclusion that, for the sake not merely of my palate but, more importantly, of *Ahavat Yisrael,* in respect for and tolerance of our differences, we should aim to create an eclectic Jewish cuisine that combines the best from each tradition (coupled with some attention to good health). With all the cookbooks that are now available, it is easy to plan holiday menus that offer a twist on the usual fare.

My hope is that, over time, such eclectic cuisine can help build bridges among Jews, forge a tighter sense of *Klal Yisrael,* enhance our observance of holidays, and enable us to appreciate the elaborate diversity contained within Jewish life. We are fortunate to have such a vast and spicy heritage.

Rabbi Joshua Elkin
Headmaster, Solomon Schechter Day School

Sutlach

 Virginia Israel

A sweet, creamy pudding from the Sephardic tradition, served before setting off to Tefillot services, or on Shavuot and other festive occasions.

4½ cups whole milk
½ cup powdered white rice
  (unsweetened rice flour)

½ cup sugar
Cinnamon

Bring 4 cups of milk to a simmer in a saucepan over medium heat.

In a bowl, mix together the remaining ½ cup milk, rice, and sugar, then stir into the simmering milk. Heat gently to a boil, stirring constantly, until mixture thickens slightly. Pour into 8 small cups and sprinkle with cinnamon. Refrigerate.

Serve chilled or at room temperature.

Serves 8

Spinach Bolemas

 Virginia Israel

An elegant appetizer, these Sephardic pastries are made by coiling a spinach-filled roll of stretched yeast or filo dough.

1 pound spinach
1 cup feta cheese, finely grated
½ cup plus 2½ tablespoons Parmesan cheese, finely grated
1 teaspoon dry yeast
½ teaspoon sugar

1⅛ teaspoons salt
1 cup warm water
3 cups plus 1½ tablespoons flour
1 teaspoon butter, plus extra for dotting cheese
1 cup vegetable oil

To prepare the filling, discard spinach stalks and wash leaves. Shred finely and pat dry. In a bowl, mix the spinach with feta, ½ cup Parmesan, and set aside while you prepare the dough.

Dissolve yeast, sugar, and ⅛ teaspoon salt in the water in a large bowl. Blend in 1 tablespoon flour and leave for 10 minutes to froth and bubble. Add 3 cups flour, remaining salt and butter. Add ½ tablespoon flour and ½ tablespoon Parmesan. Mix to form a soft dough. Knead well and shape into 20 2-inch balls.

Pour oil into a shallow pan, and place the balls in the pan in a single layer. Turn balls to coat with oil, cover, let rise about 15 minutes.

On a greased surface, flatten and stretch out each ball as thinly as possible. Fold stretched pastry into rectangles of about 3 x 10-inches. Place 1 tablespoon filling across the longer side of the pastry strip. Starting at one end of the roll, keep turning it upon itself to make a coiled, snail-shell shape, just like a coffee roll. Repeat for remaining balls of dough.

Place the pastries on an oiled pan and allow to rise for 5 to 10 minutes.

Preheat oven to 350°.

Place a dot of butter on top of each, sprinkle with remaining grated Parmesan, and bake for 20 to 25 minutes, until golden brown on the bottom.

Remove and drain on paper towels. Serve warm.

Yields 20 bolemas

Potato Borrekitas

 Virginia Israel

Small savory pastries made by Sephardic Jews of Turkish and Greek origins.

4 large potatoes, peeled, boiled, and mashed
3 eggs, beaten
1 cup feta cheese, grated
½ cup Parmesan cheese, grated

½ teaspoon salt, plus more to taste
Pepper, to taste
½ cup vegetable oil
½ cup water
2 cups all-purpose flour

To prepare filling, mix potatoes, 2 eggs, feta, Parmesan, salt and pepper, to taste, together in a large bowl, and set aside.

Mix oil, ½ teaspoon salt, and water together in a large bowl. Add flour and knead to a firm dough. Shape into balls the size of a walnut and allow to stand for 15 minutes.

Preheat oven to 350°.

Roll out each pastry ball to about 2 inches in diameter. Place 1 teaspoon of filling in center and fold dough over. (The edge can be trimmed with a glass or knife to a smooth round shape, and teased into a croissant shape if desired.)

Lightly oil a baking sheet and place borrekitas on it. Brush each one with beaten egg. Bake for 20 minutes, or until golden.

Yields 12 borrekitas

My Grandma's Yaprakes

 Judy Elkin

These Turkish-style stuffed grape leaves make a lovely appetizer and work especially well followed by salmon.

30–35 grape leaves (may be bought in jars; or if you have a vine, pick young, tender leaves)

2 large onions, minced

³/₄ cup vegetable oil

1 cup rice

2¹/₂ teaspoons salt

1 teaspoon pepper

1¹/₂ cups water

¹/₂ cup parsley, minced

Juice of 2–3 lemons, or more to taste

Parboil leaves, if fresh, then drain and separate. If using leaves in jars, rinse, drain and separate.

In a skillet, sauté minced onions in ¹/₂ cup oil until transparent, about 10 minutes. Add rice, 2 teaspoons salt, pepper, and 1 cup water and cook about 10 minutes more, or until water evaporates. Add parsley.

To fill, spread out a leaf on your work surface, shiny side facing down. Place a heaping teaspoon of rice mixture in center of leaf. Turn left side of leaf over rice mixture, then right side over left. Roll up tightly and arrange rolled leaves firmly and snugly together in a 2-quart saucepan. Add one layer of yaprakes on top of another.

Mix ¹/₄ cup oil and lemon juice, salt and water together in a small bowl. Lots of lemon can be used to make sure they're fairly tart. Pour over yaprakes. Cover with leftover leaves and put lid on. Cook on low heat until rice is tender, about 30 minutes, being careful not to burn the bottom rolls.

Cool to room temperature. Remove and serve on a platter.

Yields 30–35 yaprakes

INDIAN SHABBAT DINNER

Serves 6

Kiddush Wine

No-Knead Whole Wheat Challah (*see Erev Yom Kippur Dinner* ∿ 20)

Indian Lentil Soup ∿ 244

Shabbat Chicken — double recipe ∿ 245

Saffron Rice ∿ 246

Steamed Green Beans

Chocolate Chip Mandelbrot (*see A Mishloach Manot Basket for Purim* ∿ 110)

Fresh Fruit Salad

Indian Lentil Soup

 Linda Jacob

This soup can be somewhat time consuming but is well worth the effort. Cooking the lentils the night before can dramatically speed up the soup-making.

1 cup lentils (preferably yellow dal from an Indian grocery)
3 cups water
1 teaspoon turmeric
1 teaspoon ground coriander
1 teaspoon cumin
1 teaspoon curry powder, or more to taste

3 medium onions, chopped
5 cloves garlic, minced
Crushed red pepper, to taste
Vegetable oil, for sautéing
Fresh coriander leaves (cilantro), chopped
2 lemons, cut into wedges

Rinse lentils well and place in a large pot. Add water and tumeric, ground coriander, cumin, and curry powder. Cover and simmer about 2 hours, or until lentils are soft, stirring occasionally. If lentils are drying out, add more water.

Sauté onions, garlic, and crushed red pepper in oil over medium heat until onions are golden, about 20 minutes. Add sauté to the lentils. Cook covered for two hours more over medium heat, adding water as needed for desired thickness.

Top with coriander leaves and serve with lemon wedges (for your guests to squeeze into the soup).

Serves 4–6

Variations: For a very spicy flavor, add 1 tablespoon quick curry paste pickles (available at Indian groceries and some supermarkets) and an extra tablespoon of curry powder when adding the sauté to the lentils. The soup also tastes good with rice added to it.

Shabbat Chicken

  Linda Jacob

This is actually a Baghdadi-Jewish recipe which my mother-in-law made every week for Shabbat dinner.

2 tablespoons vegetable oil
1 small onion, sliced
2 whole cloves
1 cinnamon stick
1/2 teaspoon salt, or more to taste
1 teaspoon turmeric

1 teaspoon fresh ginger, grated, or more to taste
1 teaspoon garlic, finely minced, or more to taste
1 chicken, cut in sixths, skin removed and reserved

In a covered pan, heat oil over medium-low heat and brown the onion. Add cloves, cinnamon, salt, turmeric, ginger, and garlic. Add chicken parts plus enough skin to prevent the meat from sticking to pan. Raise heat to medium to brown meat. Mix frequently until brown.

Reduce heat to medium-low, cover, and cook until tender, about 25 minutes. Check it frequently and mix to minimize sticking. Turn the heat off, leave the top on the pan, and let it wait while you say the Shabbat blessings.

Serves 4–6

Saffron Rice

  Linda Jacob

If you can't find basmati rice at your supermarket, it's available in Indian grocery stores. If you have leftovers, this rice is also delicious with some of the Lentil Soup spooned on top, accompanied by lots of lemon.

1 cup basmati rice
2 tablespoons pareve
  margarine
2 cups boiling water or
  chicken stock

¹/₂ teaspoon saffron
Salt and pepper, to taste

Preheat oven to 350°. Grease a 1¹/₂-quart casserole.

Wash and drain rice twice. In a casserole, combine all ingredients. Cover and bake 30 minutes, or until rice is tender.

This dish can be prepared ahead and held in a warm oven for 30 minutes.

Serves 4

ORIENTAL SHABBAT DINNER

Serves 4–6

Kiddush Wine
Challah (*see Rosh Hashanah Dinner* ～ 5)
Oriental Beef and Noodle Soup ～ 248
Stir-Fry Beef with Broccoli — double recipe ～ 249
Szechuan Green Beans ～ 250
Fried Rice — halve recipe (*see Winter Shabbat Dinner* ～ 210)
Almond Cookies ～ 251
Fresh Fruit

Kiddush Wine
Challah (*see Rosh Hashanah Dinner* ～ 5)
Oriental Bluefish ～ 252
Brown Noodles ～ 253
Szechuan Green Beans ～ 250
Ginger Cucumber Salad (*see Vegetarian Barbecue* ～ 190)
Almond Cookies ～ 251
Fresh Fruit

Oriental Beef and Noodle Soup

 Roberta Hoffman

A hearty winter soup with stir-fried vegetables and oriental-flavored stock.

3 ounces bean thread or cellophane noodles, or thin spaghetti

5 cups chicken stock

2 tablespoons vegetable oil

½ pound peppersteak, cut very thinly

4 scallions, cut into thin strips

5 tablespoons fresh ginger, grated

2 large bok choy leaves, cut crosswise into 1-inch pieces

2 tablespoons tamari or soy sauce, or more to taste

1 tablespoon toasted sesame oil, or more to taste

Put bean thread noodles in a bowl. Cover with boiling water. Let stand 15 minutes. (If using spaghetti, put on to cook until al dente.)

Meanwhile, bring stock to boil in a medium saucepan. Reduce heat and keep warm.

Heat oil in wok or skillet over high heat and cook peppersteak, half the scallions, and 3 tablespoons ginger. Add bok choy and stir-fry for a minute or two until done. Add stock, remaining scallions and ginger, tamari sauce, and sesame oil and simmer for 3 minutes.

Drain noodles and divide among 4 to 6 bowls. Ladle soup on top and serve immediately.

Serves 4–6

Stir-Fry Beef With Broccoli

 Ruth Spack

1 tablespoon cornstarch	1 pound London Broil, cut into
2 tablespoons dark soy sauce	1-inch strips
1 tablespoon toasted sesame	1 pound broccoli
oil	1 tablespoon corn oil
1 tablespoon sherry	2 tablespoons water

Mix cornstarch, soy sauce, sesame oil, sherry, and London Broil together in a nonaluminum dish. Marinate 30 minutes.

Remove tough ends and leaves from broccoli. Cut florets and slice stalks.

Heat $^1/_2$ tablespoon corn oil in skillet or wok over medium-high heat. Stir-fry broccoli 1 minute. Add 2 tablespoons water and cook 2 minutes more. Remove from heat and set aside.

Heat an additional $^1/_2$ tablespoon corn oil in the skillet until hot. Stir-fry the beef mixture for 2 minutes. Add broccoli to beef mixture and stir well for 2 minutes. Serve hot.

Serves 4

Szechuan Green Beans

 Debby Zigun

This is a hot and spicy vegetable side dish.

6 cloves garlic
2 thin slices fresh ginger
2 scallions
1 teaspoon crushed red pepper, or less to taste
1 tablespoon vegetable oil

1 tablespoon soy or tamari sauce
1 tablespoon rice wine vinegar
1 pound fresh green beans, trimmed

Mince garlic, ginger, and scallions by hand or in a food processor. Combine with oil and crushed red pepper. Stir-fry in a skillet or wok over medium heat, about 3 minutes. Stir in remaining ingredients. Cook uncovered about 10 minutes, stirring occasionally, until beans are crisp-tender. Serve hot or cold.

Serves 4–6

Almond Cookies

 Debby Zigun

Delicious even without a Chinese dinner to go with them!

¹/₄ cup vegetable shortening	2 tablespoons almond extract
¹/₄ cup pareve margarine	1 egg
1 cup all-purpose flour	1 tablespoon water
¹/₂ teaspoon salt	24 whole blanched almonds
6 tablespoons sugar	

Cut together shortening, margarine, and flour in a large bowl. Add salt, sugar, and almond extract. Work together with hands until a dough forms. Shape into a long roll 1-inch in diameter. Wrap in waxed paper. Chill for 1 hour.

Preheat oven to 375°.

Cut roll into 24 slices. Place 1 inch apart on ungreased cookie sheet. Press 1 almond on top of each cookie. Bake for 5 to 8 minutes, until golden.

Yields 24 cookies

Oriental Bluefish

 Linda Novak

This is an easy recipe sure to wow your company. Serve it with rice to soak up the sauce. People who think that they don't like bluefish will be surprised when they taste this dish.

1½ pounds bluefish, swordfish, or halibut

4 scallions, minced

2 tablespoons fresh ginger, minced

2 cloves garlic, minced

3 tablespoons toasted sesame oil

4 tablespoons toasted sesame seeds

3 tablespoons tamari sauce

3 tablespoons mirin (sweet Japanese rice wine)

Juice of 1 lemon

Rinse bluefish and pat dry. Feel the fish for bones, and use pliers or tweezers to remove them.

Combine scallions, ginger, and garlic in a small bowl. Oil a baking dish (just big enough to fit the bluefish) with some of the sesame oil and spread half of the scallion mixture over the bottom of the dish. Sprinkle with sesame seeds. Arrange fish pieces on top. Sprinkle with remaining scallion mixture.

Preheat oven to 400°.

Blend remaining sesame oil, tamari sauce, mirin, and lemon juice together in a small bowl. Spoon mixture over fish. (At this point, fish can be covered and refrigerated for several hours before cooking. Return it to room temperature first.)

Bake uncovered for 20 to 25 minutes. Serve immediately or hold for up to 30 minutes in a 250° oven — baste occasionally and the fish will be more tender and the flavors even richer.

Serves 4

Brown Noodles

 Ivy Feuerstadt

This noodle dish is really simple and my kids love it. The optional ingredients make it great — but then my kids won't eat it at all!

1 pound Japanese udon noodles (you could use fettucine)

3 tablespoons toasted sesame oil

3 tablespoons tamari sauce

1/2 sweet red pepper, chopped (optional)

2 clove garlic, chopped or crushed (optional)

Bring 4 quarts of water to a boil. Drop in the noodles and cook al dente. Drain quickly and submerge in cold water, drain again.

Place noodles in a large serving bowl and stir in sesame oil and tamari sauce. Mix in optional ingredients. Refrigerate and serve cold or at room temperature.

Serves 4–6

ORIENTAL SHABBAT LUNCH

Serves 4–6

Kiddush Wine
Challah (*see Rosh Hashanah Dinner* ⌇ 5)
Hot and Sour Soup ⌇ 256
Spicy Oriental Chicken Salad ⌇ 257
with Creamy Peanut Sauce (*see Erev Yom Kippur Dinner* ⌇ 23)
Lo Mein — Pareve Variation ⌇ 258
Almond Cookies (*see Oriental Shabbat Dinner* ⌇ 251)
Fresh Fruit

Kiddush Wine
Challah (*see Rosh Hashanah Dinner* ⌇ 5)
Noodles in Spicy Peanut Sauce with Tofu ⌇ 259
Ginger Cucumber Salad (*see Vegetarian Barbecue* ⌇ 190)
Sesame Broccoli (*see July 4th Barbecue* ⌇ 180)
Hot and Sour Cabbage Salad ⌇ 260
Almond Cookies (*see Oriental Shabbat Dinner* ⌇ 251)
Fresh Fruit

Hot and Sour Soup

 Debby Zigun

This recipe was adapted for kosher cooking by a local cooking teacher and caterer. The optional unusual ingredients are available at local Oriental cooking store and make for a richer soup.

4 ounces beef or veal, thinly sliced

1 tablespoon tamari or soy sauce

1 teaspoon cornstarch

2 tablespoons vegetable oil

6 cups chicken stock

8 ounces firm tofu

1/2 cup bamboo shoots

1/2 cup golden needles, soaked and shredded (optional)

2 tablespoons wood ear, soaked and shredded (optional)

4 black mushrooms soaked and shredded (discard hard stem)

2 tablespoons light soy sauce

2 tablespoons vinegar

1 teaspoon chili oil

1/2 teaspoon black pepper

1 tablespoon fresh ginger, finely grated

1 egg, beaten

3 tablespoons cornstarch

3 tablespoons water

Garnishes:

1 teaspoon toasted sesame oil

3 tablespoons scallions, chopped

In a small bowl, marinate meat in tamari and cornstarch for 15 minutes. Heat oil in skillet over medium heat and stir-fry meat until it changes color. Set aside.

In a pot, bring chicken stock to a boil. Add tofu, bamboo shoots, golden needles, wood ear, and black mushrooms. Simmer for 3 to 5 minutes. Add meat and soy, vinegar, chili oil, pepper, and ginger. Add egg in a slow steady stream while stirring.

In a small bowl, blend the cornstarch with the water. Add to soup, stirring slowly. Cook 1 minute more and ladle into bowls.

Just before serving, drizzle sesame oil on top of each bowlful and sprinkle with chopped scallions.

Serves 4–6

Spicy Oriental Chicken Salad

 Brenda Freishtat

This is a wonderful way to use up the chicken from your chicken soup. It is a great dish for company lunch or supper.

3 quarts water

2 tablespoons peanut oil

10 ounces thin Chinese egg noodles or Italian spaghettini

1 pound cooked boneless, skinless chicken meat, chopped or shredded

2 tablespoons toasted sesame oil

1 cup bean sprouts

1 cup carrots, thinly sliced

1 cup cucumbers, thinly sliced

1 cup string beans, slightly steamed

10 ounces corn kernels, slightly steamed

1 cup scallions, thinly sliced

Creamy Peanut Sauce, page 23

In a pot, add water and 1 tablespoon peanut oil. Bring to a boil and cook noodles until al dente. Drain them well.

In the center of a serving platter, toss the chicken and noodles with remaining peanut and sesame oil. Place sprouts, carrots, cucumber, beans, and corn around the chicken. Sprinkle scallions on top. Serve with Creamy Peanut Sauce, page 23 on the side.

Serves 4–6

Lo Mein

 Debby Zigun

1 pound thin Chinese egg noodles

3 tablespoons sesame oil

6 tablespoons tamari or soy sauce

2 tablespoons sugar

2 tablespoons red wine vinegar

¹/₄ cup peanut butter

2 tablespoons peanut oil

1 tablespoon garlic, minced

1 tablespoon scallions, chopped

1 tablespoon fresh ginger, minced

1 chicken breast half, poached and shredded (optional)

Cook noodles in a pot in plenty of boiling water until al dente. Run under cold water, drain well.

Place in large bowl and toss with 2 tablespoons sesame oil.

In food processor or blender, combine soy sauce, sugar, vinegar, and peanut butter.

Heat peanut oil and remaining sesame oil in a small saucepan. Add garlic, scallions, and ginger. Stir-fry over medium-high heat for 1 minute and add soy sauce mixture. Bring to simmer and remove from heat.

Pour over noodles. If desired, add shredded chicken. Toss well.

Refrigerate and return to room temperature before serving.

Serves 4

Noodles in Spicy Peanut Sauce with Tofu

 Larry Sternberg

This good source of protein and carbohydrates is especially good in the summer.
You can prepare it without the tofu, using only half the sauce.

1 pound Chinese egg noodles
2 scant cups unsalted
  peanuts
6 tablespoons toasted sesame
  oil
4¹/₂ tablespoons peanut oil
6 tablespoons Chinese soy
  sauce
4¹/₂ tablespoons Chinese
  black vinegar
6 large cloves garlic, minced
6 teaspoons sugar
³/₄ teaspoon cayenne pepper
  (optional)

¹/₂–³/₄ cup water
1 pound firm or extra-firm tofu,
  cut into 1-inch cubes

Garnishes:
5 scallions, white parts only, cut
  lengthwise into fine strips
¹/₄ cup chopped peanuts
1 cucumber, peeled, halved
  lengthwise, seeds removed,
  and sliced

Cook noodles in a pot in plenty of boiling water until at dente. Set aside.

Finely chop the peanuts in a food processor. Set aside ¹/₄ cup for garnish. Add 4 tablespoons sesame oil, the peanut oil, soy sauce, black vinegar, garlic, sugar, and optional cayenne to the processor. Blend to a smooth, thick paste. Add water to thin so that the sauce will pour. Place the tofu in a nonaluminum dish and pour half the sauce over it. Let it marinate about 30 minutes.

Place noodles in a serving bowl, add remaining sesame oil, and toss. Add tofu and remaining sauce. Garnish with scallions, peanuts, and cucumber, if desired. Serve warm or at room temperature.

Serves 4–6

Hot and Sour Cabbage Salad

 Janet Yassen and Irle Goldman

This recipe is an instant success, easy to make, and delicious. You can make it in large quantities and adjust it according to how hot and spicy your tastes are. It works well with other Chinese dishes or just as an interesting side dish, and tastes best served cold.

2 pounds cabbage
5 tablespoons peanut oil
1 teaspoon crushed red pepper, or 2 to 4 dried chili peppers, crumbled*
2 teaspoons salt

3 tablespoons tamari or soy sauce
2 tablespoons white vinegar
2 tablespoons toasted sesame oil

Core cabbage and slice into ½-inch strips about 2-inches long.

Heat oil in wok over high heat, add crushed red pepper or crumbled chili peppers and cabbage. Stir-fry about 3 minutes or until cabbage is soft. Add salt and tamari sauce. Stir-fry for 1 minute more. Add vinegar and sesame oil. Stir until thoroughly mixed. Cool before serving.

Serves 8–10

*See Ceviche recipe on page 228 for wise advice on preparation of chili peppers.

A RUSSIAN MEAL FROM
A NEW AMERICAN FAMILY

Serves 8–10

Vodka
Bread

Butter or Shortbread Cookies
Chocolate Candies
Sweet Wine

Borscht

  Valery Spitkovsky

Borscht is a very popular first course in the Ukraine and Russia, enjoyed from high society to the working class. It is a soup made with a variety of vegetables and meat — Russians have an expression to describe borscht made without meat that translates as "empty borscht" — whose distinctive quality is its red or green color ("no color, no borscht," to quote the Russians again). Although each region has its own traditional way of preparing borscht, the Ukrainian version is considered the mother and father of them all. It is not, however, cooked in Jewish kitchens because it is always made with pork. But Jews have adapted it to kosher cooking and added a few flavors of their own. At heart, borscht is peasant food, thrown into the pot in large amounts to feed big families for a week during late autumn until early spring. The genuine article is prepared the day before it is eaten.

2 pounds soup beef (chuck or flanken)
1 pound soup bones
4 quarts water
2 bay leaves
5 peppercorns, or more to taste
2 large onions, peeled
2 large carrots, peeled
2 parsley roots
2 celery roots
1 teaspoon salt, or more to taste

3 medium beets, washed and trimmed
1 medium onion, chopped
2 large celery stalks, chopped

$^1/_2$ cup parsley, chopped
3–4 tablespoons fresh dill stems, chopped
5 large potatoes, peeled and cut into large chunks
1 medium cabbage, chopped or shredded
1 28-ounce can crushed tomatoes
Juice of $^1/_2$ lemon
2 teaspoons sugar, or more to taste
$^1/_3$ cup parsley, chopped
$^1/_3$ cup celery leaves, chopped
$^1/_3$ cup dill leaves, chopped
Salt and pepper, to taste
4 large cloves garlic, crushed, or more to taste

Place the meat and bones in a large soup pot, cover with water, and bring to a boil. Boil uncovered for 5 to 7 minutes. Drain meat and bones, rinse with fresh water, and return them to the pot. Add 4 quarts of water, bay leaves, peppercorns, whole onions, whole carrots, and parsley and celery roots. Bring to a boil, add salt, lower heat, and simmer uncovered for 1 hour.

Meanwhile, place beets in a pot, cover with water, bring to boil, lower heat to a simmer, and cook for 30 minutes. Drain, return beets to pot, and cover with cold water. When beets cool, peel and set aside.

Drain off the stock liquid and set aside. Discard cooked onions, bay leaves, peppercorns, and bones but set aside roots, carrots, and meat. Measure liquid and return to soup pot, adding boiling water so that the total liquid amount equals 4 quarts. Add onion, celery, 3 tablespoons of the parsley, and dill stems. Grate cooked beets and add to soup pot. Add potatoes and boil for 10 minutes. Add cabbage and continue to boil gently for 20 to 25 minutes until potatoes and cabbage are tender. Lower heat and add tomatoes, lemon juice, and sugar, adjusting to desired taste. Add remaining parsley, celery, and dill leaves. Turn off heat and cover pot until ready to serve.

Before serving, cut meat, carrots, and roots into bite-sized pieces and place in bowls. Add hot soup, making sure that each bowl has a chunk of cooked potato. Add salt, pepper, and crushed garlic to taste.

Serves 8–10

Variations: **Pareve Borscht** — *Omit meat. Add 2 chopped onions, lightly browned in oil, to stock in place of the whole onions. You can also serve it with a dollop of sour cream in each bowl.*

Moscovsky Borscht — *Omit meat. Add cooked beef sausage just before you turn off the heat and cover the pot.*

Uralsky Borscht — *Omit meat. Add cooked beef sausage and mushrooms just before you turn off the heat and cover the pot.*

Jewish Odessa Borscht — *Add cooked kidney beans and Greek black olives when adding the onions, carrots, and parsley to the stock. Delete the celery roots.*

Russian Vinaigrette Salad

 P Sofia Serdyuchenko

2 medium beets
4–5 medium potatoes
1 large carrot
1½ cups sauerkraut, or more
to taste

1 small onion, finely chopped
½ cup parsley, finely chopped
¼ cup sunflower or olive oil
½ cup scallions, chopped
(optional)

Wash and trim beets. Place in a pot, cover with water, and bring to a boil. Lower heat to a simmer and cook for 30 minutes, or until beets pierce easily with a fork. Drain, return beets to the pot, and cover with cold water. When beets cool, peel and cut into small cubes.

While beets are cooking, place potatoes and carrot in another pot, cover with water, and bring to a boil. Lower heat to a simmer and cook until they are soft and pierce easily with a fork, about 20 minutes. Drain, return to pot, and cover with cold water. When potatoes and carrot cool, remove potato peel and cut potatoes and carrot into 1-inch pieces. Toss beets, potatoes, and carrots with remaining ingredients and refrigerate.

Serves 8

Smoked Whitefish Salad

Sofia Serdyuchenko

3 cups flaked smoked
   whitefish
8 cups cooked white rice,
   lightly salted
1 small onion, finely
   chopped
1 cup mayonnaise

$^1/_2$ cup sour cream
Salt and pepper, to taste

Garnishes:
Chopped parsley
Sliced hard-boiled egg

Mix together fish, rice, and onion in a large serving dish. Combine
mayonnaise and sour cream in a small bowl, and blend into fish
mixture. Add salt and pepper, mix well, and refrigerate.
    Garnish before serving with parsley and egg.

Serves 8

Cheese and Egg Salad

Sofia Serdyuchenko

1 pound Cheddar or other
   mild hard cheese, grated
2 hard-boiled eggs, grated or
   chopped
1 cup walnuts, finely
   chopped

$^3/_4$ cup mayonnaise
$^1/_4$ cup sour cream
Salt and pepper, to taste
Parsley for garnish

Mix together cheese, eggs, and nuts in a serving bowl. Combine
mayonnaise and sour cream in a small bowl, and blend into cheese
mixture. Add salt and pepper, mix well, and refrigerate.
    Garnish with parsley before serving.

Serves 8

Beet Salad

  Sofia Serdyuchenko

2 medium beets
2 hard-boiled eggs, chopped
1 cup walnuts, chopped

$^1/_4$ cup parsley, finely chopped
$^3/_4$ cup mayonnaise
$^1/_4$ cup sour cream

Wash and trim beets. Place in a pot, cover with water, bring to a boil, lower heat to a simmer, and cook for 30 minutes, or until beets pierce easily with a fork. Drain, return beets to pot, and cover with cold water. When beets cool, peel and chop into small pieces.

Mix beets together with eggs, nuts, and parsley in a serving bowl. Combine mayonnaise and sour cream in a small bowl, and add slowly to beet mixture, using just enough to moisten. Add more to taste. Refrigerate and serve cold.

Serves 8

"MY CHILDREN WILL ONLY EAT..."

When we requested recipes for this cookbook, we were particularly interested in dishes that would appeal to most children. Not surprisingly, we received very few. The following recipes have been recommended by our cooks for children's ever-changing tastes.

Cauliflower Tiberias

    Smadar Babchuck

This recipe comes from my ancestors in Tiberias, Israel, who settled there in the sixteenth century. I never tasted cauliflower cooked any other way when I was growing up.

2 heads cauliflower
2 eggs, beaten
1 cup bread crumbs or flour
(use matzoh meal for
Passover)

Vegetable oil for frying
Salt and pepper, to taste
Juice of 2 lemons
1 1/2 cups water

Preheat oven to 325°.

Break apart cauliflowers into florets. Cover with water and boil for 5 minutes. Do not overcook or they will fall apart. Drain and cool.

Dip each piece in egg and then bread crumbs, and fry in oil until brown on all sides.

Place in a casserole. Salt and pepper lightly and add lemon juice and water. Cook covered for 30 minutes. Serve immediately.

Serves 8

Cinnamon Meatballs

    Lucy Tannen

My sister, Melanie Rosenbaum, and I were preparing dinner for my children and other relatives, and we were tired of the same old spaghetti and meatballs. Looking through the spices, we spotted cinnamon and thought that if the kids liked it in applesauce, they might like it with meatballs, too. After a little experimenting, we came up with this recipe. It was an instant hit.

$1/4$ teaspoon cinnamon
1 onion, chopped, or
   1 tablespoon onion flakes
1 teaspoon dried basil
1 teaspoon dried dill

Salt and pepper, to taste
2 pounds lean ground beef
Vegetable oil for frying

Mix seasonings together in a large bowl and add meat. Mix thoroughly and shape into balls, $1^{1}/_{2}$-inches in diameter. Brown in small amount of heated oil. Simmer in a pot in your favorite sauce, 40 minutes, covered.

Serve over pasta, or alone for Passover.

Serves 6–8

Fluffy Burgers

 Toby Pugh

These are very light and fluffy burgers — warm and soothing on a cold day.
After a long hard day at Yeshiva University High School for Girls, coming
home to these was heaven.

1 pound lean ground beef,
  turkey, or veal
1 egg
$^{1}/_{2}$–$^{3}/_{4}$ cup matzoh meal or
  bread crumbs
Garlic powder, to taste

Dash of parsley flakes
2–4 tablespoons tamari or soy
  sauce
Water
Vegetable oil for frying
4 cups spaghetti sauce

Mix meat and egg in a bowl. Add matzoh meal, garlic powder, a good
shake of parsley flakes, and mix well. Add tamari and enough water
to make the mixture moist and fluffy.

Heat a little oil in a large sauté pan over medium heat. With wet
hands, shape 4 thick, oval-shaped burgers. Brown both sides well in
the hot oil. When brown, pour the spaghetti sauce over them. Cover
pan tightly and continue cooking on low heat for about 15 to 20
minutes, or until burgers puff up.

Serves 4–6

Fish Casserole

 Naomi Mael Litrownik

Even the kids like fish when it is surrounded by noodles and cheese sauce. They have even been known to eat some of the spinach!

8 ounces medium egg noodles

3 tablespoons margarine or butter

3 tablespoons all-purpose flour

3 cups lowfat milk

1 tablespoon lemon juice

1 teaspoon dry mustard

1 teaspoon Worcestershire sauce

1/2 teaspoon salt, or more to taste

Dash of pepper

Dash of nutmeg

1 1/2 cups sharp Cheddar cheese, grated

2 10-ounce packages frozen chopped spinach, defrosted and squeezed dry

1 1/2 pounds cod fillets

1/4 cup slivered blanched almonds, toasted

Cook noodles until al dente in plenty of boiling water. Drain and set aside.

Preheat oven to 375°.

Melt margarine in a 4-quart pot. Blend in flour and add milk. Whisk over medium heat until smooth and thick. Stir in lemon juice, mustard, Worcestershire, salt, pepper, nutmeg, and 1 cup of cheese.

Combine cooked noodles with 1/2 the cheese sauce. Pour into 2 1/2 quart (or larger) greased baking dish. Top with spinach. Arrange fish fillets on spinach. Pour remaining sauce over fish.

Sprinkle with remaining cheese and almonds. Bake for 25 minutes or until fish is cooked through.

Serves 4–6

Green Soup

  Michael Babchuck

This wintery soup has proven a favorite with children who fuss about food, especially soups. There's something Dr. Seussy about a soup that is green, provoking the younger children to moan, groan, and giggle about being forced to eat green soup. We make the soup pareve for greater versatility and since the soup freezes so well, we make large quantities.

3 medium onions, coarsely chopped
1 tablespoon powdered ginger
1½ teaspoons dry mustard
1 tablespoon caraway seeds
1 tablespoon dried dill
Salt and pepper, to taste
⅓ cup olive oil
1 cup white wine
9 cups water
4 leek stalks, washed well and chopped

1 bunch mustard greens, rinsed and trimmed
1 small head bok choy, chopped
4 large potatoes, peeled and thinly sliced
3 tablespoons vegetable broth powder

Garnishes:
Mozzarella or Romano cheese, grated (optional)
Melba toast, nuts, or crackers (optional)

In a large pot, sauté onions, herbs, and spices in olive oil over medium heat until soft, about 20 minutes. Add wine, reduce heat, and simmer for a few minutes. Add water and vegetables and bring to a boil. Sprinkle broth powder over the surface, and stir. Reduce to a simmer and cook for 45 to 60 minutes, until all vegetables are soft. Taste and add additional spices as desired. Cool soup.

Run soup through blender or food processor, small portions at a time, until it has the consistency of cream. (It may be frozen at this point.)

Serve soup hot, topped with grated cheese for a dairy meal, or with melba rounds, soup nuts, or crackers for a meat meal.

Serves 10–12

Michelle's Gourmet Dinner

 Debby Zigun

My daughter, Michelle, spent a week with her grandparents one summer. One evening she could not find anything she wanted to eat for dinner. Her grandma suggested she make up her own recipe from things on hand in the kitchen. When she returned home, Michelle shared her creation with her family and friends. It was a great success.

1 pound ground beef
1 onion, chopped
1 clove garlic, minced
1 cup macaroni
1 tablespoon Kiddush wine
$^1/_2$ cup pareve tomato sauce

1 tablespoon ketchup
2 tablespoons tamari or soy sauce
1 cup water
$^1/_2$ cup salami, chopped (optional)

Brown beef over medium heat in a skillet, drain off fat. Add other ingredients and bring to a boil. Lower heat and simmer 20 minutes or until macaroni is cooked and liquid absorbed. Serve immediately.

Serves 4

Noah's Favorite Chicken

 Ivy Feuerstadt

I lived on Stuart Road in Newton Center, Massachusetts for about six years. It was a friendly, warm neighborhood and my friend Debbie Phillips lived right across the street. Debbie had the kind of house (or should I say kitchen) that you could breeze in and out of. Friends were always welcome to drop in and share ideas, food, or news.

I remember dropping by one winter afternoon around 5:30. I was surprised by the stillness in the kitchen, although the energy and noise upstairs certainly made up for the quiet downstairs. She told me Aliza and Noah had playovers; that it was easier, she added, if both her children had friends to play with at the same time. When Debbie gave advice, you knew to listen. She always imparted something wise and useful. What did I know? I had a one-year-old in tow and I was pregnant. Actually, Debbie was pregnant, too. I always wondered where she got her energy.

I figured they were going out for dinner since it was quickly approaching 6:00 and nothing was cooking! When I asked about dinner, she said that she was about to make Noah's favorite chicken, and it would be ready in about an hour. She said it was one of her family's favorite meals. She told me that the Spanish name was Arroz con Pollo. I couldn't believe she could do this — a very pregnant woman, four kids on the loose, and a bare kitchen.

I watched her from start to finish. She was quick and skillful. What I remember most was how happy she was cooking for her family. I only hope that when you prepare this dish, you have the same sparkle in your eyes.

1 4–4¹/₂ pound chicken, cut in eighths
¹/₂ cup olive oil
¹/₂ cup onions, chopped
1¹/₂ teaspoon salt
Dash of pepper
1 32-ounce can tomatoes, with liquid
1 bay leaf
1 cup rice, rinsed

In a large sauté pan or electric frying pan, fry chicken in oil over medium-high heat until evenly browned. Remove chicken, and cook onions until translucent, about 10 minutes. Replace chicken; add salt and pepper, tomatoes, bay leaf, and rice. Cook over low heat for about 1 hour, or until rice is fully cooked. Remove bay leaf and serve.

Serves 3–4

Pasta with Tomato Meat Sauce

 Judy Herzig-Marx

This recipe was originally made with ground beef. But like many people, our family is eating less red meat. Last year I began experimenting with ground turkey. It works best with robust, flavorful dishes and is delicious over pasta. There is so much chopping involved in this recipe that I always double it and freeze half.

2 tablespoons olive oil	$^1/_2$ cup green pepper, chopped
1 cup onion, chopped	1 teaspoon dried oregano
2 cloves garlic, minced	1 teaspoon dried basil
1$^1/_2$ cups grated carrots	1 bay leaf
1 pound ground turkey	$^1/_2$ teaspoon pepper
1 28-ounce can tomato purée	$^1/_2$ teaspoon allspice
1 cup meatless spaghetti sauce	Dash of crushed red pepper
	Salt, to taste
1 6-ounce can tomato paste	$^1/_2$ cup red wine
8 ounces mushrooms, thinly sliced (optional)	1 pound pasta

Heat oil in a heavy 4 to 5 quart saucepan over medium-high heat. Add onion and garlic, and sauté, stirring until lightly browned, about 20 minutes.

Lower heat, add carrots and cook, stirring until softened, a couple of minutes more. Add meat and cook until crumbly and liquid has evaporated.

Reduce heat to low. Add all remaining ingredients except wine and simmer uncovered 1$^1/_2$ hours, stirring occasionally. Blend in wine and simmer 30 minutes more.

Cook pasta in plenty of boiling water until al dente. Drain and place in a large serving bowl. Pour the sauce over the pasta and serve immediately.

Yields 8 cups

Rebecca's Hot Dog Casserole

 Harriet Cole

My daughter Rebecca likes to make this crazy recipe for company.

8 hot dogs, cut into bite-sized pieces

2 16-ounce cans vegetarian baked beans

2 tablespoons brown sugar

1/2 teaspoon chili powder, or more to taste

Dash of cayenne pepper, or more to taste

2 tablespoons ketchup

1 tablespoon prepared mustard

Preheat oven to 350°.

Mix all ingredients together in a baking dish. Cover and bake for 45 minutes. Serve immediately.

Serves 6

Squash and Peanut Butter Soup

 Savitri Clarke

This is one of my favorites — kids love the taste, and I like it because the peanut butter and milk make it protein-rich.

4 cups vegetable stock
1 butternut squash, peeled and cut into 2-inch pieces
1 large tart apple, cored, peeled, and sliced
1 large onion, quartered
1/2 cup peanut butter
2 teaspoons curry powder

1/2 teaspoon salt (optional if peanut butter is salted)
1/4 teaspoon pepper
3/4 cup cream, half-and-half, or milk
3 tablespoons fresh parsley, chopped, for garnish

Bring the stock to a boil in a large pan. Add squash, apple, and onion. Reduce heat and simmer until vegetables are tender, about 20 minutes. Stir in peanut butter and spices.

Purée the mixture in batches in a blender or food processor until smooth.

Return to the pot and stir in the cream. Add more if necessary to achieve desired consistency. Garnish with chopped parsley.

Serves 6

Stuffed Celery

  Smadar Babchuck

This is a Jewish-Greek recipe designed especially to break up the monotony of hamburgers day in, day out. My aunt served it to me when I announced that I hated celery. I licked my fingers then and my children do the same today.

1 bunch celery	Salt and pepper, to taste
1/2 pound ground beef	Vegetable oil for frying
2 eggs	1 1/2 cups water
1 cup bread crumbs (use matzoh meal for Passover)	Juice of 2 lemons

Cut off the wide bottom part of each celery stalk, about 4 to 5 inches long. Wash and dry.

Mix together beef, 1 egg, 1/3 cup bread crumbs, pinch of salt and pepper in a small bowl. Stuff each stalk bottom to form a small mound.

Beat the remaining egg in a dish. Dip each piece of stuffed celery in the egg, then in the bread crumbs and fry in hot oil on both sides (celery side down first) until lightly brown, about 3 to 5 minutes.

Preheat oven to 325°.

Place stuffed celery in a casserole dish. Salt lightly, and add water and juice of 2 lemons. Bake covered for 30 minutes.

Serves 4–6

Sweet and Sour Lentils

 Judy Adnepos

This recipe makes a large quantity for a buffet or potluck meal. The hardy, delicious flavor surprises non-lentil eaters and those usually suspicious of brown food. This recipe is adapted from the Zen Center in Rochester, New York.

1/4 cup tamari or soy sauce
1 large bay leaf or 2 small ones
3 tablespoons onion powder
3/4 cup vegetable oil
3/4 cup honey
1/2 cup red wine vinegar

1 teaspoon allspice
1/2 teaspoon powdered ginger
4 cups water
3 cups lentils, rinsed
Parsley leaves, chopped, for garnish (optional)

Mix the first 8 ingredients in a 4 quart pot. Add water and mix together. Add lentils. Bring to a boil, then cover, lower heat, and simmer for 1 1/2 hours. Turn off heat and leave pot covered for about 15 minutes. Uncover, remove bay leaf, and stir gently.

This dish can be served hot, room temperature, or cold. Garnish with chopped parsley.

These lentils freeze well.

Serves 10

MISCELLANEOUS GOODIES

Appetizers

Baba Ghanouj ～ 282
Nut and Mushroom Paté ～ 283

Soups

Pumpkin Soup ～ 284

Vegetables

Easy Yummy Sweet Potatoes ～ 317
Savory Beans with Tomatoes ～ 318
Stir-Fried Green Beans ～ 319

Main Dishes — Meat

Boureka ～ 289
Greek Potato Moussaka ～ 290
Kasha Meatloaf ～ 291
Marinades for Beef ～ 292
Pasta with Spicy Veal ～ 293
Polynesian Flank Steak ～ 294
Stuffed Breast of Veal ～ 295
Syrian Meatballs ～ 296
Chicken with Artichokes ～ 308
Chicken with Cashews ～ 309
Chinese Noodles with Chicken ～ 310
Low-Cholesterol Chicken Curry ～ 311
Low-Sodium Peanuty Chicken ～ 312
Stir-Fried Chicken with Peanuts and
    Hot Peppers ～ 313
Low-Cholesterol Turkey Loaf ～ 314
Oriental Turkey Stir-Fry ～ 315

Main Dishes — Dairy

Eggplant Lamaze ～ 285
Low-Cal Fettucine Alfredo ～ 286
Microwave Poached Salmon ～ 287
Poached Salmon with Yogurt Dill
    Sauce ～ 288
Oatmeal Pancakes ～ 300
Mint Pesto Pasta ～ 316
A Lighter Dairy Kugel ～ 320
Sweet Low-Cholesterol Kugel ～ 321

Main Dishes — Pareve

Tofu with Vegetables ～ 297
Chinese-Style Steamed Fish with
    Black Bean Sauce ～ 298
Spring Pancakes ～ 299
Oatmeal Pancakes ～ 300
Korean Barbecued Tofu ～ 301
Meatless Balls ～ 302
Simple Sole ～ 303
Stir-Fry Salmon ～ 304
Tofu Manicotti ～ 305
Tofu Dinner ～ 306
Tofu Loaf ～ 307

Desserts

Hot Pear Soufflé ～ 322
Easy and Delicious Chocolate
    Cake ～ 324
Pareve Banana Frappe ～ 324
Sweet Potato Pie ～ 325

Baba Ghanouj

 Miriam Hoffman

1 medium eggplant

5–6 cloves garlic, finely chopped

2 teaspoon parsley, chopped

Salt and pepper, to taste

3 tablespoons mayonnaise, or more to taste

Prick skin of eggplant with fork and bake in a glass dish in a microwave oven for 12 to 14 minutes, or in a conventional oven for about 40 minutes, or until soft. Peel when eggplant has cooled. Chop finely and add garlic, parsley, and salt and pepper. Add mayonnaise to taste.

Serves 4 as an appetizer, more as a dip

Nut and Mushroom Paté

 Ronda Jacobson

This paté can be served as a dip with crackers or fresh vegetables, or used as a filling for pastry or filo dough.

½ cup mixed nuts and seeds (cashews or almonds with sunflower or sesame seeds)
6 tablespoons olive oil
1 onion, finely chopped
1 pound mushrooms, finely chopped
½ cup crumbled firm tofu
2 tablespoons tamari or soy sauce

Juice of ½ lemon
¼ cup tahini (sesame paste)
1 clove garlic, crushed
½ teaspoon dried oregano
½ teaspoon dried tarragon
½ teaspoon mustard powder

Toast the nuts and seeds in a toaster oven or a skillet until lightly browned; set aside.

Heat 2 tablespoons oil in a skillet, and add onion and mushrooms. Cook for several minutes, stirring often, until mixture is dark brown and dry, but do not burn. Set aside.

In a blender or food processor, combine tofu, remaining oil, tamari or soy sauce, lemon juice, tahini, garlic, herbs, and mustard. Blend until smooth. Add nut mixture and blend; crunchy is fine. Stir in mushrooms and onions and transfer to a serving bowl.

Serves 4–6

Pumpkin Soup

 Joyce Bohnen

We first had this at a Bar Mitzvah in Pittsburgh. Its beauty is that it can be made in 15 minutes in a food processor. It can also be prepared a few days in advance.

1 large onion
¼ cup butter or pareve
　margarine
½ teaspoon curry powder
2 cups pumpkin purée (not
　quite 2 whole cans)

1½ teaspoons salt
2 cups light cream
2½ cups vegetable stock
Dash of cinnamon

Slice the onion thinly, or use the slicing blade of a food processor.

Melt the butter in a skillet over medium heat. Add the onions and sauté until limp, about 10 minutes. Sprinkle onions with curry powder, and sauté an additional minute or two. Put curried onions, pumpkin, and salt into the food processor and process until mixed, approximately 10 seconds. Quickly pour in cream while continuing to process. (Refrigerate the purée if it will not be served right away.)

Transfer the pumpkin purée to a large saucepan. When ready to serve, add soup stock and heat slowly to just below boiling. Sprinkle with a little cinnamon and serve.

Serves 6

Eggplant Lamaze

  Trudy Shulman Fagen

Making Eggplant Parmesan is a lot like childbirth. You labor for a long time, wonder how you could have possibly persuaded yourself to do this (more than once), are real glad when it's over and done with, and then at a moment of sheer exhaustion, invite people over to celebrate! Now, an Eggplant Parmesan made more simply and healthfully.

1–2 tablespoons oil (preferably olive oil but anything will do — the oil will make it taste like it has been fried)

2 medium eggplants or 1 very large one

2 eggs

⅓ cup water

½ cup bread crumbs* (with a dash of wheat germ for those who like to evoke the 60s, or update with oatbran), use more as needed

4 cups tomato or spaghetti sauce, homemade if you are into long labor or 2 32-ounce jars of your family's favorite

2–3 cups shredded Mozzarella, to taste, part-skim or whole, depending on your family's current cholesterol level

Preheat oven to 375° and grease a cookie sheet with 1 tablespoon oil.

Cut eggplant into ¼-inch slices. Mix 1 tablespoon oil, 1 egg, and ⅓ cup water in a bowl. Pour crumbs in another bowl. Dip eggplant slices individually into liquid mix and then into bread crumbs.

Arrange breaded eggplant on the cookie sheet in single layer. Bake about 5 minutes per side, or until brown and soft when pierced with a fork.

Layer sauce, cooked eggplant, and cheese in a deep pan (9 x 12-inch casserole or lasagna pan is good) in 2 or 3 layers, starting with sauce. Bake for 20 to 30 minutes or until cheese is melted and the top is slightly crusty.

This recipe is even good cold the next day, or it can be reheated in a microwave. It also freezes well.

Serves 6–8

*Use matzoh meal for Pesach.

Low-Cal Fettucine Alfredo

 Harriet Cole

12 ounces fettucine
1 cup skim milk
1/2 cup Romano cheese,
  grated

1/3 cup low-cal margarine
Salt and pepper, to taste

Cook fettucine in plenty of boiling water until al dente. Drain. Return to saucepot. Add all other ingredients to fettucine. Cook over low heat until margarine melts and mixture is heated through.

Serves 6

Variation: Chopped cooked broccoli or asparagus can be added.

Microwave Poached Salmon

   Elaine Pollack

I'm always looking for easy microwave recipes. It is hard to believe that for the first two years that I owned a microwave oven I used it exclusively to reheat my morning coffee and bake potatoes!

4 8-ounce salmon steaks
1 large shallot, minced
   (substitute scallion in a
   pinch)
⅓ cup dry white wine
Salt and freshly ground
   pepper, to taste
8 sprigs of dill or tarragon

Green mayonnaise:
1 scallion, cut into 1-inch
   pieces
1 bunch dill

4 sprigs parsley
1 cup mayonnaise
1 tablespoon white wine
   vinegar (use any *kosher
   l'Pesach* vinegar)
Salt and pepper, to taste

Dill sauce:
¼ cup sour cream
¼ cup mayonnaise
1–2 tablespoons dill, chopped,
   or 1–2 teaspoons dried, or
   more to taste

Carefully cut the salmon steaks in half down the middle. Remove skin and any bones. Place the shallots in a microwave-safe baking dish and put the salmon on top. Pour wine over, then season with salt and pepper to taste. Place a sprig of dill on each piece. Cover dish tightly with microwave-safe plastic wrap and place in microwave oven. Cook on high power for 5 minutes. Remove from oven and let stand 2 minutes longer before uncovering. Transfer to serving dish and serve with either green mayonnaise or dill sauce.

Serves 4

Green mayonnaise: *Place ingredients in food processor and blend for 30 seconds. Transfer to jar and refrigerate. Can be made several days in advance.*

Dill sauce: *Mix sour cream and mayonnaise in a bowl and add dill.*

Poached Salmon with Yogurt Dill Sauce

  Ruth Spack

Sauce:
1/2 cup yogurt
1 clove garlic, crushed
1/4–1/2 teaspoon dried dill

1 1/2 pounds fresh salmon
  fillets or steaks
2 cups water

3 tablespoons white vinegar
1/4 cup onions, finely cut
3 whole peppercorns
2 sprigs fresh dill or 1 teaspoon
  dried
1 bay leaf, crushed
1/4 teaspoon salt

To make sauce, combine yogurt, garlic, and dill in a small bowl and refrigerate until ready to serve.

Cut fish into 6 portions and place them in a large sauté pan. Combine all other ingredients and add to pan. Bring to boil. Cover pan and reduce heat to low. Simmer 6 to 8 minutes, or until fish flakes easily with a fork. Using a spatula, carefully lift fish out of the liquid.

Serve with a gravy boat of sauce.

Serves 6

Boureka

 Susan Milstein

Savory pastries made by Sephardic Jews of Turkish and Greek origin. Enjoy, enjoy!

3 cups all-purpose flour	¼ teaspoon black pepper
2 teaspoons salt	2 tablespoons parsley, chopped
½ cup pareve margarine	2 tomatoes, peeled and chopped
4 tablespoons vegetable oil	
½ cup water	½ cup nuts, chopped
1 onion, chopped	1 egg, beaten
1 pound ground beef	2 tablespoons sesame seeds

Blend flour, 1 teaspoon salt, and margarine in a bowl or food processor until the mixture resembles cornmeal. Mix in 2 tablespoons oil and the water until the dough starts to come together. Form into a ball, wrap in waxed paper and chill for at least 2 hours.

Meanwhile, prepare the filling. Sauté onion in remaining oil over medium heat until limp, about 10 minutes. Add beef, pepper, parsley, and tomatoes. Sauté until meat is cooked, about 10 minutes. Drain off fat and stir in nuts. Set aside to cool.

Preheat oven to 350°.

Divide dough in half. Roll out dough to fit pan (I use a 9 x 13-inch glass dish). Spread with filling. Roll out second half of dough, press gently down on top of filling. Brush with egg and sprinkle with sesame seeds. Cut into squares. Bake for about 30 minutes, until golden brown.

Serves 8–10

Greek Potato Moussaka

  Sharon Haselkorn

This casserole tastes best made ahead and reheated.

1 clove garlic, halved
2 tablespoons olive oil, or more if needed
1 pound lean ground beef or ground turkey
1 bay leaf, crumbled into small pieces
1 teaspoon dried sage

Salt and pepper, to taste (optional)
6 cups thinly sliced, peeled potatoes
1 cup onions, sliced
1 15-ounce can tomato sauce
Paprika, to taste

In a large skillet, brown half the garlic clove in the oil over medium heat. Then remove clove. In the same pan, brown the beef or turkey slowly, for about 15 minutes, with bay leaf and sage, adding salt and pepper if desired. Remove meat with a slotted spoon and set aside.

Brown the other half of garlic clove in meat drippings, adding oil if needed, then remove garlic. Add potatoes and onions to pan and cook, stirring often, for 10 to 15 minutes, until potatoes start to look translucent. (Potatoes and onions may be cooked in two batches, depending on the pan size.)

Preheat oven to 375°.

In a 4 or 5 quart casserole, layer the ingredients as follows: one-third of the potato mixture, half the beef or turkey, one-half the tomato sauce, one-third potatoes, remaining beef or turkey, potatoes, and tomato sauce. Sprinkle paprika on top and bake, covered, for 1 hour, or until potatoes are cooked.

Serves 6

Kasha Meatloaf

 Joan Gadon

1 pound extra lean ground
beef
1 cup medium kasha
2 eggs
1 small onion, chopped
2 teaspoons salt

2 cups tomato or vegetable
juice
$^1/_2$ teaspoon garlic powder
(optional)
1 teaspoon dried oregano
(optional)

Preheat oven to 350° and grease a 9 x 5-inch loaf pan.

In a large bowl, mix the first 5 ingredients. Add juice and
optional garlic powder and oregano, if desired. Mix well (mixture
will be thin) and pour into loaf pan. Bake for 1 hour. Let stand a
few minutes before serving.

Serves 6

Marinades for Beef

 Roberta Hoffman

½ cup onion, chopped
¼ cup vegetable oil
¼ teaspoon pepper
½ teaspoon dried oregano
1 clove garlic, minced
1½ teaspoons Worcestershire sauce

1 tablespoon sugar
½ cup fresh lemon juice
½ teaspoon dried thyme
½ teaspoon dried rosemary
⅓ cup tamari or soy sauce
¾ teaspoon powdered ginger

Mix all ingredients and pour over meat in a nonaluminum pan to marinate. Leave for 4 hours or overnight. Refrigerate until ready to serve.

Grill or broil meat to taste and slice thinly to absorb juices just before serving. Flavor accompanying rice or potatoes with remaining marinade.

Makes 1½ cups, or enough for 3 pounds of London broil

½ cup vegetable oil
⅓ cup tamari or soy sauce
¼ cup red wine vinegar
2 tablespoons lemon juice
1 tablespoon Worcestershire sauce

1 teaspoon dry mustard
1 clove garlic, minced
Salt and pepper, to taste

Mix all ingredients and pour over meat in a nonaluminum pan to marinate. Leave for 4 hours or overnight. Refrigerate until ready to serve.

Grill or broil meat to taste and slice thinly to absorb juices just before serving. Flavor accompanying rice or potatoes with remaining marinade.

Makes 1½ cups, or enough for 3 pounds of London broil

Pasta with Spicy Veal

 M Joan Weinstein

12 ounces angel hair or other very thin pasta

2 teaspoons toasted sesame oil

1½ pounds lean ground veal

3–4 tablespoons fresh ginger, grated

2 cloves garlic, minced

2–4 tablespoons chili sauce

4 teaspoons reduced sodium tamari or soy sauce

4 tablespoons dry sherry

3 tablespoons hoisin sauce

1½ cups chicken stock

4 scallions, chopped

Garnishes, optional:
Parsley, chopped
Slivered carrots
Red peppers, chopped

Cook pasta in plenty of boiling water until al dente.

While pasta cooks, heat oil in a wok or skillet over medium heat and sauté veal until brown, about 10 minutes. Add ginger and garlic, sauté for 30 seconds and stir. Reduce heat, add chili sauce, tamari, sherry, hoisin sauce, and mix thoroughly. Add chicken stock. Raise heat and cook quickly until liquid reduces, stirring constantly. Remove from heat and stir in scallions.

Drain pasta into a large serving bowl. Add spicy veal, toss thoroughly, and let stand covered for 20 minutes to blend flavors, stirring occasionally. Garnish if desired with parsley, carrots, and/or red peppers.

Serves 4

Polynesian Flank Steak

 Roberta Hoffman

This flank steak is marinated overnight and served with noodles.

$^1/_3$ cup soy or tamari sauce
$^1/_2$ cup orange juice
$^3/_4$ teaspoon ground ginger
2 tablespoons brown sugar
$^1/_2$ teaspoon garlic powder
$2^1/_2$–$3^1/_2$ pounds thinly sliced
   flank steak, London broil,
   or pepper steak

4 tablespoons vegetable oil
8 ounces medium egg noodles,
   cooked and drained
2 cups celery, chopped
2 onions, chopped (optional)
2 green, red or yellow peppers,
   sliced (optional)

In a small bowl, combine soy sauce, orange juice, ginger, brown sugar, and garlic powder, and pour over meat. Marinate overnight in a nonaluminum dish.

Preheat oven to 350°.

Drain off marinade and reserve.

Sear meat over high heat in a dry wok or skillet. Remove meat from wok and set aside. In the same wok, heat 1 tablespoon oil over medium heat, add noodles and toss to coat with oil. Remove from wok and set aside.

Heat remaining oil in wok and sauté celery and optional onions and peppers. Add them to noodles and toss together.

Place noodles on bottom of a 9 x 12-inch baking dish, cover with meat slices, and spread reserved marinade over the top. Bake until meat is tender, about 20 minutes.

Serves 6–8

Variation: Cook meat in wok until tender, and combine with noodles and vegetables without baking.

Stuffed Breast of Veal

  Chana Meyer

This is one of my family's favorite main courses, which, unfortunately, they only get when we have company. This recipe is made the day before. Slice the veal cold and reheat in the gravy half an hour before serving.

8 ounces mushrooms
1 tablespoons vegetable oil
3 scallions, minced
3 cloves garlic
1 10-ounce package frozen spinach, defrosted and squeezed dry
1/4 cup bread crumbs (use matzoh meal for Pesach)
1 egg, beaten
1/2 teaspoon dried basil
1/2 teaspoon dried thyme

Salt and pepper, to taste
1/4 cup pine nuts (optional)
4–5 pound veal breast with pocket
Vegetable oil for frying
1 cup white wine
1 cup chicken stock
1 bay leaf
1 carrot, sliced
1 onion, sliced

Preheat broiler.

Chop mushrooms into very small pieces in a food processor. Wrap mushroom pieces in a clean dish towel and squeeze out juices. Sauté in a skillet in oil over medium-high heat, stirring until pieces start to brown slightly. Remove from pan. Sauté scallions for 2 minutes. Crush 1 clove garlic and add it and spinach and sauté until liquid has evaporated. Remove the pan from the heat and mix in mushrooms, bread crumbs, egg, basil, thyme, salt, pepper, and nuts. Stuff mixture into pocket of veal and either sew or skewer closed.

Place veal in a casserole and baste top and bottom with oil. Using broiler, brown the top.

Preheat oven to 350°.

Add remaining ingredients to casserole, cover with foil and bake for 2 hours. Allow to cool, remove bay leaf, and refrigerate overnight.

The next day, cut veal off the bones. Slice as you would a roast and heat in a little of the gravy. Heat the additional gravy and pass it around the table.

Serves 8–10

Syrian Meatballs

  Susie Jacobs

1 pound ground beef
1 egg
2 tablespoons matzoh meal, plus a little extra for dredging
2 tablespoons walnuts, finely chopped
Salt and pepper, to taste

2 tablespoons vegetable oil
1 16-ounce can tomato sauce
Juice of 1 lemon
$^1/_2$ teaspoon kosher coarse salt
1 tablespoon sugar
1 cup water

In a large bowl, mix together beef, egg, matzoh meal, walnuts, and seasonings, and shape into walnut-sized balls. Roll meatballs in extra matzoh meal. Heat oil in large saucepan and fry the balls over medium heat until browned. Add remaining ingredients, and mix. Bring to a boil, reduce heat, and simmer covered for 30 to 40 minutes.

Serves 4–6

Tofu with Vegetables

 P Margery Gann

A quick dinner, good for those who work late. Hint: to keep ginger root fresh for a long time, put it in a jar, cover with sherry, and refrigerate. An added benefit is that you always have flavored sherry for cooking!

1/2 cup water
2 tablespoons tamari or soy sauce
2 tablespoons dry sherry
1 teaspoon sugar
2 teaspoons cornstarch
1/4 teaspoon toasted sesame oil

1 pound firm tofu
4 tablespoons salad oil
1 clove garlic, crushed
2 slices fresh ginger, crushed
1 pound bean sprouts and broccoli, in any combination

In a bowl, mix the water, tamari, 1 tablespoon sherry, cornstarch, and sesame oil together well to make a cooking sauce.

Drain tofu and pat dry. Cut into 1/2-inch cubes.

Rinse bean sprouts. Cut broccoli into florets. Heat 2 tablespoons of salad oil in a wok or skillet. Add garlic and ginger, and sauté over medium heat. Add remaining sherry, and continue cooking until sherry evaporates. Add broccoli and bean sprouts and stir-fry for a few minutes. Remove from pan. Add remaining oil and brown tofu. Add cooking sauce to pan, cook until thick. Add cooked vegetables. Toss gently to heat and mix. Serve over rice.

Serves 4–6

Chinese-Style Steamed Fish with Black Bean Sauce

 Marlene Leffell

1–3 pounds fish (sole, flounder, halibut, or snapper)

2 teaspoons fresh ginger, minced

1 scallion, finely chopped

3 cloves garlic, minced

2 tablespoons Chinese salted black beans (available in Chinese grocery stores)

5 tablespoons sherry or Chinese wine

1 tablespoon vegetable oil for 1 pound fish, 2 tablespoons for 2–3 pounds fish (optional)

Lay fish in greased pie plate or casserole. Sprinkle with ginger, scallion, and garlic. For a light sauce, sprinkle on black beans left whole. For a darker and stronger sauce, chop black beans coarsely before sprinkling over fish. Pour sherry and optional oil over fish.

Select a wok or covered pot large enough to hold the pie plate or casserole. Invert a heatproof saucer into the bottom of the wok. Add ³/₄ cup water for 1 to 1¹/₂ pounds fish or 1 scant cup for up to 3 pounds fish. Bring water to a boil. Carefully place pie plate on top of saucer and steam the smaller quantity of fish for 12 minutes, the larger for 14 minutes. Fish stays moist if cooked slightly longer.

Serves 2–4

Variations: You can steam other fish such as salmon, with toppings such as white wine, onion, herbs, lemon slices or lemon juice, fresh ground black pepper, or peppercorns.

Spring Pancakes

   Judy Adnepos

2 bunches parsley, finely
   chopped
5 ounces spinach, chopped
1 bunch scallions, chopped
5 eggs, beaten
$1/2$–1 teaspoon salt, or more
   to taste

$1/4$ teaspoon pepper
$1/4$ teaspoon garlic powder
1 teaspoon dried basil
Vegetable oil for frying

Place parsley, spinach, and scallions in a large bowl. Add eggs, basil, and spices. In a large, heavy skillet heat $1/4$ inch of oil over medium heat. With a slotted spoon, place $1/4$ cup of the mixture into the hot oil. Cook on both sides until brown, about 2 minutes on each side. Drain on paper towels and keep warm while you repeat for the remaining pancakes.

Yields 12 pancakes

Oatmeal Pancakes

  Allen Spivack

I wanted a good, healthy pancake that the whole family could tolerate and prefer to make everything from scratch — it keeps you in touch with the food. This batter is best chilled a few hours before cooking, and it can be made as far as a week ahead and stored in the refrigerator.

3/4 cup corn meal
3 teaspoons baking powder
2 teaspoons cinnamon
1/4 cup molasses
1 cup hot water
3/4 cup oats (or 1/2 cup oatbran and 1/4 cup wheat germ), soaked for a few minutes in enough hot water to cover

1/2 cup ground walnuts or pecans
1/2 cup whole wheat flour
1/4 cup safflower oil
3/4 cup lowfat yogurt (optional)
1 egg (optional)

In a large bowl, combine the corn meal, baking powder, cinnamon, molasses, and water, and stir until the batter is nice and thick. Add soaked oatmeal and ground nuts. Mix well and add flour, oil, and optional yogurt and/or egg. Add water to adjust the consistency to that of cooked oatmeal.

Use a light coat of oil in the skillet or hot griddle. Spoon in batter for pancakes with a diameter of 3 to 4 inches. Turn pancakes when bubbles start to break on top of pancakes and bottom is golden brown. Turn and brown on the other side.

Yields about 15 pancakes

Variation: Add fruits such as chopped cranberries, blueberries, strawberries, or peaches.

Korean Barbecued Tofu

 P   Diane Levine

Marinade:
$^1/_2$ cup tamari or soy sauce
6 tablespoons sugar
2 teaspoons dry mustard
$^1/_2$ teaspoon garlic powder or
   4 cloves garlic, minced
2 teaspoons onion powder

$1^1/_2$ pounds firm tofu, cut into
   $^1/_4$–$^1/_2$ inch slices
2 tablespoons vegetable oil

Combine marinade ingredients and marinate tofu for 2 hours in a nonaluminum dish. Make sure all sides of tofu are covered with marinade.

Heat oil in large skillet. Drain tofu and add it to the pan. Cook over medium-high heat until the sides are brown, about 10 minutes. Serve hot or at room temperature.

Serves 4–6

Meatless Balls

P   Susan L. Weiss

2 cups eggplant, peeled and
finely chopped

1 pound tofu

2 cups whole wheat pastry
flour

1 cup onion, minced

1 cup bread crumbs or 2
pieces of whole wheat
matzoh, ground

¹/₂ cup walnuts, finely
chopped (optional)

¹/₂ teaspoon salt

Dash of black pepper

¹/₄ cup fresh parsley, minced

¹/₄–¹/₃ cup tamari sauce

2 eggs, beaten

¹/₂ teaspoon dried oregano

¹/₂ teaspoon dried marjoram

¹/₂ teaspoon dried thyme

Vegetable oil for frying

Steam eggplant over boiling water until tender, about 10 minutes. In a large bowl, mash tofu, add eggplant, 1 cup flour, and all other ingredients except for oil. Mix well. Mixture should be somewhat soft and moist but hold together. Add more bread crumbs or flour as needed. Roll balls about the size of a walnut and dip in remaining flour.

Heat oil in a skillet and sauté the balls over medium heat until cooked through, about 5 minutes. Drain on paper towels. Serve plain or on pasta, with your favorite tomato sauce, or any sauce you wish.

Yields 32–34 balls, serves 8–10

Simple Sole

  Ivy Feuerstadt

5 tablespoons olive oil
1 large onion, thinly sliced
2 cloves garlic, chopped
2 teaspoons dried oregano,
  or more to taste
2 tablespoons capers, rinsed
  (omit for Pesach)

1 scant cup canned whole
  tomatoes with juice
Salt and pepper, to taste
2 pounds sole fillets, washed
  and patted dry

Preheat oven to 450°.

Heat oil in a large skillet over medium heat. Add onion and garlic and cook until soft, about 10 minutes — do not burn the garlic. Add oregano and capers, and mix. Add tomatoes with their juice, salt, and pepper. Simmer uncovered for about 20 minutes.

Put a little sauce on the bottom of an ovenproof serving dish that is large enough to hold the fillets in a single layer. Arrange the fillets on top. Pour remaining sauce over everything. Bake on top rack of oven about 8 minutes until cooked through, depending on the thickness of the fish.

Serves 4

Stir-Fry Salmon

 Arlene R. Remz

1 tablespoon vegetable oil

1 medium onion, thinly sliced

1 green, red, or yellow pepper, cut into strips (or even better, a mixture of colors)

1 large tomato, chopped

2 tablespoons capers, rinsed

2 teaspoons garlic, minced

2 tablespoons fresh thyme or 2 teaspoons dried

Freshly ground pepper, to taste

$1/4$ cup plus up to 2 tablespoons more balsamic, red wine, or herbed vinegar

$3/4$ cup 1-inch salmon fillet strips

Heat oil in a skillet over medium heat. Add onion, pepper strips, tomato, capers, garlic, thyme, and pepper, and cook for 1 minute. Add vinegar and cook for 5 minutes, covered.

Move the vegetables to the sides of the pan and add fish. If most of the vinegar has evaporated, add 1 to 2 tablespoons more. Cook until fish is just barely done and loses its translucent color. If using small stir-fry pieces, it will take only 1 to 2 minutes per side. Thicker fillets will take a few minutes longer. Serve immediately.

Serves 2

Tofu Manicotti

 P   Judy Adnepos

This is a wonderful alternative for those who cannot enjoy dairy products.

12–14 large manicotti shells

Filling:
1 10-ounce package frozen chopped spinach, defrosted and squeezed dry
1/4 cup olive oil
2 cups (about 1 pound) tofu, mashed
2 eggs, beaten
2 cloves garlic, crushed
Salt and pepper, to taste
2 tablespoons Parmesan soy cheese (optional)
Dried basil, to taste
Dried oregano, to taste

Sauce:
1 large onion, chopped
2 cloves garlic, minced
1/4 cup olive oil
2 28-ounce cans tomatoes with juice
1/2 cup red wine
1 tablespoon dried basil
1 teaspoon salt
1 teaspoon dried oregano
1 teaspoon dried thyme

Garnishes:
Fresh parsley, chopped
Parmesan soy cheese

Partially cook manicotti shells according to package directions.

In a large bowl, combine all the filling ingredients. Set aside.

To prepare the sauce, sauté the onion and garlic in oil in a large skillet over medium heat for a few minutes. Do not let them brown. Add the tomatoes with juice, and break up with a spoon. Add the rest of the ingredients and simmer 20 to 25 minutes.

Preheat oven to 350°.

Meanwhile, fill the partially cooked manicotti shells with the filling. Set aside. Pour about 1 cup sauce on the bottom of a 9 x 13-inch baking pan. Place filled shells on sauce. Pour rest of the sauce over the shells. Cover tightly with foil. Bake for 35 to 45 minutes.

Sprinkle with garnishes and serve.

Serves 4–5

Tofu Dinner

 P Melinda Strauss

This marinated tofu can be served cold in a pasta salad or barbecued as part of a vegetarian kebob. Although it is served hot, the leftovers taste good cold. The tofu can be marinated overnight, and the whole dish prepared in advance.

Marinade:
2 tablespoons tamari sauce
3 tablespoons miso (traditional red miso is fine,
   found at natural food
   stores)
2 tablespoons honey
2 tablespoons tahini (sesame
   paste)
3 drops Tabasco sauce
1 tablespoon onion, chopped
2 large cloves garlic, crushed
1 tablespoon fresh ginger,
   grated

2 tablespoons corn oil
1/2 cup water

3 medium carrots, sliced
2 cups broccoli
1 pound extra-firm tofu
1 tablespoon corn oil
2 large onions, chopped
2 cups cooked brown rice

Garnishes:
Carrot, grated
Parsley, chopped

To prepare the marinade, blend tamari, miso, honey, tahini, and Tabasco sauce in a small bowl. In a skillet, gently sauté onion, garlic, and ginger in oil over medium heat, until it starts to brown, then add to miso mixture, adding all the oil from the pan. Blend together, then add water a little at a time, mixing thoroughly.

Rinse tofu, wrap in a thick towel and gently squeeze, without crumbling, to remove excess water. Repeat with another dry towel. Slice the tofu horizontally through the middle, then cut vertically to form 3/4-inch rectangles. Place them in an 8 x 8-inch nonaluminum pan or a ziplock bag. Pour marinade over tofu, cover, and refrigerate at least 3 hours or overnight, turning once or twice to marinate evenly.

Steam carrots and broccoli until slightly softened (broccoli should be bright green). Sauté onions in a lightly oiled skillet over medium heat, until they just begin to brown. Set vegetables aside.

Drain tofu, reserving marinade, and sauté it in oil in a large skillet (cast iron works well) over medium heat. Tofu will turn golden brown, and bits of garlic, etc., will turn dark brown. Try to get tofu browned on most sides by frequent turning; this will take about 20 minutes.

At this point the tofu dinner can be prepared two ways. Add the vegetables and rice to the pan with the tofu, heat through, pour enough marinade to moisten over all and heat for a few more minutes.

Or place the browned tofu, steamed broccoli and carrots, browned onions, and rice on a large platter, and reheat briefly in a microwave oven.

Garnish with grated carrot and parsley. Pass the marinade, heated, as a sauce.

Serves 4

Tofu Loaf

 Diane Levine

1 1/2 pounds tofu, well
    mashed
1/3 cup ketchup
1/3 cup (scant) tamari sauce
2 tablespoons Dijon mustard
1/2 cup fresh parsley, chopped

Dash or 2 of black pepper
1/4 teaspoon garlic powder
1 cup whole grain bread crumbs
2 tablespoons vegetable oil
2 tablespoons orange juice
    (optional)

Preheat oven to 350°.

Mix everything together except oil in a large bowl. Oil a 9 x 5-inch loaf pan, then press mixture into pan. Bake for 40 to 45 minutes, until browned on top. Let cool 10 to 15 minutes before removing from pan and slicing.

Serves 6–8

Variation: Add 2 tablespoons orange juice.

Chicken with Artichokes

 Helen Flusberg

1 cup all-purpose flour	8 chicken breast halves
2 tablespoons dried oregano	$1/3$ cup olive oil
2 tablespoons dried basil	2 cups mushrooms
1 tablespoon dried parsley	1 can artichoke hearts in water, drained
Garlic powder, to taste	
Salt and pepper, to taste	$1/2$ cup white wine

Preheat oven to 350°.

Mix flour, herbs, and spices together, and dip chicken into flour. Sauté in olive oil in a skillet over medium heat until chicken is browned. (You may have to do this in batches.) Remove chicken from skillet and place in a baking dish. Sauté mushrooms and artichoke hearts in skillet with remaining oil, add wine, and pour mixture over chicken. Bake for 30 minutes until chicken is tender and cooked through.

Serves 8

Chicken with Cashews

 Ruth Spack

2 boned and skinned whole
  chicken breasts, cut in
  strips
1 tablespoon hoisin sauce
2 tablespoons soy sauce
2 teaspoons sherry
2 teaspoons cornstarch
Dash of white pepper
1/2 teaspoon toasted sesame
  oil

1 egg white
3 tablespoons vegetable oil
1 cup dry roasted cashews
 2 scallions, minced
1 clove garlic, crushed
1/2 cup bamboo shoots, chopped
1/2 cup chicken stock (optional)

In a bowl, mix chicken with hoisin sauce, soy sauce, sherry, cornstarch, pepper, sesame oil, and egg white. Marinate 30 minutes.

Heat 1 1/2 tablespoons oil in a wok or skillet for 30 seconds over
high heat. Add cashews. Stir-fry them for 30 seconds and set them
aside.

Heat remaining oil in the wok for 30 seconds. Add scallions and
garlic; stir-fry 10 seconds. Add chicken mixture; stir-fry until chicken
browns slightly. Add cashews and bamboo shoots. Heat through. For
a more saucy dish, add 1/2 cup chicken stock and heat through.

Serve immediately.

Serves 4

Chinese Noodles with Chicken

 Roberta Hoffman

3 whole chicken breasts, skinned

1 small onion, sliced

1 carrot, sliced

Celery leaves

$^{1}/_{2}$ cup white wine

Salt and pepper, to taste

2 red bell peppers, cut into strips, or mixture of other fresh vegetables, such as broccoli or cauliflower, cut into pieces

$^{1}/_{2}$ pound pea pods

$^{1}/_{3}$–$^{1}/_{2}$ cup vegetable oil

2 tablespoons toasted sesame oil, or to taste

1 scant teaspoon hot oriental chili oil

$^{3}/_{4}$ cup tamari or soy sauce

2 teaspoons sesame seeds, lightly toasted or sautéed in sesame oil (optional)

1 pound cooked vermicelli, angel hair pasta, or linguine

To poach chicken, place in a large saucepan, cover with water and add onion, carrot, celery leaves, wine, salt, and pepper. Bring to a boil and cook until chicken is white and tender, about 10 minutes. Remove chicken, let cool, and cut into strips or cubes.

Blanch remaining vegetables by placing them in boiling water for less than a minute. Drain and rinse with cold water to cool. In a large serving bowl, toss cooked chicken with vegetables, oils, tamari, and optional sesame seeds. Add noodles and toss well. Serve cold or at room temperature.

Serves 6–8

Low-Cholesterol Chicken Curry

 Relly Dibner

This chicken can sit for a day in the refrigerator to enhance the taste.

8 chicken breast halves,
skinned and boned
1 onion, chopped
2 tablespoons curry powder
$^1\!/_2$ teaspoon black pepper
1 teaspoon garlic powder (or
2 or 3 cloves, minced)
2 cups unsweetened apple
sauce
1 cup mango chutney, or less
to taste
1 red or green pepper, cut
into small pieces

Tabasco sauce or chili powder, to
taste (optional)

Garnishes:
$^1\!/_2$ cup shelled peanuts
$^1\!/_2$ cup raisins
Pineapple chunks (optional)
Shredded coconut (optional)
Cut bananas (optional)
Peach slices (optional)

Cook chicken and onion for 20 minutes in a large pot over medium
heat, with just enough water to cover bottom of pot so chicken
doesn't stick. Add remaining ingredients, mix, and cook on low heat
for 45 minutes more. Cool and refrigerate. Reheat and garnish as
desired.

Serves 8

Low-Sodium Peanuty Chicken

 Lois Gordon

This is a Szechuan dish, tasty but low in sodium.

1 cup unsalted chicken stock
3 tablespoons unsalted
    peanut butter
2 tablespoons peanut oil
4 whole chicken breasts,
    skinned, boned, and cut
    into 1-inch chunks
1/2 green pepper, chopped
Dash of crushed red pepper

4 cloves garlic, minced
2 tablespoons dry sherry
1 tablespoon red wine vinegar
2 teaspoons sugar
2 tablespoons raisins
6 scallions, chopped

In a small saucepan, heat stock to a simmer and cook 5 minutes. Add peanut butter and simmer 5 minutes, stirring often.

In wok or skillet, heat oil over low heat. Add chicken, green pepper, crushed red pepper, and garlic. Stir-fry 2 minutes, or until chicken turns white.

Stir in sherry, vinegar, sugar, and 2 tablespoons stock mixture. Heat 1 minute. Stir in raisins and cook 2 minutes. Add remaining stock mixture and scallions. Cook 2 minutes more, stirring frequently. Serve immediately.

Serves 4

Stir-Fried Chicken with Peanuts and Hot Peppers

  Debby Zigun

This is my family's favorite Friday night chicken dish. Serve it with white rice to temper the hot and spicy flavor. Each cook will want to season the dish to the degree of hotness desired.

2 whole boneless chicken breasts, about ¾ pound each

2 teaspoons cornstarch

1 egg white

½ cup bamboo shoots

2 teaspoons fresh ginger, finely shredded

½ cup unsalted peanuts

3 small dried chili peppers,* crumbled, or to taste

1 tablespoon cornstarch

½ cup cold water

2 tablespoons dry sherry

¼ cup low-salt soy or tamari sauce

½ teaspoon sugar

4 tablespoons vegetable oil

Cube chicken breasts into ½-inch pieces and place in a large bowl. Toss with cornstarch until the pieces are lightly coated. Add egg white, and stir to mix. Add bamboo shoots, ginger, peanuts, and chili peppers.

In a small bowl, dissolve cornstarch in water, add sherry, soy sauce, and sugar. Heat oil in wok or large skillet. Add chicken mixture and stir-fry until chicken pieces are no longer translucent. Stir soy sauce mixture and pour over chicken. Stir-fry until sauce thickens, just a few minutes more. The thickness of the sauce depends on the amount of cornstarch added and can be varied according to taste.

Serves 6

* See Ceviche, page 228, for note on preparation of chili peppers.

Low-Cholesterol Turkey Loaf

 Jeanne Weil

1 tablespoon vegetable or olive oil

2 large cloves garlic, minced

1 cup celery, chopped

1/2–3/4 cup onion, chopped

2 medium red peppers, chopped

8 ounces mushrooms, thinly sliced

1 1/4 pounds ground turkey

1 egg white

1/2 teaspoon ground black pepper

1/2 teaspoon salt (optional)

Dash of nutmeg

1/2 cup bread crumbs

1/2 cup fresh parsley, minced

Preheat oven to 375° and grease a 8 x 4-inch loaf pan.

Heat oil in a non-stick skillet. Add garlic, celery, onion, and red peppers. Sauté until vegetables are slightly softened, about 3 to 5 minutes. Add mushrooms, stirring until liquid has evaporated. Remove from heat and set aside.

In a large bowl, combine turkey, egg white, seasonings, bread crumbs, and parsley. Add sautéed vegetables and combine ingredients well. Pack into prepared loaf pan. Bake for 1 hour and 15 minutes.

Serves 6

Oriental Turkey Stir-Fry

 Judy Herzig-Marx

1 pound firm tofu	1 teaspoon hot chili-garlic paste
1 pound broccoli florets	8 ounces ground turkey
1 tablespoon vegetable oil	4 teaspoons cornstarch
2 large cloves garlic, minced	1⅓ cup chicken stock
2 teaspoons fresh grated ginger	¼ cup hoisin sauce

Drain tofu and press between paper towels to remove moisture. Cut into small cubes.

Cut broccoli florets into bite-sized pieces.

Heat oil in a wok or large skillet over high heat. Add garlic, ginger, and chili paste and stir 30 seconds. Reduce heat and add tofu. Stir for 2 minutes.

Add turkey and cook just until it loses its pink color. Add broccoli and cook for 2 minutes.

In a small bowl, mix cornstarch with a little of the stock. Combine with remaining stock and hoisin sauce, and stir into broccoli mixture. Cover, reduce heat, and simmer 3 to 5 minutes, or until broccoli is cooked but still crisp.

Serves 4 generously

Mint Pesto Pasta

 Varda E. Farber

Mint tends to grow like a weed. This year it took over my vegetable patch. I was looking for a way to use it up, and this wonderful mint pesto did the trick. My family loves it at room temperature over bow-tie pasta. Add salad and you have a great summer meal.

2–3 cups fresh mint leaves, washed and dried

2 cups freshly grated Parmesan cheese

1 cup olive oil

½ cup canola oil

1½ cups walnuts, coarsely chopped

2 pounds bow-tie pasta, cooked and drained

Combine the mint, cheese, and oils in a food processor. Blend to a paste and pour into a large serving bowl.

Place nuts in a heavy ungreased skillet and toast on all sides over medium heat, stirring constantly. Stir walnuts into pesto.

Toss cooked pasta with pesto to coat thoroughly.

Serves 6–8

Easy Yummy Sweet Potatoes

Lois Nadel

This is an after-work quickie-but-goody. Holds well if dinner is delayed.

2 sweet potatoes (long and narrow rather then round and fat)
2 tablespoons pareve margarine

¹/₄ cup honey
¹/₄ cup orange marmalade

Peel sweet potatoes and slice into ¹/₄-inch slices. In a skillet, melt margarine and sauté sweet potatoes, covered, for about 15 minutes over medium heat. Lower heat and add honey and marmalade. Leave cover off and turn slices often to coat well. Cook until slightly crispy and serve.

Serves 4

Savory Beans with Tomatoes

 P   Lois Nadel

You can use broccoli florets instead of beans.

1 pound green beans, cut
   into 2-inch pieces
4 tablespoons pareve
   margarine
1 small onion, chopped
1 large shallot, sliced
2 cloves garlic, crushed
8 ounces mushrooms, sliced
1 tablespoon fresh basil or
   1 teaspoon dried

1 tablespoon fresh oregano or
   1 teaspoon dried
$^1/_2$ teaspoon salt
1 large tomato or 4 plum
   tomatoes, cut into $^1/_4$-inch
   slices
Sliced almonds or pimiento, to
   taste (use almonds for
   Pesach)

Steam beans for 5 minutes. Plunge in ice water and drain — this will keep the beans bright green.

Melt margarine in a skillet over medium heat and sauté the onions, shallot, garlic, and mushrooms until slightly brown, stirring often, about 15 minutes. Add herbs and salt; stir; add beans and cook 2 minutes to blend. Add tomatoes and nuts or pimiento, stir and cook 2 more minutes. Serve immediately

Serves 4 generously

Stir-Fried Green Beans

 Marlene Leffell

2 tablespoons olive or canola oil

1 pound green beans, trimmed

1 clove garlic, minced

1 teaspoon fresh ginger, minced

2 tablespoons water

1/2 cup chicken stock

1 tablespoon soy or tamari sauce

1 tablespoon cornstarch

1 teaspoon sugar

1 teaspoon grated orange zest

1 teaspoon toasted sesame oil

1 tablespoon toasted sesame seeds

Heat oil in a wok or skillet over medium-high heat. Stir-fry beans, garlic, and ginger for 2 minutes. Add water, cover, and cook 1 to 2 minutes until beans are crisp-tender. Stir together chicken stock, soy sauce, cornstarch, and sugar, and pushing beans aside, pour mixture into pan, stirring until it thickens, about 30 seconds. Stir in beans, orange zest, sesame oil, and sesame seeds. Serve hot.

Serves 4–6

Hints: To store ginger, wrap in double brown bags, and store in refrigerator for 1–2 weeks, or place in freezer to store longer. To toast sesame seeds, heat in small skillet over low heat for 5 minutes, or place under broiler or in toaster oven for approximately 1 minute.

A Lighter Dairy Kugel

 Varda E. Farber

1 pound medium noodles, cooked and drained

4 tablespoons butter or margarine, melted

$^1/_2$ cup granulated sugar

1 cup light sour cream

2 cups milk

1 pound low-fat cottage cheese

1 pound low-fat ricotta cheese

$^1/_2$ teaspoon salt

1 teaspoon vanilla extract

6 eggs, beaten

Topping:

2 tablespoons butter, melted

$^1/_4$ cup granulated sugar

$^1/_4$ cup brown sugar

$^1/_4$ cup slivered almonds

Preheat oven to 350°. Place aluminum foil on bottom of the oven to catch drips. Butter a 9 x 13-inch casserole dish.

Mix together in a large bowl, butter, sugar, sour cream, milk, cottage cheese, ricotta cheese, salt, vanilla, and eggs. Fold in the noodles. Pour into the casserole dish. Combine topping ingredients in a small bowl. Spread on noodles. Bake for 1$^1/_2$ hours.

Serves 10–12

Sweet Low-Cholesterol Kugel

 Melinda Strauss

I have adapted traditional kugel recipes to my family's need for low-cholesterol eating. Don't be put off by the tofu — it's too subtle a taste to notice in a sweet kugel. The texture of the tofu changes once the kugel has been frozen and defrosted, but the taste is still good. It must be assembled several hours before cooking. Please note that some egg substitute products contain additives.

12 ounces yolk-free egg noodles
1 pound soft or silken tofu
Equivalent to 4 eggs of a yolk-free egg substitute
2 egg whites
2 cups 1 percent milkfat cottage cheese
$1/2$ cup granulated sugar
$1/2$ cup brown sugar
2 teaspoons vanilla extract
$3/4$ cup margarine, melted

Topping:
$1/4$ cup margarine, melted
$1/3$ cup sugar
1 tablespoon cinnamon
2 cups bran cereal (any kind), ground in a blender or food processor

Grease 9 x 13-inch glass baking dish.

Cook noodles al dente in plenty of boiling water. While noodles cook, blend tofu in food processor or blender until smooth. Add egg substitute and egg whites. Pour into a very large mixing bowl. Add cottage cheese, sugars, and vanilla, and stir until blended. Drain noodles, add melted margarine, and stir. Add noodles to mixture in bowl, mix, and pour into prepared pan. Cover and refrigerate for several hours or overnight.

Preheat oven to 325°.

Before baking, mix topping ingredients together, spread evenly in a thick layer over cold noodles. Bake for $1^{1}/4$ hours. Serve warm.

Serves 12

Hot Pear Soufflé

Lora Brody. A variation of this recipe is published in *Indulgences* by Lora Brody (Little, Brown and Company, 1987).

While I am usually associated with chocolate desserts, I sometimes get a craving for something non-chocolate, especially when I am watching my weight. The following soufflé is sophisticated, yet simple to make, especially because the base can be prepared well ahead of time and refrigerated or frozen. Low in cholesterol, this dessert soufflé rises dramatically and makes a spectacular presentation. You can make individual soufflés or one large one. You can also substitute ripe peaches, and peach brandy for the pear liqueur.

1 16-ounce can pears in heavy syrup
1 tablespoon lemon juice
½ cup granulated sugar, plus extra for dusting
½ cup water
2 tablespoons cornstarch
¼ cup ice water
⅓ cup pear brandy
2 tablespoons unsalted butter, softened

1 cup egg whites (about 8 large eggs), at room temperature
Pinch of cream of tartar
3 tablespoons confectioners sugar, sifted
¾ cup fresh or previously frozen raspberries, blackberries, or blueberries, drained of their liquid if previously frozen
Confectioners sugar for garnish

Prepare the soufflé base. Purée the pears with ½ cup of syrup and lemon juice in a food processor or blender.

Combine the sugar and ½ cup water in a skillet and cook over medium heat. Stir until the sugar dissolves, raise the heat, and boil for 3 minutes. Combine the pear purée and sugar syrup in the skillet, and cook over medium heat; simmer for 5 minutes, stirring frequently.

Combine the cornstarch and ¼ cup ice water in a small bowl. Whisk to a smooth paste, stir into the pear purée, return to a boil, and simmer 4 to 5 minutes, stirring occasionally until the mixture reduces somewhat and is very thick. The base should be the consistency of pudding. Stir in the brandy and cook for 1 minute.

Preheat oven to 450° with the rack in the upper third, but not in the highest position.

Use the butter to generously coat six 1-cup soufflé dishes or one 6-cup soufflé dish. Sprinkle generously with granulated sugar.

In a large bowl, beat the egg whites with the cream of tartar until soft peaks form, adding the confectioners sugar gradually during the beating process. Continue beating until the egg whites are firm but not dry. Add a generous spoonful of the whites to the base and stir to lighten. Fold all the whites into the base.

For individual soufflés, fill each dish about $1/3$ full and sprinkle on a tablespoon of the berries. Divide the remaining mixture among the dishes, filling them to just below the rim. Smooth the tops gently with a rubber spatula. Place the dishes on a heavy-duty baking sheet and bake for 15 to 20 minutes.

For a large soufflé, fill the bottom $1/3$ full, add the entire cup of berries and fill with the rest of the mixture, smoothing the top. Place the dish on a heavy-duty baking sheet. Bake 15 minutes, then reduce the oven to 350° and bake another 15 minutes.

The soufflés are done when they have risen up out of the dishes (1 inch for the little ones and 2 inches for the big one) and the tops are well browned. The soufflé(s) should be fairly firm and not wiggle very much when moved. Hold a strainer filled with a little confectioners sugar over the hot soufflé(s) and dust lightly. Serve immediately.

Serves 6

Easy and Delicious Chocolate Cake

 Ruth Kopelman

½ cup butter, softened
1 cup sugar
4 eggs
2 cups chocolate syrup

1¼ cups all-purpose flour
1 teaspoon baking powder
1 teaspoon vanilla extract

Grease a 9 x 13-inch baking pan and preheat oven to 350°.

Beat butter and sugar together in a large bowl, add eggs thoroughly one at a time, and add chocolate syrup.

In a separate bowl, sift together flour and baking powder, and add to mixture with vanilla.

Pour into the baking pan and bake for 30 to 40 minutes or until a toothpick inserted in the center comes out clean. This cake can be served plain or frosted.

Serves 12–15

Pareve Banana Frappe

 Melinda Strauss

This is a treat for people who are lactose intolerant, but it is also an easy way to get a lot of protein out of a snack that can be used as a small, quick meal. To make frozen bananas, peel ones that are overripe, wrap tightly in plastic, and freeze.

1 frozen banana

1 generous cup vanilla soy milk

Break frozen banana into a few pieces. Place in blender with soy milk, and blend at low speed until smooth.

Serves 1

Variations: Plain, chocolate, or coffee soy milk can be used. Use 1 percent soy milk for fewer calories. Chocolate syrup can be added before blending.

Sweet Potato Pie

 Carol Killian

5–6 medium sweet potatoes,
   boiled and skinned or
   1 17-ounce can sweet
   potatoes
3 eggs
1/2 cup sugar
1/4 cup butter, melted and
   cooled
1/2 teaspoon ginger

1/2 teaspoon cinnamon
1/2 teaspoon nutmeg
1/2 teaspoon baking powder
1 teaspoon vanilla extract
Dash of ground cloves
1/2 cup evaporated milk
1 9-inch deep-dish pie crust,
   pre-baked for 10 minutes

Preheat oven to 400°.

Combine all the ingredients except the milk and pie crust in a
food processor or blender. Blend milk in slowly. Pour into pie shell.
Bake for 45 minutes to 1 hour, or until the filling is firm.

Serves 6

INDEX

Bold type denotes the recipe reference, italics refer to essays.

Q

INGREDIENTS FOR GREAT COOKING

Moosewood Cookbook

by Mollie Katzen

The top-to-bottom revision of our best-selling cookbook retains all the old favorites and adds twenty-five new recipes. Every one is as delicious as ever, and reflects today's lighter eating tastes.

"One of the most attractive, least dogmatic meatless cookbooks printed . . . an engaging blend of hand-lettered care and solid food information."

—The New York Post

$16.95 paper, $19.95 cloth, 256 pages

The Enchanted Broccoli Forest

by Mollie Katzen

Two hundred and fifty more great vegetarian recipes from the author of *Moosewood. "An imaginative, witty book, a real charmer."* —Library Journal

$16.95 paper, $19.95 cloth, 320 pages

Still Life with Menu

by Mollie Katzen

Dozens of delicious, meatless menus—over two hundred recipes in all—each gloriously illustrated with a full-color still life painted by the author.

$19.95 paper, $34.95 cloth, 352 pages

Mollie Katzen's Still Life Sampler

With twenty of the most popular paintings from the *Still Life with Menu* cookbook, along with sixteen recipe cards, this is the perfect gift. Either give the *Sampler* itself, or frame and share the easily removed still lifes.

$12.00 paper, 48 pages

The New Laurel's Kitchen

by Laurel Robertson, Carol Flinders & Brian Ruppenthal

Millions of people have enjoyed this cookbook for its warm tone, lovely art, and, of course, fantastic recipes. This new edition contains updated nutritional information and hundreds of healthful recipes.

$24.95 paper, $27.95 cloth, 512 pages

Fog City Diner Cookbook

by Cindy Pawlcyn

Sit back and enjoy one hundred and fifty recipes from one of the nation's most famous diners. Familiar diner favorites and a sparkling array of inventive new recipes make this book *"relaxed, refreshing, and just plain fun."*

—William Rice, Chicago Tribune

$24.95 cloth, 224 pages

The Uncommon Gourmet

by Ellen Helman

The rich variety of these three hundred-plus recipes will please the most discriminating palate, yet proves that gourmet food need not be elaborate and difficult to be flavorful, fresh, and uncommonly delicious.

$16.95 paper, 416 pages

Recipes from a Kitchen Garden

by Renee Shepherd and Fran Raboff

From the founder of Shepherd's Garden Seeds comes a bumper crop of three hundred or so recipes, strewn with charming illustrations, for garden-fresh vegetables, fragrant herbs, and edible flowers.

$11.95 paper, 176 pages